why meditate?

why meditate?

—◇—

edited by Clint Willis

ILLUMINA™

A BALLIETT & FITZGERALD BOOK

MARLOWE & COMPANY
NEW YORK

Published by
Marlowe & Company
An Imprint of Avalon Publishing Group Incorporated
841 Broadway, 4th Floor
New York, NY 10003

Library of Congress Catalog-in-Publication Data

Why Meditate?: The Essential Book About How Meditation Can Enrich
Your Life / edited by Clint Willis.
    p. cm.
  ISBN 1-56924-586-X
    1. Meditation. I. Willis, Clint.

BL627.W495 2001
158.1'2—dc21   2001030055

9   8   7   6   5   4   3   2   1

Book design:Sue Canavan

Manufactured in the United States of America

Distributed by Publishers Group West

For Jennifer Schwamm Willis
with thanks and love

contents

INTRODUCTION x

BEGINNINGS
from *The Accidental Buddhist*
by Dinty W. Moore 1

SEEING
from *Pilgrim at Tinker Creek*
by Annie Dillard 29

TRUE LOVE
from *Teachings on Love*
by Thich Nhat Hanh 57

BASKETBALL
from *Sacred Hoops*
by Phil Jackson and Hugh Delehanty 67

GRIEF
from *Nine-Headed Dragon River*
by Peter Matthiessen 87

WRITING
from *Long Quiet Highway*
by Natalie Goldberg 99

DYING
from *The Tibetan Book of Living and Dying*
by Sogyal Rinpoche 127

SIMPLICITY
from *Voluntary Simplicity*
by Duane Elgin   141

FORGIVENESS
from *Lovingkindness*
by Sharon Salzberg   159

CHILDREN
from *Everyday Blessings*
by Myla and Jon Kabat-Zinn   181

FEAR
from *When Things Fall Apart*
by Pema Chödrön   201

THERAPY
from *Awakening the Heart*
by John Welwood   231

TIME
from *Full Catastrophe Living*
by Jon Kabat-Zinn   247

PAIN
from *Who Dies?*
by Stephen Levine   265

ENLIGHTENMENT
from *The Three Pillars of Zen*
by Roshi Philip Kapleau   273

SPONTANEITY
from *The Way of Zen*
by Alan Watts   279

MOTIVATION
from *Zen Mind, Beginner's Mind*
by Shunryu Suzuki   303

MINDFULNESS
from *Wherever You Go, There You Are*
by Jon Kabat-Zinn   329

ANSWERS
from *The Miracle of Mindfulness*
by Thich Nhat Hanh   335

ACKNOWLEDGEMENTS   343

BIBLIOGRAPHY   346

introduction

—◇—

Certain moments from my past insist upon my attention. One moment in particular tugs at me. I was 12 or 13 years old, so this was 1969 or 1970. I was growing up in South Louisiana, in a small city that served as a kind of hub for more rural communities with names like New Iberia and Abbeville and Opelousas.

My father was an attorney. Once or twice a month he would drive 20 or 30 miles to one of those little towns. When he got there, he'd visit the local courthouse in search of a particular set of documents. Sometimes he would meet with other lawyers, usually men he had come to know over the years.

I occasionally would go on these trips with my father. We set out early, just as the heat and humidity of the day began to gather momentum. We often drove part of our way on old roads and quiet blacktop highways, past sugarcane or cotton fields. Every so often, we'd pass an abandoned shack with a tarpaper roof and a falling-down porch.

We usually brought our lunch with us in a small Styrofoam ice chest. We would look for a place to stop on the way home and have a kind of picnic. One day my father pulled off of one of those little back roads and parked in front of an empty house. It had a high porch and enough paint on it to seem almost like a former home for a property owner rather than a shack for servants or share-croppers. We ate our sandwiches on the sagging porch, with a view across the empty asphalt road to a field that went back to some oak or pecan trees.

My father stepped into the house through a low window on the porch. I followed him. The rooms were musty and drab and very dark after the glare of the almost tropical sun that in those parts oversaw the sky all summer long. The house was not furnished, but soggy cardboard boxes and old newspapers in stacks and other objects (a pair of pliers, a broken picture frame) brought to my mind the people who might have lived there once. I felt dimly afraid and sorry for them; they were gone.

Someone must have owned the land and the house. But when I went back outside and wandered around to the back of the house I could see empty fields all the way to the horizon. The land around the house was utterly unpopulated and in my memory remains entirely silent.

This is the moment that tugs at me: Something shifted. Matters like property rights fell away as they might at the edge of a desert or perhaps at the moment of death. I was alone in a landscape that in some mysterious way seemed to represent the true inside of my mind. It might be better to say that I stopped living in my mind for that moment and instead lived in the landscape in all its scale and quiet.

I should mention that things at home were not going well. My family had lived in New Orleans and we were snobs about that; we pretended to ourselves that we were better than our neighbors. But our family seemed to be falling apart in ways that contradicted any notion that we were superior. My older brother was flunking out of the local college and it seemed possible or even likely that he would be drafted and go to Vietnam. He spent his time at his fraternity house so that I rarely saw him anymore. My sister had run away to marry a divorced Vietnam veteran who worked as a mechanic at Sears. My father viewed the marriage as a social and personal catastrophe.

I carried these troubles around in my head much of the time, trying to sort them out one way or another, as if my behavior and my thinking were crucial to resolving matters. But as I stood at the edge of the field my thoughts and the mind that carried them seemed suddenly to stop. There was nothing familiar about me; I was no longer a creature with particular views or duties. It seemed to me that I was a dream creature in a dream landscape.

My father came around the house and spoke to me. Thoughts and ideas came back, and the day resumed its ordinary shape. But I carried away that moment of quiet; I tucked it away like a twenty-dollar bill one of my grandmothers used to safety-pin to her slip.

Why Meditate? The title acknowledges that there are many good reasons to sit on a cushion or chair and go about the work of trying to be present for your experience. The headings that introduce each piece in this anthology—words such as children, dying, basketball—are concessions to the fact that people bring to meditation such agendas.

Eventually, though, you will want to let go of your motives and practice meditation for its own sake. You don't have to do that now or worry about how to do it. Meditation will teach you. Here is Annie Dillard at Tinker Creek:

> My God, I look at the creek. It is the answer to Merton's prayer, "Give us time!" It never stops. If I seek the sense and skill of children, the information of a thousand books, the innocence of puppies, even the insights of my own city past, I do so only, solely and entirely that I might look well at the creek. You don't run down the present, pursue it with baited hooks and nets. You wait for it, empty-handed, and you are filled.

Or listen to Lao Tzu:

> The master doesn't seek fulfillment,
> Not seeking, not expecting,
> She is present, and can welcome all things.

Welcome all things. This is not as easy as it sounds. I am a veteran of more than a decade of psychotherapy. After several years of that work, I began to believe that I would face anything—go through any door—to be happy. But where was the door?

One day I found myself riding a train through the countryside north of New York City, heading home from a weekend at a friend's house. I was reading a paperback novel, and I was working hard to wish myself into the story—I didn't want to go back to my job in the city—but I kept looking up from my book to stare out of the train window.

The country going by was pretty; mostly fields and woods with an occasional building or farmhouse. A deer stepped out of some trees in the near distance, and I saw it and imagined myself into the deer's perspective. I believed that I knew what it was like to be that deer standing there with no particular expectations or plans for the week; a creature without notions or words. I wanted to be like that.

More time passed. Again, I carried the moment with me. One day my therapist gave me Jon Kabat-Zinn's second book, *Wherever You Go, There You Are.* The book read as if some kinder, wiser version of myself—the person I wanted to be—had written it; it felt familiar as well as true. The second page of Kabat-Zinn's introduction to the book offered this assertion:

> We usually fall, quite unawares, into assuming that what we are thinking—the ideas and opinions that we harbor at any given time—are the 'truth' about what is 'out there' in the world and 'in here' in our minds. Most of the time, it just isn't so.

I knew that! I knew I was at least partly wrong about everything. Kabat-Zinn went on to describe the cramped, uncomfortable world of illusion that I was increasingly tired of inhabiting:

> We may never quite be where we actually are, never quite touch the fullness of our possibilities. Instead, we lock ourselves into a personal fiction that we already know who we are, that we know where we are and where we are going, that we know what is happening—all the while remaining enshrouded in thoughts, fantasies, and impulses, mostly about the past and about the future, about what we want and

like, and what we fear and don't like, which spin out
continuously, veiling our direction and the very
ground we are standing on.

Better yet, Kabat-Zinn offered a prescription: Meditate. Sit quietly. Watch your breathing and whatever else comes up. If you
think, take note of your thought and then let it go. Return to your
breathing.

I began my meditation practice. It was very quiet; things shim-
mered the way they do when a child has a high fever and everyone
is quiet and careful. At the same time, I became aware of a tiresome
and astonishing array of voices, worries, wishes, threats, fears,
reminders and other noise that occupied my energy and most of
my time.

I watched it all. The voices faded a little and at moments gave way
to something more pleasant and more interesting—a sense of seeing the world with some clarity and finding myself at home in it.
This clarity was a great surprise and relief to me.

Meditation is in part a matter of faith, and intelligent faith is a
matter of trust. Reading this book you may come upon voices that
you can believe. One voice I trust belonged to Shunryu Suzuki, who
helped bring Zen to America before dying at his Zen Center in San
Francisco almost thirty years ago. Before I ever read Suzuki's words
or heard his name, someone sent me a picture of him on the front
of a postcard. I scotch-taped the picture to my wall because I love
his posture—he sits erect and cross-legged on his pillow—and the
look of delight on his face. This image of the late teacher smiles at
me now and makes me smile, too. Can I be that happy?

A week or so ago I rode my bicycle to the beach on a Sunday morning. It was cold the way early December in Maine is cold, so that you can tell that later on it will be colder. I rode down a hill from the highway to the beach. The outgoing tide had polished the sand to a perfect flat glistening band; the sun painted streaks of fire in the wet sand like flint striking a stone. The sand carried right on to the water, which carried on to the sky. The water also was flat except for one or two rows of perfect little curlers at the shore.

Two or three young men in black wetsuits waded in the surf wearing neoprene hoods that made me think of aliens at some pointless, brainy kind of play that they'd invented or—better— otters, sleek and quick and interesting. The young men held surf- boards under their arms, and a few of their friends straddled their boards just past those little breakers, waiting for a wave big enough to ride. The flat sea and the sky were parallel to one another like floor-and-ceiling mirrors; they carried on farther out than I could begin to see as I stood straddling my bike, a little jealous of the surfers, smitten by the view and their part in it and also by my own role in inventing this spectacle—in being the one to notice it.

Everyone has theories, and this is one of mine: We live inside poems, pictures, songs and stories. But we live in them only to the extent that we make them, and we make them by paying attention. These poems, pictures, songs and stories show us things as they are: a musty old abandoned home that stinks of death; evening light from a train; the December ocean off the coast of Maine. The only way to see this world is to show yourself to it. You must step out from behind the rocks or trees where you are hiding if you want to get the view. That is what a practice like meditation (or walking by creeks like Annie Dillard) is for.

I want to be like the boy I was standing in the South Louisiana sunlight; the deer I saw stepping into the field; the men at play in the cold water and the man watching them. I want to step out to where I can see more of the world, because the more I see of the world the better I like it—and the better it likes me. Sometimes on my meditation pillow or at my desk or anywhere, I feel something watching me back, taking in me precisely the same pleasure that I take in it.

I mean to say that meditation is a way to love the world. And why do that? Because the world will love you back.

—Clint Willis

beginnings

—◇—

from
THE ACCIDENTAL BUDDHIST
by Dinty W. Moore

Dinty W. Moore (born 1955) was born a
Catholic, but in 1995 found himself at a Zen
monastery, taking his first steps along the
Buddhist path. Moore isn't quite sure why he is
taking this journey, and he takes an amusingly
skeptical view of things. Still, some people and
practices stand up to his doubts, and offer
inspiration for his next step.

—◇—

Z en Mountain Monastery is an impressive stone structure
tucked neatly onto the side of Tremper Mountain, in the
Catskills, in eastern New York State.

I arrive there with a fair degree of trepidation on a Friday
evening and am directed to a second-floor dorm room. There are
eight bunk beds and a sink crammed into the small area. When I
stumble in, Harold, a sixty-something attorney with a neatly
trimmed white beard, has already marked out his territory by
spreading his expensive luggage in a wide circle.

He introduces himself amicably enough, but only as an excuse,
it seems, to make it clear to me within seconds that he knows more
about Zen, Buddhism, and meditation than anyone, other than
perhaps the Buddha himself. He mentions the many *zendos* where
he has studied, the Zen *koans* (riddles, more or less) he has con-
templated, the teachers he has spoken with, and throws around an
impressive array of foreign-sounding words.

I am stuck listening to the boasting because Harold has blocked my way to where I hope to make my bunk, and because Wayne, the only other roommate to have arrived at this point, has wisely retreated to his bed, where he quietly reads a book.

It takes some work, but I manage to extricate myself from Harold's lecture and find a corner bed. From there, all I have to do is watch the room fill up and wonder what the heck I am doing in a monastery anyway. It has been ages since Brother Damien took me aside, and it feels odd to be back.

Sometime after dark, I join a handful of other spiritual green-horns for dinner, a tasty assortment of vegetables, spiced and stir-fried, served over rice. We are next herded into the Buddha Hall, a small room with no chairs, no tables, no real furniture, just an altar topped with framed photos of old Asian men, probably deceased Buddhist teachers, and lots of round black pillows scattered across the carpet.

There is discernible anxiety in the room, though we have all come willingly—in fact, we have paid for the privilege. Many in attendance have come from New York City, just a few hours to the east. Other have come across state from Ithaca, Albany, or Rochester. I have driven six hours from Central Pennsylvania.

We range in age from early twenties to mid-sixties, and except for our loose cotton clothing, it strikes me that we would not look much different if we had come for a business seminar, or a week-end of bird-watching.

With our shoes left out in the hall, we sit on the thin carpet and nervously check out one another's socks, lost in our individual fears. How long, I wonder, can I sit in silent meditation without going totally nuts?

At the front of the room, a Japanese woman settles onto a pillow, carefully arranges the hems of her flowing black robes, then slowly tucks the hems under her knees. She is quite compact, barely more than four feet tall, but sturdily built. Her head is shaved.

"My name is Jimon," she says, in a soft, pleasant voice. There is no trace of an accent, so she probably isn't Japanese after all. She is probably Japanese-American. It doesn't matter, of course, except that I am full of curiosity. Buddhism is an Asian religion, the monastery is run for American students, and I'm already wondering where the two cultures are going to gently intersect and where they are going to slam right into one another.

"I'm here to introduce you to Zen practice," the woman continues. "The most important part of that practice is sitting, and there are a few good ways to do this."

. She tells us that the round pillows on the floor are called *zafus*, and describes the various ways they can be used for support, then outlines the different postures—full lotus, half lotus, and kneeling. For those of us who can't handle the pillows, she points to small, individual wooden benches—you sit on the slanted bench, and tuck your legs underneath, so there is less pressure on the knees. She calls them *seiza* benches.

"And for anyone who can't handle that," Jimon says, smiling, "you can sit on a chair."

The weekend newcomers breathe a collective sigh of relief. Jimon's voice, her very manner in fact, is reassuring, and now that she has promised us that we won't be forced to dislocate our knees, we are feeling pretty good. *Gee*, I can almost hear a few people behind me thinking, *who said this was going to be hard?*

"More important than how you sit is what you do with your mind," she informs us, and that turns out to be the difficult part.

During meditation, the mind is supposed to be still. But the mind doesn't want to be still. In fact, left to its own devices, the mind would prefer to babble, jabber, and prattle all day—rushing from thought to thought, worry to worry, and generally keeping us as far away from enlightenment as possible. Buddhists call this Monkey Mind, Jimon says. The path of human thinking can be thought of as being like a monkey in the jungle, constantly swinging from vine to vine, tree to tree, seldom lighting for more than a second before it is off again.

She suggests we count our breaths as a way to combat the mental anarchy. If you focus on the count, she promises, it will distract you from the inner dialogue. And if that doesn't work, she adds, there is always the stick.

"During the long periods of sitting tomorrow, if you feel that your shoulders are too tight, someone will come along with a stick, and you can request that they hit your accupressure points," she explains softly. "You make this request by bringing the hands together in the prayer position and bowing."

The anxiety in the room instantly resurfaces. Someone behind me whispers "Ouch" at the thought of being smacked with a long piece of lumber. A small, nervous laugh ripples from pillow to pillow. We have probably all read stories along the way about Zen masters who punch their students in the nose, cut off their ears, or somehow do them bodily harm because they lack diligence.

Jimon, though, just smiles her reassuring smile.

"Oh, it doesn't hurt," she promises. "The *kyosaku* stick is made of soft wood."

We are released to our bedrooms with that thought on our minds. Tomorrow we will "sit *zazen*"—meditate—in earnest, so for now, we all need a good night's sleep.

.   .   .

Saturday

Thanks to Harold, though, I barely sleep at all.

He is tucked into a Polartek sleeping bag barely two feet from my metal bunk, and all through the long chilly night, he chants "*Zaaaaazzzzeeeeeeen . . . zaaaazzzzeeeeen.*"

The snoring is insistent, steady, as if the glottal vibrations were his secret mantra. If I was any sort of Buddhist at all, I probably would not have spent the wee hours entertaining so many murderous thoughts about the man, but I'm not any sort of Buddhist, and I want to choke him.

At precisely five a.m., a sudden bell clangs along the darkened hallways. Wayne fights himself free of his covers first, then shakes the still-snoring Harold by the shoulders. Wake-up time.

We have been told to maintain full silence until after the dawn meditation session, and everyone in my room complies. There is no time for small talk anyway. No time even for a morning shower. Like *zazen* zombies, we pull on our cold, wrinkled clothes and spill out into the monastery's massive meditation hall.

Then we sit.

In a big open room, on squat black pillows, with incense swirling past our noses and all manner of cluttered thoughts jumping through our unaccustomed brains, we sit.

And sit some more.

The sitting part does not turn out to be particularly difficult. So early in the morning, my bones are more than happy to hold perfectly still. My brain, though, is another story.

Jimon warned us about Monkey Mind, and she was right on the money. My inner dialogue erupts almost before my bottom hits the *zafu: Oh, I am doing meditation, how relaxing, oops, I shouldn't be thinking so much, my knee hurts, wait, just focus on the breath, is that a woman in front of me or a guy* with long hair, pretty hair anyway, wonder what's for lunch, hey, wait, count your breath, one, two, three, four, did I turn off my car lights?

Jimon not only warned us that our minds might do this, she also warned us that we would find it discouraging. This racing mind stuff trips up many beginning meditators. They find that they can't quiet the stream of distraction, and so, discouraged, they give up on meditation altogether.

Stick with it, she advised.

So I persist, but the truth is, I turn out to have a particularly unrelenting monkey. He not only swings from tree to tree, he rips off big green leaves and chatters at the top of his monkey lungs, an angry baboon somehow set loose in an espresso bar.

Following Jimon's instructions, I try to bypass the monkey by counting my breaths. The first "in" breath is one, the second is two, the third is three, but my Monkey Mind is stubbornly unco-operative. More often than not, I lose track around five or seven. Needless to say, *nirvana* completely eludes me.

The sitting meditation ends eventually, and we all stand by our pillows. Pretty soon, a bell rings.

Along with the thirty or so of us newcomers, thirty or so others in long gray robes are seated further toward the middle of the monastery's large meditation hall. They are the advanced students, I assume. Most of those in gray robes don't have shaved heads, but a handful of more serious-seeming types in black robes, *with* shaved heads, sit in the front rows. I'm focusing on hairstyles here, because I am still trying to figure out who is a monk, who is not, and where it all fits together. None of this has been explained.

Suddenly, those in the know begin chanting in Japanese: *"No mo san man da moto nan oha ra chi koto sha sono nan to ji to en gya gya gya ki gya."*

I am handed a card with the words, so that I can chant, too, though I have no idea what the words mean, and no one attempts to explain.

Off and on during the ensuing service, we bow from the waist, and then, following the gray robes in the row ahead of me, I learn the full prostration bow—falling to the knees and bowing on the floor.

At various points, assorted black robes and gray robes approach the main altar, then back away. Sometimes they carry incense boxes, other times they carry items I can't identify.

It begins to seem awfully familiar: the seemingly pointless walking back and forth, the retrieval of various objects only to put them right back where they started out, the chanting in a foreign tongue—it reminds me of morning mass at Good Shepherd Catholic Church when I was a boy. I never understood what was being said then either, not knowing Latin, and though I knew what the priests were up to in a vague sort of way—they were consecrating the bread and wine into the body and blood of Christ—they seemed to have found perhaps the most inefficient manner imaginable to accomplish this sacred task. The old priests reminded me of amnesiacs in a kitchen, always turning back to the cupboard to get something they forgot, putting things down in the wrong place, and then later having to cross the room to get those same things.

To say this about Catholic Mass is a sacrilege, and if I had expressed these thoughts in front of one of my grade school nuns, I surely would have felt a sharp rap, and not from the soft wood of the *kyosaku* stick, either.

I don't know enough about Buddhism yet to know if I'm being sacrilegious here, too, or, if so, what I'm supposed to do, or say, or think about it. Jimon has mentioned nothing about venial sin.

Eventually, though, I relax and begin to enjoy the Zen liturgy for what it is—rather interesting, exotic, and nonthreatening. No one is going to make me take communion. No one is going to force me into the confessional. Sister Mary Catherine is not coming up behind me to pull my ear.

And anyway, the chants are invigorating, and we are able to move around finally—stand and bow, stand and bow twice, turn, stand and bow, deep bow—instead of just staring at a blank wall.

When the ceremony finally concludes—for no reason clear to me except that another bell rings and everyone stops—we are herded down narrow, winding steps to the monastery's massive dining hall. Our breakfast is steaming on long tables, but first the head cook lights incense at another small altar and leads us in yet another chant, this time in English:

First, seventy-two labors brought us this food
We should know how it comes to us
Second, as we receive this offering
We should consider
Whether our virtue and practice deserve it

My virtue and practice have been pretty inconsequential to this point, but I'm hungry. The oatmeal is hot, and we are finally allowed to talk.

Five of us end up at one table, including Harold, my snoring roommate, complaining that, in fact, it was he who didn't get much sleep at all.

"Someone's watch was going off all night," he says, looking pointedly in my direction, raising a gray eyebrow. "Does anyone know whose watch that might have been?"

We all shrug.

"Kept me awake," Harold complains, shaking his head from side to side. "Damn thing beeped all through the night."

He looks around the table at each of us, again resting his eyes on me a bit longer than on the others. "Anybody know whose watch that was?"

I am truly and absolutely clueless. My watch did beep, as a matter of fact, once every hour, but not only was the sound nearly imperceptible, especially when hidden under a pillow and squashed by my large Irish head, but I know for a fact, since I was wearing the watch, and checking it on occasion, that old Harold was snoring from two-thirty to five a.m., uninterrupted snoring of the deepest and most annoying kind. He wouldn't have heard a bomb go off. He didn't even hear the loud bell that was supposed to awaken us before dawn.

Yet he heard my Timex?

It was my first Zen *koan*.

After seeking the tranquillity that comes through Buddhist meditation for roughly half a day or so, only one conclusion makes any sense: I have Attention Deficit Disorder. I am too scattered, too undisciplined, too easily distracted, to focus on anything.

True of me certainly, this is true as well of most of the people I know. One uniting characteristic of our times is that we skitter from thing to thing, eating while we talk, reading while we eat, chatting on the phone while we watch TV, thinking about work while we dress our kids for school, daydreaming about our weekend while we work. We put phones in our cars, install televisions in our bathrooms, pipe music into every shopping mall and public space, erect flashing signs along every roadway. We seem to be fleeing stillness as if it were some curse, yet ironically, many of us are starting to actively seek it out.

from The Accidental Buddhist

I am not the only one exploring Buddhism right now—there is, in fact, a modest surge underway. The interest that has been rooted for quite some time in cultural centers such as New York, Los Angeles, and San Francisco is starting to spread inward. *Zendos,* monasteries, and meditation centers are popping up in every state, in the cities, in the college towns, and even in rural corners such as Floyds Knobs, Indiana, and High View, West Virginia. Start paying attention, and you'll notice more and more references to Buddhism, Zen, and mindfulness on television, in the news, in the casual speech of those around you. Vice President Al Gore visited a California monastery just before the last election, though he may regret it now.

Hollywood is playing its part with a string of recent and upcoming movies, such as *Little Buddha, Seven Years in Tibet,* and *Kundun.* Richard Gere is a Buddhist, and makes it known. So are Tina Turner, Oliver Stone, and Chicago Bulls head coach Phil Jackson. Rocker/actress Courtney Love took the ashes of her dead husband, Kurt Cobain, to India, to be embedded in a Buddhist shrine. Walk the streets of any medium to large city these days, and you will see faddish Buddha T-shirts, *om mani padme om* tattoos, and Tibetan folk-art boutiques.

While a good number of Americans are embracing serious religious Buddhist practice, many, many others are engaging in "vaguely" Buddhist practice, much of it part of the New Age movement. *Business Week* hails meditation as "the new balm for corporate stress." Even beat cops are being taught to breathe, for relaxation. Beermaker Adolph Coors reports that meditation has helped lower the company's mental health costs 27 percent since 1987.

And still other Americans are engaged in wildly shallow and seemingly absurd Buddhist practice. *Elle* magazine, of all places, ran a recent series of articles promoting the meditative lifestyle. In one article, Buddhist psychiatrist Mark Epstein endorses a group of New Yorkers who have begun chanting for parking spaces. "It definitely works," he offered. "I always get a parking place that way, just by asking for one."

Even Bart Simpson, the cartoon character, has taken up the subject, finally determining just exactly what "one hand clapping" sounds like. He may be our first animated Zen master.

Buddhism is a religion with a sense of humor, and I'm guessing the Buddha liked a good laugh as well. I don't know for sure what all this scattered interest in Buddhism means exactly, but I do know that our interest is growing.

Why?

Yankelovich Partners, Inc., the polling firm, occasionally asks Americans how many think that life has become too complicated. In 1985, just over half said yes. At the end of 1996, that proportion had climbed to 73 percent. Many of us are beginning to realize that we need *some* tranquillity, or we are going to explode.

Perhaps our flirtation with Buddhism as the twenty-first century fast approaches is a cry for help from a chronically active culture. We are truly the Distracted Generation. It is hard to hear your own heartbeat when your pager is beeping, your car phone is ringing, and a stream of faxes is pouring out of your Danka.

Did someone say mindfulness?

Did someone suggest meditation?

Hell, we can hardly breathe.

As for myself, I had toyed with Buddhist philosophy in my young adulthood. Like millions of other college kids, I read Pirsig's *Zen and the Art of Motorcycle Maintenance* in one long weekend, put it down thinking my life had been forever transformed, then promptly forgot about it. I even took a meditation class once, but never got past how to fold my legs.

One day, many years later, though, I chanced upon a book called *Being Peace* by a Vietnamese monk named Thich Nhat Hanh, and something was awakened in me. Not any deep faith in God, to be honest, but just enough curiosity to start me thinking again. What was it that these Buddhists had discovered? What was I missing?

Most striking to me about Nhat Hanh's book was the fact that the Zen monk didn't talk about man's shortcomings, our undeservedness, or the necessity of suffering. He talked about being happy. He talked about how if we were happy and kind, we would pass this happiness and kindness on to the people around us, and they would be happier and kinder, too. Simple as that. He said that this was the heart of Buddhism.

Well, over the years, that rocklike ball of anger first identified by Brother Damien had dissipated a good bit. I wasn't exactly ticked off at the world anymore, but unfortunately, I wasn't particularly happy either. I was just getting along. My anger had mellowed to what might best be described as persistent dissatisfaction. Some gloom, maybe. No matter where I went, what I did, I always felt a little bit empty. I have spoken to enough other people to know I am not alone in this feeling.

"Many of us worry about the situation of the world," Thich Nhat Hanh wrote. "We don't know when the bombs will explode. We feel that we are on the edge of time. As individuals we feel helpless, despairing."

I recognized more of myself in his description than I am comfortable admitting. The low-level agitation, the sense of just holding on, was familiar. Nhat Hanh said the answer was at hand, however—that relief from this despair was as simple as breathing.

. . .

Breathing? It seemed too simple.

Then I had this bright idea—the best way to learn about Buddhism would be to see it in action, the best way to imagine how it might fit into my hectic life would be to see how other Americans are fitting it into their busy American lives. I was always a big fan of quests and adventures, and here was a chance to have my own. Buddhism has long thrived in Asian-American communities, of course, but I was most interested in searching out the homegrown kind, the American Buddhism springing up among those with no Buddhist background. I called it my American Buddhism Project, and immediately subscribed to every Buddhist newspaper and magazine I could put my hands on. I imagined myself the Ponce de Leon of American *dharma,* and set off with pen and pad.

That was my idea.

And that's how I ended up, three months later, sitting on a round black cushion on Monkey Mind Mountain, trying my best not to scream and run off.

After breakfast on Saturday, each of us at Zen Mountain Monastery is given a work assignment. Work, Jimon explains, is part of Zen practice, a way to integrate meditative concentration into our everyday tasks. It is also, clearly, an efficient way to keep the monastery clean.

Everyone works, we are told, from the lowliest weekend visitor like myself to the highest-ranking monk. Even the abbot of the monastery, John Daido Loori, works, though I don't see him sweeping floors anywhere near me. In fact, we have yet to see him at all.

I am paired with Tom, an affable glassblower from New Jersey, and we are instructed to merge our Buddha selves with a ten-pound bag of onions, to dice diligently until we completely fill a giant wooden bowl, and to talk as little as possible in the process.

Tom and I don't talk at all. We are high achievers. Instead, we chop like skilled chefs, running through the heap of onions in record time. And a lesson is learned. It is easier, more efficient, to chop onions when you are only chopping onions, not conversing, checking up on the rest of the kitchen, answering the phone, flirting with the young lady scouring the coffeepot, or whatever.

When done, Tom and I wash up the knives and cutting board with a bottle of Big Top blue dish detergent, and the head cook gives us a second chore: hauling a forty-gallon plastic garbage can of kitchen waste out to a well-composted compost pile the size of a Plymouth minivan. As a gardener, I am well impressed.

When the work is done, we return to the main hall, meditate some more, then have instruction in Zen painting, the practice of catching an image in a single brush stroke. The lesson is so brief that all we really learn is that Zen painting looks simple but is deceptively difficult. Then a quick lunch, during which Harold, at my table again, lets us all know just how much of what we are learning he knew already, and complains about his aching back. I've noticed over the course of the morning that he has developed a minor limp, and my compassion is tested. I don't much like the guy, and I'm of the opinion that he deserves a pain in the back now and then, but I'm also beginning to sense that this is not a very Buddhist thought.

The monastery building is an impressive maze of rooms and hallways, but they are mainly small and dark, so in the break after lunch, I head outside for some fresh air.

The Zen Mountain grounds include 230 acres of nature preserve, and though a sign has been posted on the main bulletin board warning us that a hungry bear has been spotted in the area, I don't see one.

Instead, after a ten-minute climb straight uphill past cabins that house some of the longer-term residents, I run into three whitetail deer—does, nice-sized, very much alert and mindful.

Mindfulness is what we are focusing on this weekend: the unwavering concentration that comes from stillness. When we are sitting on the *zafu* pillow, we should just be sitting. When we are chopping onions, we should be chopping onions only, right there, right then, at the chopping board, as if the onions, the knife, and our hands were all that existed. Later, as we return to our lives as doctors, lawyers, Indian chiefs, we should ideally bring that mindfulness with us as well, and as a result, we should be far better able to focus clearly on whatever task comes to hand. Mindfulness is the antithesis of Monkey Mind. Turtle Mind, maybe.

Or Doe Mind. The does are totally concentrated, it seems, on the sounds, the sights, the odors, that surround them in the woods, are absolutely focusing on the moment at hand, not worrying ahead to the next hour or the next day or whether they'll have the money they need for retirement. They are sniffing the tall weeds, looking for tasty clumps of grass, and listening sharply, ever alert for change or danger.

Just then, amazingly, I am mindful, too, for what seems like an uncommonly long time, as I do nothing more than simply watch them stray nearer and nearer to where I crouch frozen behind a small stand of dry late-autumn brush. Watching the thin, sleek, elegant creatures, I lose track of why I am there or where I am going. The winter sun is shining on my back, and it all feels rather magical.

from The Accidental Buddhist

I suppose it is a Zen moment, but the quibbling monkey voices in my head start almost immediately to ruin it. *How trite!* the monkeys giggle. *City boy merges with nature. He sees a few cute, dumb animals and imagines he has achieved some spiritual plateau. Had a cheeseburger lately, animal lover? Okay, bonehead, you paid your money, you saw the deer, now why don't you go write a poem about it.* If you haven't yet noticed, my brain is home to some particularly skeptical, sarcastic, and mean-spirited monkeys. Blame it on the nuns.

Distracted by all of this, and with my leg muscles beginning to ache, I shift my weight, snap a branch under my right foot, and the does are off like lightning into the forest.

Walking back, I am filled with fresh misgivings. Remembering the hyperactivity of my mind during morning *zazen*, my discourteous questioning of the Zen liturgy, my distinct lack of Buddhist compassion toward my fussy roommate with the bad back, my natural mistrust of all things spiritual, I begin giving serious thought to the notion that perhaps I am being a fool. This Project I have concocted may be dead before it even gets off the ground. Perhaps my true nature is too frantic, cynical, volatile, and mundane for anything good to ever happen.

Back at the meditation hall, though, on the pillow again for the afternoon session, I have a meditative breakthrough. After sitting for fifteen minutes in total stillness and total silence, looking at nothing more than the gray robe of the stick-thin monk one row of *zafus* ahead of me, thinking of nothing but my breath, I lose track. I actualy stop thinking for a moment.

Then of course, I have this thought:

Look, I'm not thinking.

And the bubble bursts.

But for that brief fragment of time, there was no real time, because I was not keeping track, because I had forgotten to grasp greedily at every moment and analyze every twitch and twitter of my life, and it was a remarkable feeling.

I could very well have been spaced out on my *zafu* for an hour or more, though in all honesty it was probably no more than a few minutes. What I experienced was not *samadhi*, the Zen state of "no mind"—or maybe it was. But whatever it was, it felt good. And immediately I want to get the feeling back.

Wanting that feeling to return is attachment, of course, and Buddhists say that attachments are bad, that as soon as I attach to a feeling and pursue it, it will elude me all the more. Our minds are tricky. If we want something, we can't get it. Once we stop wanting it, it comes. This is why Zen is so hard.

I am not at all sure why I experience this mini-*samadhi*, if I may call it that. Perhaps it is just the wonderful excess of fresh, clean mountain air that I have inhaled over the lunch break, or perhaps it is a timely answer to the doubts that washed over me on my walk back down the mountain, or perhaps it is random and meaningless.

I just don't know, but during the instructional session that follows, I find myself sincerely wishing the various black robes would talk less and let me sit some more.

In the late afternoon, Jimon takes a seat at the head *zafu* to prepare us for face-to-face teaching by Abbot John Daido Loori. Loori, an American-born scientist and photographer, is founder and director of the monastery. The students call him Daido-shi.

I know all of this from the brochure that came when I registered, though I have yet to see the man, and face-to-face teaching, it turns out, is not so simple as going into a room and asking Daido-shi a question.

Smiling her lovely smile, Jimon tells us the rules:

During sitting meditation that evening, we are to listen for an announcement. When we hear a voice saying, "All weekend retreat participants who desire *dokusan* now enter the line, we are to spring from our *zafus* and race for the hallway just outside the meditation hall. First come, first served.

But this is just the beginning. Once we reach the hallway, we are to wait in line, sitting in half lotus or whatever position our legs are able to accomplish, until a bell is rung. That bell, coming from an inside room where Daido-shi is waiting, signals the first person on line to approach and enter his chamber.

When the first person goes into *dokusan*, the formal name for the face-to-face encounter, the rest of the hallway line moves up one space. When it is our turn, and we enter the *dokusan* room, we are to put our hands together, bow twice, then step forward, then bow again, then do a full prostration bow, dropping to our knees and bowing until our foreheads hit the floor, then another half bow, then we should sit about a foot from Daido-shi's knees and introduce ourselves, first name only, and tell Daido-shi what kind of practice we do ("If you don't know," Jimon tutors us, "just say that you count breaths," and then we can ask Daido a question.

He will answer the question, or else he won't.

We can ask a follow-up question, perhaps, but as soon as Daidoshi rings the bell again, we are to spring to our feet, bow like mad, and get the heck out of there, because our turn is over.

"*Dokusan* is an important part of the teaching," Jimon warns us gently. "Don't waste this opportunity. Think, if you could ask a question of the Buddha, what would you ask?"

Geez wheez, how intimidating. Daido-shi, we are told, has learned his Zen Buddhism from another teacher, and that teacher had a teacher before him, and that teacher can trace his Buddhism back to yet another teacher, and then another, and another, and another, centuries back, an unbroken string of face-to-face teaching, theoretically returning all the way to the historic Shakyamuni Buddha, also known as Siddhartha Gautama, the good fellow who started all of this. Direct transmission, it is called.

Zen is not learned from books, Jimon tells us, it is learned from teachers, and for a teacher to be legitimate, his or her transmission lines should be intact, and John Daido Loori is the real thing.

So because of this direct transmission, teachers of the lineage are sometimes referred to as "living Buddhas." *Dokusan* will be our chance to meet with a living Buddha, but we have to remember the rules.

The weekend training participants seem clearly unsettled by this prospect, and they pepper Jimon with worried questions. How exactly do we know when to get in the line? Which bow comes first? Are there two small bows and then a big one, or one small and then two big ones? What do we do after the third bow?

As for myself, I am beginning to feel skeptical again. Back in the old days, I never much liked the deference we were expected to pay our parish priests, or the idea that they were God's hand-picked representatives. They were just guys who had volunteered—I knew that, even as a kid. Anyone with a working brain had to question the idea that priests were special emissaries of God, worthy of so many exceptional privileges, because it was the priests themselves who had decided this, and kept reminding us of it. As the comedian says, isn't that a little too convenient?

So here is Jimon, touting Daido-shi's special standing in the Buddhist world, and it brings up all my deep-rooted cynicism. I haven't even met the guy yet, and I'm beginning to dislike him.

"Daido-shi is not a guru," Jimon says, as if reading my thoughts.

"He is a teacher, with a deep understanding of the *dharma*, of the teachings."

Well, here is another fine Zen contradiction. If the man is not to be treated as a guru, why all the fuss, ceremony, and complex choreography just to ask him a question? I'm a college professor— I have office hours. Just knock on my door.

"Can we rehearse the bows?" a young woman named Connie asks.

"No," Jimon answers with her calm, quiet smile, a smile that I'm noticing is actually common among the black robes. "I don't think so."

We have an open hour before dinner.

Many of the weekend participants settle on the couches in the dining hall, busily reading magazines that have been left on a big table. Aren't we supposed to be emptying our minds?

Apparently not. One of the resident staff opens the Monastery Store, and we are allowed to do some shopping practice. The small shop is filled with books, tapes, clothing, incense, and Buddha statues. I am mindful of not buying too much, but come away with a nifty sweatshirt, a coffee mug, and two postcards.

Supper is black bean soup, salad, corn bread. One consistent aspect of the retreat is the excellent food.

Our dinner-table conversations are dominated by more nervous speculation and anxiety over *dokusan*. I can tell from the strained voices that many of my fellow newcomers are as confused and intimidated as I am. Eventually we move on though, to a discussion of our healthy, tasty meal, which segues easily into talk about our various obsessions with losing weight and our nasty eating habits back in our real lives.

A few of us have young daughters, it turns out, and weight and body image leads naturally to a discussion of Barbie dolls, and how it is that after concerted efforts to shield our daughters from the anorexic Barbie culture, they still come home one day wanting nothing more than tiny clothes and a pink plastic Corvette. Direct transmission, obviously. The teachings are directly transmitted from one four-year-old girl to another, in an unbroken chain of Barbie *dharma*.

Later, we sit *zazen* again, and all I can think about is what I will ask Daido-shi, whether I will even get the chance to ask him anything, and whether his exalted self will immediately sense my wobbly soul and impure motives. I am ready to spring from my seat at the first hint that newcomers are being called to the *dokusan* line, knocking people over if need be, just to get it over with, so that I can concentrate on my meditation again.

But Jimon's voice calls new students on the north end of the meditation hall first. And, as promised, they *do* sprint. It is a full-out footrace, fairly dangerous on the slippery wood floor, and raucously loud. The springing and racing part is a disconcerting contrast to the slow, deliberate stillness that accompanies every other activity here, but Jimon said it is a way to show our eagerness.

I am stuck on my *zafu* listening to the bell ring, calculating by the bell's interval just how long Daido-shi is taking with each student, sneaking a peek to count the number in line, and quietly figuring the math of whether he will even get to those of us sitting on the south end. Not what the Buddha had in mind, probably.

To distract myself from my *dokusan*-anxiety, when I sense Jimon behind me, I bow, and slant my head to one side.

Thwack!

The pine *kyosaku* slams down on one shoulder. I slant my head to other side.

Thwack!

from The Accidental Buddhist

Jimon never mentioned the evening before that she was the one who would be wielding the *kyosaku* stick, but she is.

The points on my back where I have been struck burn, then ache, but it is very effective. I feel my obdurate, unyielding shoulders begin to melt down in a way they never have before. My body begins to relax, and my mind, well, it does, too, just a little.

Sometime later, another announcement is made. "Weekend retreat participants on the south end . . . "

With every non-Buddhist competitive American Yankee Doodle capitalist fiber of my being, I spring and bound, overtaking five fellow students who are nearer to the line but slower getting up from the pillow, and end up in the *dokusan* queue with just three people ahead of me.

But then, before my turn actually comes, a different bell rings, signaling that time is up. Jimon instructs me and six disappointed newcomers directly behind me to return to our places in the meditation hall for the evening's closing ceremony.

And soon after this, we are back in our dorm rooms for lights out. The beds are small, uncomfortable, squeaky, the heat uncertain, the room frigid. I stare at the wire frame of the bunk above me for about ten minutes, frustrated and unsure why I ever thought I would want to spend a weekend with Buddhists, why I ever imagined Thich Nhat Hanh's advice applied to me, where I ever got the idea that a consummate unadulterated nerve-ending like myself could find peace anywhere.

Then I drift into the deepest *zazen* possible.

. . .

Sunday

The bell wakes us again before dawn. Harold dozes right through it, of course, snoring like a rusty sump pump, until Wayne compassionately shakes him awake.

Slipping on my new black ZMM sweatshirt, I notice out of the corner of my eye that the freshly awakened Harold's first act is to pull two rubber earplugs out of his ears. He heard my watch through earplugs?

Breakfast is scrambled eggs and bagels, and once again everything tastes better than expected. Perhaps it isn't that the food is so awfully good—I mean, scrambled eggs are scrambled eggs. Maybe the truth is that all of this meditating does something agreeable to the taste buds.

After breakfast we have another hour of work practice. In my case, I do Scrubbing Out the Industrial Refrigerator *zazen*. It is a big refrigerator, a walk-in closet really, with crates of fresh produce and jars of various sauces. I mindfully remove all the food, take out the wire racks, wash the racks, wipe out the inside of the refrigerator with baking soda, clean the insides of the doors, replace the racks, replace the food, wipe off the outside until it sparkles. I am awfully proud of my work, but when I turn to the long-term resident who acts as crew chief, she unaffectedly tells me to sweep the dining room.

Apparently, no one here ever says "Job well done" or "You clean a refrigerator better than anyone, big guy." And perhaps that is deliberate. Perhaps I should be cleaning the refrigerator simply so that the refrigerator will be clean, not to prove what an anal-compulsive wonder I can be. No ego, no praise, no need for praise. Just a clean refrigerator.

During the meditation session that follows, I begin to notice much less pain in my legs and ankles, though they now tend to fall asleep faster. After the first thirty minutes of quiet sitting, we rise for a brief period of walking meditation. I stand, my legs numb and unsupportive below me, and lurch wildly forward, nearly toppling two senior students who seem in no way amused.

I have been obsessing off and on about *dokusan* again, but not quite as much as the evening before. Shortly after we finish walking and sit again, a voice calls "all those participating in the training weekend who have not yet sat *dokusan* may now . . ."

Bouncing from my *zafu* as if my buttocks were metal springs and sprinting for the line once more, I come in second, just behind Wayne. I sense my competitiveness is not pure Zen mind, but they *did* encourage us to hurry.

The bell rings. I am at the front of the line for three minutes, while Wayne has private face-to-face teaching, and then the bell rings again. It is my turn, finally.

I stand and enter the *dokusan* room, do a series of bows, though not the series we were taught, then totally forget to introduce myself or to mention what sort of practice I am doing. ("I obsess a lot," I would have said. "Then I get distracted.")

None of this matters, however, because Daido-shi isn't even looking at me when I enter. I could have done an Irish jig with my tongue out. Eventually though, sensing my presence, or smelling my fear, he looks up from his meditative reverie. At first, his meticulously shaved head and ornate chestnut robes, as well as the exotic trapping of the *dokuan* room, make him seem vaguely Asian, but he is not, and once you look closely, the fact is obvious. He is a large man, tall and big-shouldered, American, and I spend a moment ruminating as to whether he looks more like the actor Telly Savalas or the actor Ernest Borgnine.

He smiles a very warm, very sleepy, amused smile, and I wonder if he's reading my mind.

"Do you have a question?" he asks.

I spit out what I have silently rehearsed: "How do I diligently pursue what Zen has to offer, without grasping?"

It seems like a dumb question before it is even off my lips.

"Just sit." He smiles with his eyes, then nods.

The response seems too simple, so I repeat the question, trying somewhat different words but asking essentially the same thing. "How can I be deliberate about seeking Buddhism and yet not be too attached?"

"Practice is enlightenment," Daido answers this time. "Enlightenment is practice. Just sit."

He flashes his beatific smile again. Though I am trying, he is fairly hard not to like. When I attempt to ask the same question a third time, however, he shakes his head and rings the bell—the signal that the face-to-face teaching is over, for me at least.

I spring up, still unsure how many bows I am supposed to do, but no matter—despite all our preparation, he isn't watching.

Practice makes perfect. Is that it? Is that my message from the Buddha-heir?

In Zen, it begins to seem, simplicity is profundity. That is a hard concept for someone like me to accept, though. Perhaps I have seen too many *New Yorker* cartoons about going to the mountaintop and learning the meaning of life from the meditating mystic. I thought Daido-shi would say something profound.

He probably has.

Our final lunch, oddly enough, is spaghetti with meat sauce. But this is an *American* Buddhist monastery, so why not?

Harold does not sit with the rest of us at the newcomers' table.

He is across the room, at a table dominated by monks and long-term monastery residents. Perhaps he is offering to teach them a thing or two.

And perhaps he is the reason I must come back.

It occurs to me that I have focused far too much on my snoring, limping, bragging nemesis this weekend, and not enough on myself. Whatever brought me here, whatever precipitated my brief spiritual foray, that ball of dissatisfaction that has lingered on since Brother Damien called me a rock, is probably all tied up with this—with my critical Monkey Mind voice, and my facility for blaming everyone else.

Before I can wonder any more about that, lunch is ended, we rinse our dishes, and my first Zen Retreat weekend is unceremoniously brought to a halt. There is nothing to do but drive home.

Just sit, Daido-shi told me.

For the next six hours, I do, because I am stuck behind the wheel of my car. I sit and wonder.

What would Brother Damien say?

seeing

—◇—

from
PILGRIM AT TINKER CREEK
by Annie Dillard

Annie Dillard (born 1945) was in her late twenties when she went to live near Tinker Creek. She spent her time reading and walking—trying hard to observe and experience the raw facts of the world that surrounded her. Early in her book about the sojourn, Dillard describes the experience of a young patient's visit to a garden after her sight is restored: "She is greatly astonished . . . stands speechless in front of the tree, which she only names after taking hold of it, as the tree with the lights in it.'"

—◇—

C atch it if you can.

It is early March. I am dazed from a long day of interstate driving homeward; I pull in at a gas station in Nowhere, Virginia, north of Lexington. The young boy in charge ("Chick 'at oll?") is offering a free cup of coffee with every gas purchase. We talk in the glass-walled office while my coffee cools enough to drink. He tells me, among other things, that the rival gas station down the road, whose FREE COFFEE sign is visible from the interstate, charges you fifteen cents if you want your coffee in a Styrofoam cup, as opposed, I guess, to your bare hands.

All the time we talk, the boy's new beagle puppy is skidding around the office, sniffing impartially at my shoes and at the wire rack of folded maps. The cheerful human conversation wakes me, recalls me, not to a normal consciousness, but to a kind of energetic readiness. I step outside, followed by the puppy.

I am absolutely alone. There are no other customers. The road vacant, the interstate is out of sight and earshot. I have hazarded into a new corner of the world, an unknown spot, a Brigadoon. Before me extends a low hill trembling in yellow brome, and behind the hill, filling the sky, rises an enormous mountain ridge, forested, alive and awesome with brilliant blown lights. I have never seen anything so tremulous and live. Overhead, great strips and chunks of cloud dash to the northwest in a gold rush. At my back the sun is setting—how can I not have noticed before that the sun is setting? My mind has been a blank slab of black asphalt for hours, but that doesn't stop the sun's wild wheel. I set my coffee beside me on the curb; I smell loam on the wind; I pat the puppy; I watch the mountain.

My hand works automatically over the puppy's fur, following the line of hair under his ears, down his neck, inside his forelegs, along his hot-skinned belly.

Shadows lope along the mountain's rumpled flanks; they elongate like root tips, like lobes of spilling water, faster and faster. A warm purple pigment pools in each ruck and tuck of the rock; it deepens and spreads, boring crevasses, canyons. As the purple vaults and slides, it tricks out the unleafed forest and rumpled rock in gilt, in shape-shifting patches of glow. These gold lights veer and retract, shatter and glide in a series of dazzling splashes, shrinking, leaking, exploding. The ridge's bosses and hummocks sprout bulging from its side; the whole mountain looms miles closer; the light warms and reddens; the bare forest folds and pleats itself like living protoplasm before my eyes, like a running chart, a wildly scrawling oscillograph on the present moment. The air cools; the puppy's skin is hot. I am more alive than all the world.

This is it, I think, this is it, right now, the present, this empty gas station, here, this western wind, this tang of coffee on the tongue, and I am patting the puppy, I am watching the mountain.

And the second I verbalize this awareness in my brain, I cease to see the mountain or feel the puppy. I am opaque, so much black asphalt. But at the same second, the second I know I've lost it, I also realize that the puppy is still squirming on his back under my hand. Nothing has changed for him. He draws his legs down to stretch the skin taut so he feels every fingertip's stroke along his furred and arching side, his flank, his flung-back throat.

I sip my coffee. I look at the mountain, which is still doing its tricks, as you look at a still-beautiful face belonging to a person who was once your lover in another country years ago: with fond nostalgia, and recognition, but no real feeling save a secret astonishment that you are now strangers. Thanks. For the memories. It is ironic that the one thing that all religions recognize as separating us from our creator—our very self-consciousness—is also the one thing that divides us from our fellow creatures. It was a bitter birthday present from evolution, cutting us off at both ends. I get in the car and drive home.

Catch it if you can. The present is an invisible electron; its lightning path traced faintly on a blackened screen is fleet, and fleeing, and gone.

That I ended this experience prematurely for myself—that I drew scales over my eyes between me and the mountain and gloved my hand between me and the puppy—is not the only point. After all, it would have ended anyway. I've never seen a sunset or felt a wind that didn't. The levitating saints came down at last, and their two feet bore real weight. No, the point is that not only does time fly and do we die, but that in these reckless conditions we live at all, and are vouchsafed, for the duration of certain inexplicable moments, to know it.

Stephen Graham startled me by describing this same gift in his antique and elegant book, *The Gentle Art of Tramping.* He wrote, "And as you sit on the hillside, or lie prone under the trees of the forest, or sprawl wet-legged on the shingly beach of a mountain stream, the great door, that does not look like a door, opens." That great door opens on the present, illuminates it as with a multitude of flashing torches.

I had thought, because I had seen the tree with the lights in it, that the great door, by definition, opens on eternity. Now that I have "patted the puppy"— now that I have experienced the present purely through my senses—I discover that, although the door to the tree with the lights in it was opened *from* eternity, as it were, and shone on that tree eternal lights, it nevertheless opened on the real and present cedar. It opened on time: Where else? That Christ's incarnation occurred improbably, ridiculously, at such-and-such a time, into such-and-such a place, is referred to—with great sincerity even among believers—as "the scandal of particularity." Well, the "scandal of particularity" is the only world that I, in particular, know. What use has eternity for light? We're all up to our necks in this particular scandal. Why, we might as well ask, not a plane tree, instead of a bo? I never saw a tree that was no tree in particular; I never met a man, not the greatest theologian, who filled infinity, or even whose hand, say, was undifferentiated, fingerless, like a griddlecake, and not lobed and split just so with the incursions of time.

I don't want to stress this too much. Seeing the tree with the lights in it was an experience vastly different in quality as well as in import from patting the puppy. On that cedar tree shone, however briefly, the steady, inward flames of eternity; across the mountain by the gas station raced the familiar flames of the falling sun. But on both occasions I thought, with rising exultation, this is it; this is it; praise the lord; praise the land. Experiencing the present purely is being emptied and hollow; you catch grace as a man fills his cup under a waterfall.

Consciousness itself does not hinder living in the present. In fact, it is only to a heightened awareness that the great door to the present opens at all. Even a certain amount of interior verbalization is helpful to enforce the memory of whatever it is that is taking place. The gas station beagle puppy, after all, may have experienced those same moments more purely than I did, but he brought fewer instruments to bear on the same material, he had no data for comparison, and he profited only in the grossest of ways, by having an assortment of itches scratched.

Self-consciousness, however, does hinder the experience of the present. It is the one instrument that unplugs all the rest. So long as I lose myself in a tree, say, I can scent its leafy breath or estimate its board feet of lumber, I can draw its fruits or boil tea on its branches, and the tree stays tree. But the second I become aware of myself at any of these activities—looking over my own shoulder, as it were—the tree vanishes, uprooted from the spot and flung out of sight as if it had never grown. And time, which had flowed down into the tree bearing new revelations like floating leaves at every moment, ceases. It dams, stills, stagnates.

Self-consciousness is the curse of the city and all that sophistication implies. It is the glimpse of oneself in a storefront window, the unbidden awareness of reactions on the faces of other people—the novelist's world, not the poet's. I've lived there. I remember what the city has to offer: human companionship, major-league baseball, and a clatter of quickening stimulus like a rush from strong drugs that leaves you drained. I remember how you bide your time in the city, and think, if you stop to think, "next year . . . I'll start living; next year . . . I'll start my life." Innocence is a better world.

Innocence sees that this is it, and finds it world enough, and time. Innocence is not the prerogative of infants and puppies; and far less of mountains and fixed stars, which have no prerogatives at all. It is not lost to us; the world is a better place than that. Like any other of the spirit's good gifts, it is there if you want it, free for the asking, as has been stressed by stronger words than mine. It is possible to pursue innocence as hounds pursue hares: single-mindedly, driven by a kind of love, crashing over creeks, keening and lost in fields and forests, circling, vaulting over hedges and hills wide-eyed, giving loud tongue all unawares to the deepest, most incomprehensible longing, a root-flame in the heart, and that warbling chorus resounding back from the mountains, hurling itself from ridge to ridge over the valley, now faint, now clear, ringing the air through which the hounds tear, open-mouthed, the echoes of their own wails dimly knocking in their lungs.

What I call innocence is the spirit's unself-conscious state at any moment of pure devotion to any object. It is at once a receptiveness and total concentration. One needn't be, shouldn't be, reduced to a puppy. If you wish to tell me that the city offers galleries, I'll pour you a drink and enjoy your company while it lasts; but I'll bear with me to my grave those pure moments at the Tate (was it the Tate?) where I stood planted, open-mouthed, born, before that one particular canvas, that river, up to my neck, gasping, lost, receding into watercolor depth and depth to the vanishing point, buoyant, awed, and had to be literally hauled away. These are our few live seasons. Let us live them as purely as we can, in the present.

The color-patches of vision part, shift, and reform as I move through space in time. The present is the object of vision, and what I see before me at any given second is a full field of color-patches scattered just so. The configuration will never be repeated. Living is moving; time is a live creek bearing changing lights. As I move, or as the world moves around me, the fullness of what I see shatters. This second of shattering is an *augenblick,* a particular configuration, a slant of light shot in the open eye. Goethe's Faust risks all if he should cry to the moment, the *augenblick,* "Verweile doch!" "Last forever!" Who hasn't prayed that prayer? But the *augenblick* isn't going to *verweile.* You were lucky to get it in the first place. The present is a freely given canvas. That it is constantly being ripped apart and washed downstream goes without saying; it is a canvas, nevertheless.

I like the slants of light; I'm a collector. That's a good one, I say, that bit of bank there, the snakeskin and the aquarium, that patch of light from the creek on bark. Sometimes I spread my fingers into a viewfinder; more often I peek through a tiny square or rectangle—a frame of shadow—formed by the tips of index fingers and thumbs held directly before my eye. Speaking of the development of *papier collé* in late Cubism, Picasso said, "We tried to get rid of *trompe-l'oeil* to find a *trompe-l'esprit.*" Trompe-l'esprit! I don't know why the world didn't latch on to the phrase. Our whole life is a stroll—or a forced march—through a gallery hung in trompes-l'esprit.

Once I visited a great university and wandered, a stranger, into the subterranean halls of its famous biology department. I saw a sign on a door: ichthyology department. The door was open a crack, and as I walked past I glanced in. I saw just a flash. There were two white-coated men seated opposite each other on high lab stools at a hard-surfaced table. They bent over identical white enamel trays. On one side, one man, with a lancet, was just cutting into an enormous preserved fish he'd taken from a jar. On the other side, the other man, with a silver spoon, was eating a grapefruit. I laughed all the way back to Virginia.

Michael Goldman wrote in a poem, "When the Muse comes She doesn't tell you to write;/ She says get up for a minute, I've something to show you, stand here." What made me look up at that roadside tree?

The road to Grundy, Virginia, is, as you might expect, a narrow scrawl scribbled all over the most improbably peaked and hunched mountains you ever saw. The few people who live along the road also seem peaked and hunched. But what on earth—? It was hot, sunny summer. The road was just bending off sharply to the right. I hadn't seen a house in miles, and none was in sight. At the apogee of the road's curve grew an enormous oak, a massive bur oak two hundred years old, one hundred and fifty feet high, an oak whose lowest limb was beyond the span of the highest ladder. I looked up: there were clothes spread all over the tree. Red shirts, blue trousers, black pants, little baby smocks—they weren't hung from branches. They were outside, carefully spread, splayed as if to dry, on the outer leaves of the great oak's crown. Were there pillowcases, blankets? I can't remember. There was a gay assortment of cotton underwear, yellow dresses, children's green sweaters, plaid skirts. . . . You know roads. A bend comes and you take it, thoughtlessly, moving on. I looked behind me for another split second, astonished; both sides of the tree's canopy, clear to the top, bore clothes. Trompe!

But there is more to the present than a series of snapshots. We are not merely sensitized film; we have feelings, a memory for information and an eidetic memory for the imagery of our own pasts.

Our layered consciousness is a tiered track for an unmatched assortment of concentrically wound reels. Each one plays out for all of life its dazzle and blur of translucent shadow-pictures; each one .hums at every moment its own secret melody in its own unique key. We tune in and out. But, moments are not lost. Time out of mind is time nevertheless, cumulative, informing the present. From even the deepest slumber you wake with a jolt—older, closer to death, and wiser, grateful for breath. You quit your seat in a darkened movie theatre, walk past the empty lobby, out the double glass doors, and step like Orpheus into the street. And the cumulative force of the present you've forgotten sets you reeling, staggering, as if you'd been struck broadside by a plank. It all floods back to you. Yes, you say, as if you'd been asleep a hundred years, this is it, this is the real weather, the lavender light fading, the full moisture in your lungs, the heat from the pavement on your lips and palms—not the dry orange dust from horses' hooves, the salt sea, the sour Coke—but this solid air, the blood pumping up your thighs again, your fingers alive. And on the way home you drive exhilarated, energized, under scented, silhouetted trees.

I am sitting under a sycamore by Tinker Creek. It is early spring, the day after I patted the puppy. I have come to the creek—the backyard stretch of the creek—in the middle of the day, to feel the delicate gathering of heat, real sun's heat, in the air, and to watch new water come down the creek. Don't expect more than this, and a mental ramble. I'm in the market for some present tense; I'm on the lookout, shopping around, more so every year. It's a seller's market—do you think I won't sell all that I have to buy it? Thomas Merton wrote, in a light passage in one of his Gethsemane journals: "Suggested emendation in the Lord's Prayer: Take out 'Thy Kingdom come' and substitute 'Give us time!'" But time is the one thing we have been given, and we have been given to time. Time gives us a whirl. We keep waking from a dream we can't recall, looking around in surprise, and lapsing back, for years on end. All I want to do is stay awake, keep my head up, prop my eyes open, with toothpicks, with trees.

Before me the creek is seventeen feet wide, splashing over random sandstone outcroppings and scattered rocks. I'm lucky; the creek is loud here, because of the rocks, and wild. In the low water of summer and fall I can cross to the opposite bank by leaping from stone to stone. Upstream is a wall of light split into planks by smooth sandstone ledges that cross the creek evenly, like steps. Downstream the live water before me stills, dies suddenly as if extinguished, and vanishes around a bend shaded summer and winter by overarching tulips, locusts, and Osage orange. Everywhere I look are creekside trees whose ascending boles against water and grass accent the vertical thrust of the land in this spot. The creek rests the eye, a haven, a breast; the two steep banks vault from the creek like wings. Not even the sycamore's crown can peek over the land in any direction.

My friend Rosanne Coggeshall, the poet, says that "sycamore" is the most intrinsically beautiful word in English. This sycamore is old; its lower bark is always dusty from years of floodwaters lapping up its trunk. Like many sycamores, too, it is quirky, given to flights and excursions. Its trunk lists over the creek at a dizzying angle, and from that trunk extends a long, skinny limb that spurts high over the opposite bank without branching. The creek reflects the speckled surface of this limb, pale even against the highest clouds, and that image pales whiter and thins as it crosses the creek, shatters in the riffles and melds together, quivering and mottled, like some enormous primeval reptile under the water.

I want to think about trees. Trees have a curious relationship to the subject of the present moment. There are many created things in the universe that outlive us, that outlive the sun, even, but I can't think about them. I live with trees. There are creatures under our feet, creatures that live over our heads, but trees live quite convincingly in the same filament of air we inhabit, and, in addition, they extend impressively in both directions, up and down, shearing rock and fanning air, doing their real business just out of reach. A blind man's idea of hugeness is a tree. They have their sturdy bodies and special skills; they garner fresh water; they abide. This sycamore above me, below me, by Tinker Creek, is a case in point; the sight of it crowds my brain with an assortment of diverting thoughts, all as present to me as these slivers of pressure from grass on my elbow's skin. I want to come at the subject of the present by showing how consciousness dashes and ambles around the labyrinthine tracks of the mind, returning again and again, however briefly, to the senses: "If there were but one erect and solid standing tree in the woods, all creatures would go to rub against it and make sure of their footing." But so long as I stay in my thoughts, my foot slides under trees; I fall, or I dance.

Sycamores are among the last trees to go into leaf; in the fall, they are the first to shed. They make sweet food in green broadleaves for a while—leaves wide as plates—and then go wild and wave their long white arms. In ancient Rome men honored the sycamore—in the form of its cousin, the Oriental plane—by watering its roots with wine. Xerxes, I read, "halted his unwieldly army for days that he might contemplate to his satisfaction" the beauty of a single sycamore.

You are Xerxes in Persia. Your army spreads on a vast and arid peneplain . . . you call to you all your sad captains, and give the order to halt. You have seen the tree with the lights in it, haven't you? You must have. Xerxes buffeted on a plain, ambition drained in a puff. That fusillade halts any army in its tracks. Your men are bewildered; they lean on their spears, sucking the rinds of gourds. There is nothing to catch the eye in this flatness, nothing but a hollow, hammering sky, a waste of sedge in the lee of windblown rocks, a meagre ribbon of scrub willow tracing a slumbering watercourse . . . and that sycamore. You saw it; you still stand rapt and mute, exalted, remembering or not remembering over a period of days to shade your head with your robe.

"He had its form wrought upon a medal of gold to help him remember it the rest of his life." Your teeth are chattering; it is just before dawn and you have started briefly from your daze. "Goldsmith!" The goldsmith is sodden with sleep, surly. He lights his forge, he unrolls the dusty cotton wrapping from his half-forgotten stylus and tongs, he waits for the sun. We all ought to have a goldsmith following us around. But it goes without saying, doesn't it, Xerxes, that no gold medal worn around your neck will bring back the glad hour; keep those lights kindled so long as you live, forever present? Pascal saw it. He grabbed pen and paper; he managed to scrawl the one word, FEU; he wore that scrap of paper sewn in his shirt the rest of his life. I don't know what Pascal saw. I saw a cedar. Xerxes saw a sycamore.

These trees stir me. The past inserts a finger into a slit in the skin of the present, and pulls. I remember how sycamores grew— and presumably still grow—in the city, in Pittsburgh, even along the busiest streets. I used to spend hours in the backyard, thinking God knows what, and peeling the mottled bark of a sycamore, idly, littering the grass with dried lappets and strips, leaving the tree's trunk at eye level moist, thin-skinned and yellow—until someone would catch me at it from the kitchen window, and I would awake, and look at my work in astonishment, and think oh no, this time I've killed the sycamore for sure.

Here in Virginia the trees reach enormous proportions, especially in the lowlands on banksides. It is hard to understand how the same tree could thrive both choking along Pittsburgh's Penn Avenue and slogging knee-deep in Tinker Creek. Of course, come to think of it, I've done the same thing myself. Because a sycamore's primitive bark is not elastic but frangible, it sheds continuously as it grows; seen from a distance, a sycamore seems to grow in pallor and vulnerability as it grows in height; the bare uppermost branches are white against the sky.

The sky is deep and distant, laced with sycamore limbs like a hatching of crossed swords. I can scarcely see it; I'm not looking. I don't come to the creek for sky unmediated, but for shelter. My back rests on a steep bank under the sycamore; before me shines the creek—the creek which is about all the light I can stand—and beyond it rises the other bank, also steep, and planted in trees.

I have never understood why so many mystics of all creeds experience the presence of God on mountaintops. Aren't they afraid of being blown away? God said to Moses on Sinai that even the priests, who have access to the Lord, must hallow themselves, for fear that the Lord may break out against them. This is *the* fear. It often feels best to lay low, inconspicuous, instead of waving your spirit around from high places like a lightning rod. For if God is in one sense the igniter, a fireball that spins over the ground of continents, God is also in another sense the destroyer, lightning, blind power, impartial as the atmosphere. Or God is one "G." You get a comforting sense, in a curved, hollow place, of being vulnerable to only a relatively narrow column of God as air.

In the open, anything might happen. Dorothy Dunnett, the great medievalist, states categorically: "There is no reply, in clear terrain, to an archer in cover." Any copperhead anywhere is an archer in cover; how much more so is God! Invisibility is the all-time great "cover"; and that the one infinite power deals so extravagantly and unfathomably in death—death morning, noon, and night, all manner of death—makes that power an archer, there is no getting around it. And we the people are so vulnerable. Our bodies are shot with mortality. Our legs are fear and our arms are time. These chill humors seep through our capillaries, weighting each cell with an icy dab of nonbeing, and that dab grows and swells and sucks the cell dry. That is why physical courage is so important—it fills, as it were, the holes—and why it is so invigorating. The least brave act, chance taken and passage won, makes you feel loud as a child.

But it gets harder. The courage of children and beasts is a function of innocence. We let our bodies go the way of our fears. A teen-aged boy, king of the world, will spend weeks in front of a mirror perfecting some difficult trick with a lighter, a muscle, a tennis ball, a coin. Why do we lose interest in physical mastery? If I feel like turning cartwheels—and I do—why don't I learn to turn cartwheels, instead of regretting that I never learned as a child? We could all be aerialists like squirrels, divers like seals; we could be purely patient, perfectly fleet, walking on our hands even, if our living or stature required it. We can't even sit straight, or support our weary heads.

When we lose our innocence—when we start feeling the weight of the atmosphere and learn that there's death in the pot—we take leave of our senses. Only children can hear the song of the male house mouse. Only children keep their eyes open. The only thing they *have* got is sense; they have highly developed "input systems," admitting all data indiscriminately. Matt Spireng has collected thousands of arrowheads and spearheads; he says that if you really want to find arrowheads, you must walk with a child—a child will pick up *everything*. All my adult life I have wished to see the cemented case of a caddisfly larva. It took Sally Moore, the young daughter of friends, to find one on the pebbled bottom of a shallow stream on whose bank we sat side by side. "What's this?" she asked. That, I wanted to say as I recognized the prize she held, is a memento mori for people who read too much.

Annie Dillard

• • •

We found other caddisfly cases that day, Sally and I, after I had learned to focus so fine, and I saved one. It is a hollow cylinder three quarters of an inch long, a little masterpiece of masonry consisting entirely of cemented grains of coarse sand only one layer thick. Some of the sand grains are red, and it was by searching for this red that I learned to spot the cases. The caddisfly larva will use any bits it can find to fashion its house; in fact, entomologists have amused themselves by placing a naked larva in an aquarium furnished only with, say, red sand. When the larva has laid around its body several rows of red sand, the entomologist transfers it to another aquarium in which only white bits are available. The larva busily adds rows of white to the red wall, and then here comes the entomologist again, with a third and final aquarium full of blue sand. At any rate, the point I want to make is that this tiny immature creature responds to an instinct to put something between its flesh and a jagged world. If you give a "masonry mosaic" kind of caddisfly larva only large decayed leaves, that larva, confronted by something utterly novel, will nevertheless bite the leaves into shreds and rig those shreds into a case.

The general rule in nature is that live things are soft within and rigid without. We vertebrates are living dangerously, and we vertebrates are positively piteous, like so many peeled trees. This oft was thought, but ne'er so well expressed as by Pliny, who writes of nature, "To all the rest, given she hath sufficient to clad them everyone according to their kind: as namely, shells, cods, hard hides, pricks, shags, bristles, hair, down feathers, quills, scales, and fleeces of wool. The very trunks and stems of trees and plants, she hath defended with bark and rind, yea and the same sometimes double, against the injuries both of heat and cold: man alone, poor wretch, she hath laid all naked upon the bare earth, even on

44

his birthday, to cry and wraule presently from the very first hour that he is born into the world."

I am sitting under a sycamore tree: I am soft-shell and peeled to the least puff of wind or smack of grit. The present of our life looks different under trees. Trees have dominion. I never killed that backyard sycamore; even its frailest inner bark was a shield. Trees do not accumulate life, but deadwood, like a thickening coat of mail. Their odds actually improve as they age. Some trees, like giant sequoias, are, practically speaking, immortal, vulnerable only to another ice age. They are not even susceptible to fire. Sequoia wood barely burns, and the bark is "nearly as fireproof as asbestos. The top of one sequoia, struck by lightning a few years ago during a July thunderstorm, smoldered quietly, without apparently damaging the tree, until it was put out by a snowstorm in October." Some trees sink taproots to rock; some spread wide mats of roots clutching at acres. They will not be blown. We run around under these obelisk-creatures, teetering on our soft, small feet. We are out on a jaunt, picnicking, fattening like puppies for our deaths. Shall I carve a name on this trunk? What if *I* fell in a forest: Would a tree hear?

I am sitting under a bankside sycamore; my mind is a slope. Arthur Koestler wrote, "In his review of the literature on the psychological present, Woodrow found that its maximum span is estimated to lie between 2.3 and 12 seconds." How did anyone measure that slide? As soon as you are conscious of it, it is gone. I repeat a phrase: the thin tops of mountains. Soon the thin tops of mountains erupt, as if volcanically, from my brain's core. I can see them; they are, surprisingly, serrate—scallopped like the blade of a kitchen knife—and brown as leaves. The serrated edges are so thin they are translucent; through the top of one side of the brown ridge I can see, in silhouette, a circling sharp-shinned hawk;

through another, deep tenuous veins of metallic ore. This isn't Tinker Creek. Where do I live, anyway? I lose myself, I float. . . . I am in Persia, trying to order a watermelon in German. It's insane. The engineer has abandoned the control room, and an idiot is splicing the reels. What could I contribute to the "literature on the psychological present"? If I could remember to press the knob on the stopwatch, I wouldn't be in Persia. Before they invented the unit of the second, people used to time the lapse of short events on their pulses. Oh, but what about that heave in the wrist when I saw the tree with the lights in it, and my heart ceased, but I am still there?

Scenes drift across the screen from nowhere. I can never discover the connection between any one scene and what I am more consciously thinking, nor can I ever conjure the scene back in full vividness. It is like a ghost, in full-dress regalia, that wafts across the stage set unnoticed by the principle characters. It appears complete, in full color, wordless, though already receding: the tennis courts on Fifth Avenue in Pittsburgh, an equestrian statue in a Washington park, a basement dress shop in New York city—scenes that I thought meant nothing to me. These aren't still shots; the camera is always moving. And the scene is always just slipping out of sight, as if in spite of myself I were always just descending a hill, rounding a corner, stepping into the street with a companion who urges me on, while I look back over my shoulder at the sight which recedes, vanishes. The present of my consciousness is itself a mystery which is also always just rounding a bend like a floating branch borne by a flood. Where am I? But I'm not. "I will overturn, overturn, overturn, it: and it shall be no more. . . .

. . .

from Pilgrim at Tinker Creek

All right then. Pull yourself together. Is this where I'm spending my life, in the "reptile brain," this lamp at the top of the spine like a lighthouse flipping mad beams indiscriminately into the darkness, into the furred thoraxes of moths, onto the backs of leaping fishes and the wrecks of schooners? Come up a level; surface.

I am sitting under a sycamore by Tinker Creek. I am really here, alive on the intricate earth under trees. But under me, directly under the weight of my body on the grass, are other creatures, just as real, for whom also this moment, this tree, is "it." Take just the top inch of soil, the world squirming right under my palms. In the top inch of forest soil, biologists found "an average of 1,356 living creatures present in each square foot, including 865 mites, 265 springtails, 22 millipedes, 19 adult beetles and various numbers of 12 other forms. . . . Had an estimate also been made of the microscopic population, it might have ranged up to two billion bacteria and many millions of fungi, protozoa and algae—in a mere *teaspoonful* of soil." The chrysalids of butterflies linger here too, folded, rigid, and dreamless. I might as well include these creatures in this moment, as best I can. My ignoring them won't strip them of their reality, and admitting them, one by one, into my consciousness might heighten mine, might add their dim awareness to my human consciousness, such as it is, and set up a buzz, a vibration like the beating ripples a submerged muskrat makes on the water, from this particular moment, this tree. Hasidism has a tradition that one of man's purposes is to assist God in the work of redemption by "hallowing" the things of creation. By a tremendous heave of his spirit, the devout man frees the divine sparks trapped in the mute things of time; he uplifts the forms and moments of creation, bearing them aloft into that rare air and hallowing fire in which all clays must shatter and burst. Keeping the subsoil world under trees in mind, in intelligence, is the *least* I can do.

Earthworms in staggering processions lurch through the grit underfoot, gobbling downed leaves and spewing forth castings by the ton. Moles mine intricate tunnels in networks; there are often so many of these mole tunnels here by the creek that when I walk, every step is a letdown. A mole is almost entirely loose inside its skin, and enormously mighty. If you can catch a mole, it will, in addition to biting you memorably, leap from your hand in a single convulsive contraction and be gone as soon as you have it. You are never really able to see it; you only feel its surge and thrust against your palm, as if you held a beating heart in a paper bag. What could I not do if I had the power and will of a mole! But the mole churns earth.

Last summer some muskrats had a den under this tree's roots on the bank; I think they are still there now. Muskrats' wet fur rounds the domed clay walls of the den and slicks them smooth as any igloo. They strew the floor with plant husks and seeds, rut in repeated bursts, and sleep humped and soaking, huddled in balls. These, too, are part of what Buber calls "the infinite ethos of the moment."

I am not here yet; I can't shake that day on the interstate. My mind branches and shoots like a tree.

Under my spine, the sycamore roots suck watery salts. Root tips thrust and squirm between particles of soil, probing minutely; from their roving, burgeoning tissues spring infinitesimal root hairs, transparent and hollow, which affix themselves to specks of grit and sip. These runnels run silent and deep; the whole earth trembles, rent and fissured, hurled and drained. I wonder what happens to root systems when trees die. Do those spread blind networks starve, starve in the midst of plenty, and dessicate, clawing at specks?

from Pilgrim at Tinker Creek

Under the world's conifers—under the creekside cedar behind where I sit—a mantle of fungus wraps the soil in a weft, shooting out blind thread after frail thread of palest dissolved white. From root tip to root tip, root hair to root hair, these filaments loop and wind; the thought of them always reminds me of Rimbaud's "I have stretched cords from steeple to steeple, garlands from window to window, chains of gold from star to star, and I dance." King David leaped and danced naked before the ark of the Lord in a barren desert. Here the very looped soil is an intricate throng of praise. Make connections; let rip; and dance where you can.

The insects and earthworms, moles, muskrats, roots and fungal strands are not all. An even frailer, dimmer movement, a pavane, is being performed deep under me now. The nymphs of cicadas are alive. You see their split skins, an inch long, brown, and translucent, curved and segmented like shrimp, stuck arching on the trunks of trees. And you see the adults occasionally, large and sturdy, with glittering black and green bodies, veined transparent wings folded over their backs, and artificial-looking, bright red eyes. But you never see the living nymphs. They are underground, clasping roots and sucking the sweet sap of trees.

In the South, the periodical cicada has a breeding cycle of thirteen years, instead of seventeen years as in the North. That a live creature spends thirteen consecutive years scrabbling around in the root systems of trees in the dark and damp—thirteen years! —is amply boggling for me. Four more years—or four less—wouldn't alter the picture a jot. In the dark of an April night the nymphs emerge, all at once, as many as eighty-four of them digging into the air from every square foot of ground. They inch up trees and bushes, shed their skins, and begin that hollow, shrill grind that lasts all summer. I guess as nymphs they never see the sun. Adults lay eggs in slits along twig bark; the hatched nymphs drop to the ground and burrow, vanish from the face of the earth, biding their time, for thirteen years. How many are under me now, wishing what? What would I think about for thirteen years? They curl, crawl, clutch at roots and suck, suck blinded, suck trees, rain or shine, heat or frost, year after groping year.

And under the cicadas, deeper down than the longest taproot, between and beneath the rounded black rocks and slanting slabs of sandstone in the earth, ground water is creeping. Ground water seeps and slides, across and down, across and down, leaking from here to there minutely, at the rate of a mile a year. What a tug of waters goes on! There are flings and pulls in every direction at every moment. The world is a wild wrestle under the grass: earth shall be moved.

What else is going on right this minute while ground water creeps under my feet? The galaxy is careening in a slow, muffled widening. If a million solar systems are born every hour, then surely hundreds burst into being as I shift my weight to the other elbow. The sun's surface is now exploding; other stars implode and vanish, heavy and black, out of sight. Meteorites are arcing to earth invisibly all day long. On the planet the winds are blowing: the polar easterlies, the westerlies, the northeast and southeast trades. Somewhere, someone under full sail is becalmed, in the horse latitudes, in the doldrums; in the northland, a trapper is maddened, crazed, by the eerie scent of the chinook, the snoweater, a wind that can melt two feet of snow in a day. The pampero blows, and the tramontane, and the Boro, sirocco, levanter, mistral. Lick a finger: feel the now.

Spring is seeping north, towards me and away from me, at sixteen miles a day. Caribou straggle across the tundra from the spruce-fir forests of the south, first the pregnant does, hurried, then the old and unmated does, then suddenly a massing of bucks, and finally the diseased and injured, one by one. Somewhere, people in airplanes are watching the sun set and peering down at clustered houselights, stricken. In the montana in Peru, on the rain-forested slopes of the Andes, a woman kneels in a dust clearing before a dark shelter of overlapping broadleaves; between her breasts hangs a cross of smooth sticks she peeled with her teeth and lashed with twistings of vine. Along estuary banks of tidal rivers all over the world, snails in black clusters like currants are gliding up and down the stems of reed and sedge, migrating every moment with the dip and swing of tides. Behind me, Tinker Mountain, and to my left, Dead Man Mountain, are eroding one thousandth of an inch a year.

The tomcat that used to wake me is dead; he was long since grist for an earthworm's casting, and is now the clear sap of a Pittsburgh sycamore, or the honeydew of aphids sucked from that sycamore's high twigs and sprayed in sticky drops on a stranger's car. A steer across the road stumbles into the creek to drink; he blinks; he laps; a floating leaf in the current catches against his hock and wrenches away. The giant water bug I saw is dead, long dead, and its moist gut and rigid casing are both, like the empty skin of the frog it sucked, dissolved, spread, still spreading right now, in the steer's capillaries, in the windblown smatter of clouds overhead, in the Sargasso Sea. The mockingbird that dropped furled from a roof . . . but this is no time to count my dead. That is nightwork. The dead are staring, underground, their sleeping heels in the air.

The sharks I saw are roving up and down the coast. If the sharks cease roving, if they still their twist and rest for a moment, they die. They need new water pushed into their gills; they need dance. Somewhere east of me, on another continent, it is sunset, and starlings in breathtaking bands are winding high in the sky to their evening roost. Under the water just around the bend downstream, the coot feels with its foot in the creek, rolling its round red eyes. In the house a spider slumbers at her wheel like a spinster curled in a corner all day long. The mantis egg cases are tied to the mock-orange hedge; within each case, within each egg, cells elongate, narrow, and split; cells bubble and curve inward, align, harden or hollow or stretch. The Polyphemus moth, its wings crushed to its back, crawls down the driveway, crawls down the driveway, crawls. . . . The snake whose skin I tossed away, whose homemade, personal skin is now tangled at the county dump—that snake in the woods by the quarry stirs now, quickens now, prodded under the leafmold by sunlight, by the probing root of May apple, the bud of bloodroot. And where are you now?

I stand. All the blood in my body crashes to my feet and instantly heaves to my head, so I blind and blush, as a tree blasts into leaf spouting water hurled up from roots. What happens to me? I stand before the sycamore dazed; I gaze at its giant trunk.

Big trees stir memories. You stand in their dimness, where the very light is blue, staring unfocused at the thickest part of the trunk as though it were a long, dim tunnel—: the Squirrel Hill tunnel. You're gone. The egg-shaped patch of light at the end of the blackened tunnel swells and looms; the sing of tire tread over brick reaches an ear-splitting crescendo; the light breaks over the hood, smack, and full on your face. You have achieved the past.

Eskimo shamans bound with sealskin thongs on the igloo floor used to leave their bodies, their skins, and swim "muscle-naked" like a flensed seal through the rock of continents, in order to pla-

from Pilgrim at Tinker Creek

cate an old woman who lived on the sea floor and sent or withheld game. When he fulfilled this excruciating mission, the Eskimo shaman would awake, returned to his skin exhausted from the dark ardors of flailing peeled through rock, and find himself in a lighted igloo, at a sort of party, among dear faces.

In the same way, having bored through a sycamore trunk and tunneled beneath a Pennsylvania mountain, I blink, awed by the yellow light, and find myself in a shady side of town, in a stripped dining room, dancing, years ago. There is a din of trumpets, upbeat and indistinct, like some movie score for a love scene played on a city balcony; there is an immeasurably distant light glowing from half-remembered faces. . . . I stir. The heave of my shoulders returns me to the present, to the tree, the sycamore, and I yank myself away, shove off and moving, seeking live water.

Live water heals memories. I look up the creek and here it comes, the future, being borne aloft as on a winding succession of laden trays. You may wake and look from the window and breathe the real air, and say, with satisfaction or with longing, "This is it." But if you look up the creek, if you look up the creek in any weather, your spirit fills, and you are saying, with an exulting rise of the lungs, "Here it comes!"

Here it comes. In the far distance I can see the concrete bridge where the road crosses the creek. Under that bridge and beyond it the water is flat and silent, blued by distance and stilled by depth. It is so much sky, a fallen shred caught in the cleft of banks. But it pours. The channel here is straight as an arrow; grace itself is an archer. Between the dangling wands of bankside willows, beneath the overarching limbs of tulip, walnut, and Osage orange, I see the creek pour down. It spills toward me streaming over a series of sandstone tiers, down, and down, and down. I feel as though I stand at the foot of an infinitely high staircase, down which some exuberant spirit is flinging tennis ball after tennis ball, eternally, and the one thing I want in the world is a tennis ball.

There must be something wrong with a creekside person who, all things being equal, chooses to face downstream. It's like fouling your own nest. For this and a leather couch they pay fifty dollars an hour? Tinker Creek doesn't back up, pushed up its own craw, from the Roanoke River; it flows down, easing, from the northern, unseen side of Tinker Mountain. "Gravity, to Copernicus, is the nostalgia of things to become spheres." This is a curious, tugged version of the great chain of being. Ease is the way of perfection, letting fall. But, as in the classic version of the great chain, the pure trickle that leaks from the unfathomable heart of Tinker Mountain, this Tinker Creek, widens, taking shape and cleaving banks, weighted with the live and intricate impurities of time, as it descends to me, to where I happen to find myself, in this intermediate spot, halfway between here and there. Look upstream. Just simply turn around; have you no will? The future is a spirit, or a distillation of *the* spirit, heading my way. It is north. The future is the light on the water; it comes, mediated, only on the skin of the real and present creek. My eyes can stand no brighter light than this; nor can they see without it, if only the undersides of leaves.

Trees are tough. They last, taproot and bark, and we soften at their feet. "For we are strangers before thee, and sojourners, as were all our fathers: our days on the earth are as a shadow, and there is none abiding." We can't take the lightning, the scourge of high places and rare airs. But we can take the light, the reflected light that shines up the valleys on creeks. Trees stir memories; live waters heal them. The creek is the mediator, benevolent, impartial, subsuming my shabbiest evils and dissolving them, transforming them into live moles, and shiners, and sycamore leaves. It is a place even my faithlessness hasn't offended; it still flashes for me, now and tomorrow, that intricate, innocent face. It waters an undeserving world, saturating cells with lodes of light. I stand by the creek over rock under trees.

It is sheer coincidence that my hunk of the creek is strewn with boulders. I never merited this grace, that when I face upstream I scent the virgin breath of mountains, I feel a spray of mist on my cheeks and lips, I hear a ceaseless splash and susurrus, a sound of water not merely poured smoothly down air to fill a steady pool, but tumbling live about, over, under, around, between through an intricate speckling of rock. It is sheer coincidence that upstream from me the creek's bed is ridged in horizontal croppings of sandstone. I never merited this grace, that when I face upstream I see the light on the water careening towards me, inevitably, freely, down a graded series of terraces like the balanced winged platforms on an infinite, inexhaustible font. "Ho, if you are thirsty, come down to the water; ho, if you are hungry, come and sit and eat." This is the present, at last. I can pat the puppy any time I want. This is the now, this flickering, broken light, this air that the wind of the future presses down my throat, pumping me buoyant and giddy with praise.

My God, I look at the creek. It is the answer to Merton's prayer, "Give us time!" It never stops. If I seek the senses and skill of children, the information of a thousand books, the innocence of puppies, even the insights of my own city past, I do so only, solely, and entirely that I might look well at the creek. You don't run down the present, pursue it with baited hooks and nets. You wait for it, empty-handed, and you are filled. You'll have fish left over. The creek is the one great giver. It is, by definition, Christmas, the incarnation. This old rock planet gets the present for a present on its birthday every day.

Here is the word from a subatomic physicist: "Everything that has already happened is particles, everything in the future is waves." Let me twist his meaning. Here it comes. The particles are broken; the waves are translucent, laving, roiling with beauty like sharks. The present is the wave that explodes over my head, flinging the air with particles at the height of its breathless unroll; it is the live water and light that bears from undisclosed sources the freshest news, renewed and renewing, world without end.

true love

—◇—

from

TEACHINGS ON LOVE

by Thich Nhat Hanh

Vietnamese monk Thich Nhat Hanh's (born 1926) peace efforts during the Vietnam War led Martin Luther King to nominate him for the Nobel Peace Prize in 1967. Thich Nat Hanh's Buddhist brand of activism combines meditation with non-violent civil disobedience. Here he explores the nature of love.

—◇—

Trrue love contains respect. In the Vietnamese tradition, husband and wife always respect each other as honored guests. When you practice this, your love will last for a long time. In Vietnamese, the words *tinh* and *nghiã* both mean love. Tinh contains a lot of passion. Nghiã is calmer, more understanding, more faithful. You are not as passionate, but your love is deeper and more solid. You are more willing to sacrifice to make the other person happy. Nghiã is the result of sharing difficulties and joys over a long period of time.

You begin with passion, but, living with each other, you learn to deal with difficulties, and your love deepens. The passion diminishes, but nghiã increases all the time. You understand the other person better, and you feel a lot of gratitude: "Thank you for being my husband (my wife), for having chosen me as your companion to share your best qualities, as well as your suffering. While

58

I was having difficulty and remained awake deep into the night, you took care of me. You showed me that my well-being is your own well-being. You did the impossible to help me get well. I am deeply grateful." When a couple stays together for a long time, it is because of nghiã. Nghiã is the kind of love we really need for our family and for our society. With nghiã, you are sure the other person will love you and take care of you "until your hair becomes white and your teeth fall out." Nghiã is built by both of you in your daily life.

Look deeply to see which of these elements are in your love. You cannot say love is one hundred percent tinh or one hundred percent nghiã. Both are in it. Look into the eyes of your beloved and ask deeply, "Who are you, my love, who has come to me and taken my suffering as your suffering, my happiness as your happiness, my life and death as your life and death? Who are you whose self has become my self? Why aren't you a dewdrop, a butterfly, a bird, a pine tree?" Ask with your whole body and mind. Later, you will have to ask the person who causes you the most suffering the same questions: "Who are you who brings me such pain, who makes me feel so much anger and hatred?" To understand, you have to become one with your beloved, and also one with your so-called enemy. You have to worry about what they worry about, suffer their suffering, appreciate what they appreciate. You and the object of your love cannot be two. They are as much you as you are yourself.

Continue until you see yourself in the cruelest person on Earth, in the child starving, in the political prisoner. Practice until you recognize yourself in everyone in the supermarket, on the street corner, in a concentration camp, on a leaf, in a dewdrop. Meditate until you see yourself in a speck of dust in a distant galaxy. See and listen with the whole of your being. If you are fully present, the rain of the Dharma will water the deepest seeds in your store of consciousness, and tomorrow, while you are washing the dishes or looking at the blue sky, that seed will spring forth, and love and understanding will appear as a beautiful flower.

Being rock, being gas, being mist, being mind,
being the mesons traveling among the galaxies
at the speed of light,
you have come here, my beloved.
And your blue eyes shine, so beautiful, so deep.
You have taken the path traced for you
from the non-beginning and the never-ending.
You say that on your way here
you have gone through
many millions of births and deaths.
Innumerable times you have been transformed
into firestorms in outer space.
You have used your own body
to measure the age of the mountains and rivers.
You have manifested yourself
as trees, grass, butterflies, single-celled beings,
and as chrysanthemums.
But the eyes with which you look at me this morning
tell me that you have never died.
Your smile invites me into the game
whose beginning no one knows,
the game of hide-and-seek.

O green caterpillar, you are solemnly using your
body
to measure the length of the rose branch that grew
up last Summer.

Everyone says that you, my beloved, were just born
this Spring.
Tell me, how long have you been around?
Why wait until this moment to reveal yourself to me,
carrying with you that smile which is so silent and so
deep?
O caterpillar, suns, moons, and stars flow out
each time I exhale.
Who knows that the infinitely large must be found
in your tiny body?
Upon each point on your body,
thousands of Buddha fields have been established.
With each stretch of your body, you measure time
from the non-beginning to the never-ending.
The great mendicant of old is still there on Vulture
Peak,
contemplating the ever-splendid sunset.

Gautama, how strange!
Who said that the Udumbara flower blooms
only once every 3,000 years?

The sound of the rising tide—you cannot help
hearing it
if you have an attentive ear.

If you really love someone, you have to be fully present for him or
her. A ten-year-old boy I know was asked by his father what he
wanted for his birthday, and he said, "Daddy, I want you!" His
father was too busy. He had no time for his family. His son knew
that the greatest gift his father could offer was his true presence.

When you are concentrated—mind and body at one—anything you say can be a mantra. It does not have to be spoken in Sanskrit. It can be uttered in your own language: "Darling, I am here for you." If you are fully present, this mantra will produce a miracle. You become real, the person you say it to becomes real, and life becomes real in that moment. You bring happiness to yourself and to the other person. This is the greatest gift you can offer your loved one. To love is to be there for him, for her, and for them.

"I know you are there, and I am very happy" is a second mantra. When I look deeply at the moon, I breathe in and out deeply and say, "Full moon, I know you are there, and I am very happy." I do the same when I see the morning star. Walking among the beautiful spring magnolia trees in Korea, I looked at the beautiful flowers and said, "I know you are there, and I am very happy." To be truly present and know that the other is also there is a miracle. Whenever you are really there, you are able to recognize and appreciate the presence of the other—the full moon, the morning star, the magnolia flowers, the person you love the most. First practice breathing in and out mindfully to recover yourself. Then sit close to the one you love and, in that state of deep concentration, pronounce the second mantra. You will be happy, and the person you love will be happy at the same time. These mantras can be practiced in daily life. To be a true lover, you have to practice mindful breathing in order to produce your true presence.

There is a third mantra: "Darling, I know you are suffering. That is why I am here for you." If you are mindful, you will notice when your beloved is suffering. Sit close to him and say, "Darling, I know you are suffering. That is why I am here for you." That alone will bring a lot of relief.

There is a fourth mantra you can practice when you yourself suffer: "Darling, I am suffering. Please help." Only six words, but sometimes they are difficult to say because of the pride in our hearts, especially if it was the person we love whom we believe caused us to suffer. If it had been someone else, it would not be so hard. But because it was him, we feel deeply hurt. We want to go to our room and weep. But if we really love him, when we suffer like that, we have to ask for help. We must overcome our pride.

There is a story that is well-known in my country about a young couple who suffered deeply because of pride. The husband had to go off to war, and he left his pregnant wife behind. Three years later, when he was released from the army, his wife came to the village gate to welcome him, and she brought along their little boy. When the young couple saw each other, they could not hold back the tears of joy. They were thankful to their ancestors for protecting them, and the young man asked his wife to go to the marketplace to buy some fruit, flowers, and other offerings to place on the ancestors' altar.

While she was shopping, the young father asked his son to call him Daddy, but the little boy refused. "Sir, you are not my daddy! My daddy used to come every night, and my mother would talk to him and cry. When mother sat down, daddy also sat down. When mother lay down, my daddy lay down." Hearing these words, the young father's heart turned to stone.

When his wife returned, he could not even look at her. The young man offered fruit, flowers, and incense to the ancestors, made prostrations, and then rolled up the bowing mat and did not allow her to do the same. He believed that she was not worthy to present herself in front of the ancestors. Then he walked out of the house and spent his days drinking and walking about the village. His wife could not understand why he was acting like that. Finally, after three days, she could bear it no longer, and she jumped into the river and drowned herself.

The evening after the funeral, when the young father lit the kerosene lamp, his little boy shouted, "There is my daddy!" He pointed to his father's shadow projected on the wall and said, "My daddy used to come every night just like that, and my mother would talk to him and cry a lot. When my mother sat down, he sat down. When my mother lay down, he lay down." "Darling, you have been away for too long. How can I raise our child alone?" she cried to her shadow. One night the child asked her who and where his father was. She pointed to her shadow on the wall and said, "This is your father." She missed him so much.

Suddenly the young father understood, but it was too late. If he had gone to his wife and asked, "Darling, I suffer so much. Our little boy said a man used to come every night and you would talk to him and cry with him, and every time you sat down, he also sat down. Who is that person?" she would have had an opportunity to explain and avert the tragedy. But he did not because of the pride in him.

The lady behaved the same. She was deeply hurt because of her husband's behavior, but she did not ask for his help. She should have practiced the fourth mantra, "Darling, I suffer so much. Please help. I do not understand why you will not look at me or talk with me. Why didn't you allow me to prostrate before the ancestors? Have I done anything wrong?" If she had done that, her husband could have told her what the little boy said. But she, too, was caught in pride.

In true love, there is no place for pride. When you are hurt by the person you love, when you suffer and believe that your suffering has been caused by the person you love the most, remember this story. Do not act like the father or the mother of the little boy. Do not let pride stand in your way. Practice the fourth mantra:

"Darling, I am suffering. Please help." If you really consider him to be the one you love the most in this life, you have to do that. When he hears your words, he will come back to himself and practice looking deeply. Then the two of you will be able to sort things out, reconcile, and dissolve the wrong perception.

Buddhist meditation aims, first of all, at restoring communication with ourselves. We are seldom there for ourselves. We run away from ourselves, because we are afraid to go home and face the fear and suffering in our wounded child who has been ignored for such a long time. But it is wonderful to return home and say, "Little boy or little girl, I am here for you. Don't worry. I will take care of you." This is the first step. You are the deeply wounded child waiting for you to come home. And you are the one who has run away from home, who has neglected your child.

Go back and take care of yourself. Your body needs you, your feelings need you, your perceptions need you. The wounded child in you needs you. Your suffering, your blocks of pain need you. Your deepest desire needs you to acknowledge it. Go home and be there for all these things. Practice mindful walking and mindful breathing. Do everything in mindfulness so you can be really there, so you can love.

basketball

—◇—

from

Sacred Hoops

by Phil Jackson and Hugh Delehanty

Phil Jackson (born 1945) has played for or coached eight NBA championship teams. Jackson meditates daily, and has used the concept of mindful basketball to guide players such as Shaquille O'Neil, Michael Jordan, Kobe Bryant and Dennis Rodman.

—◇—

B asketball is a complex dance that requires shifting from one objective to another at lightning speed. To excel, you need to act with a clear mind and be totally focused on what *everyone* on the floor is doing. Some athletes describe this quality of mind as a "cocoon of concentration." But that implies shutting out the world when what you really need to do is become more acutely aware of what's happening right now, *this very moment.*

The secret is *not thinking.* That doesn't mean being stupid; it means quieting the endless jabbering of thoughts so that your body can do instinctively what it's been trained to do without the mind getting in the way. All of us have had flashes of this sense of oneness—making love, creating a work of art—when we're completely immersed in the moment, inseparable from what we're doing. This kind of experience happens all the time on the basketball floor; that's why the game is so intoxicating. But if you're really paying attention, it can also occur while you're performing the most mundane tasks. In *Zen and the Art of Motorcycle Maintenance*, Robert Pirsig writes about cultivating "the peace of mind which does not separate one's self from one's surroundings" while working on his bike. "When that is done successfully," he writes, "then everything else follows naturally. Peace of mind produces right values, right values produce right thoughts. Right thoughts produce right actions and right actions produce work which will be a material reflection for others to see of the serenity at the center of it all." This is the essence of what we try to cultivate in our players.

In Zen it is said that all you need to do to reach enlightenment is "chop wood, carry water." The point is to perform every activity, from playing basketball to taking out the garbage, with precise attention, moment by moment. This idea became a focus for me while I was visiting my brother Joe's commune in Taos, New Mexico, in the late seventies. One day I noticed a banner flying near the dining hall that read simply "Remember." It made such an impression on me that I hung a replica of the flag outside my home in Montana. Now, faded and weather-beaten, it still calls out for total attention.

For some people, notably Michael Jordan, the only impetus they need to become completely focused is intense competition. But for most of us, athletes and nonathletes alike, the battle itself is not enough. Many of the players I've worked with tend to *lose* their equanimity after a certain point as the level of competition rises, because their minds start racing out of control.

When I was a player, not surprisingly, my biggest obstacle was my hyperactive critical mind. I'd been trained by my Pentecostal parents to stand guard over my thoughts, meticulously sorting out the "pure" from the "impure." That kind of intense judgmental thinking—*this* is good, *that's* bad—is not unlike the mental process most professional athletes go through every day. Everything they've done since junior high school has been dissected, analyzed, measured, and thrown back in their faces by their coaches, and, in many cases, the media. By the time they reach the pros, the inner critic rules. With the precision of a cuckoo clock, he crops up whenever they make a mistake. *How did that guy beat me? Where did that shot come from? What a stupid pass!* The incessant accusations of the judging mind block vital energy and sabotage concentration.

Some NBA coaches exacerbate the problem by rating every move players make with a plus-minus system that goes far beyond conventional statistics. "Good" moves—fighting for position, finding the open man—earn the player plus points, while "bad" moves—losing your man, fudging your foot work—show up as debits. The problem is: a player can make an important contribution to the game and still walk away with a negative score.

That approach would have been disastrous for a hypercritical player like me. That's why I don't use it. Instead, we show players how to quiet the judging mind and focus on what needs to be done at any given moment. There are several ways we do that. One is by teaching the players meditation so they can experience stillness of mind in a low-pressure setting off the court.

Venturing into the Here and Now

The meditation practice we teach players is called *mindfulness*. To become mindful, one must cultivate what Suzuki Roshi calls "beginner's mind," an "empty" state free from limiting self-centered thoughts. "If your mind is empty," he writes in *Zen Mind, Beginner's Mind*, "it is always ready for anything; it is open to everything. In the beginner's mind there are many possibilities; in the expert's mind there are few."

When I was coaching in Albany, Charley Rosen and I used to give a workshop called "Beyond Basketball" at the Omega Institute in Rhinebeck, New York. The workshop served as a laboratory where I could experiment with a number of spiritual and psychological practices I'd been itching to try in combination with basketball. Part of the program involved mindfulness meditation, and it worked so well I decided to use it with the Bulls.

We started slowly. Before tape sessions, I'd turn down the lights and lead the players through a short meditation to put them in the right frame of mind. Later I invited George Mumford, a meditation instructor, to give the players a three-day mindfulness course during training camp. Mumford is a colleague of Jon Kabat-Zinn, executive director of the Center for Mindfulness in Medicine at the University of Massachusetts Medical Center, who has had remarkable results teaching meditation to people coping with illness and chronic pain.

Here's the basic approach Mumford taught the players: Sit in a chair with your spine straight and your eyes downcast. Focus your attention on your breath as it rises and falls. When your mind wanders (which it will, repeatedly), note the source of the distraction (a noise, a thought, an emotion, a bodily sensation), then gently return the attention to the breath. This process of noting thoughts and sensations, then returning the awareness to the breath is repeated for the duration of the sitting. Though the practice may sound boring, it's remarkable how any experience, including boredom, becomes interesting when it's an object of moment-to-moment investigation.

Little by little, with regular practice, you start to discriminate raw sensory events from your reactions to them. Eventually, you begin to experience a point of stillness within. As the stillness becomes more stable, you tend to identify less with fleeting thoughts and feelings, such as fear, anger, or pain, and experience a state of inner harmony, regardless of changing circumstances. For me, meditation is a tool that allows me to stay calm and centered (well, most of the time) during the stressful highs and lows of basketball and life outside the arena. During games I often get agitated by bad calls, but years of meditation practice have taught me how to find that still point within so that I can argue passionately with the refs without being overwhelmed by anger.

How do the players take to meditation? Some of them find the exercises amusing. Bill Cartwright once quipped that he liked the sessions because they gave him extra time to take a nap. But even those players who drift off during meditation practice get the basic point: *awareness is everything.* Also, the experience of sitting silently together in a group tends to bring about a subtle shift in consciousness that strengthens the team bond. Sometimes we extend mindfulness to the court and conduct whole practices in silence. The deep level of concentration and nonverbal communication that arises when we do this never fails to astonish me.

More than any other player, B. J. Armstrong took meditation to heart and studied it on his own. Indeed, he attributes much of his success as a player to his understanding of *not thinking, just doing.* "A lot of guys second-guess themselves," he says. "They don't know whether to pass or shoot or what. But I just go for it. If I'm open, I'll shoot, and if I'm not, I'll pass. When there's a loose ball, I just go after it. The game happens so fast, the less I can think and the more I can just react to what's going on, the better it will be for me and, ultimately, the team.". . .

. . .

A Jab for a Jab

It was no coincidence that the players had a hard time staying focused against Detroit. The Pistons' primary objective was to throw us off our game by raising the level of violence on the floor. They pounded away at the players ruthlessly, pushing, shoving, sometimes even headbutting, to provoke them into retaliating. As soon as this happened, the battle was over.

The Bulls had a long, ugly history of battling the Pistons. In 1988 a brawl erupted during a game when Detroit's Rick Mahorn, a 6'10", 260-pound bruiser, fouled Jordan hard on his way to the hoop. Head coach Doug Collins, who weighed in at 195 pounds, tried to quell the disturbance by jumping on Mahorn's back and attempting to wrestle him to the floor. But Mahorn spun around and sent Collins crashing into the scorers' table. During another game in 1989, Isiah Thomas slugged Bill Cartwright in the head after running into one of Bill's elbows. Cartwright, who had never been punched before in a game, hit back, and both players were fined and suspended. Isiah fractured his left hand and missed a good part of the season.

Scottie Pippen had the most punishing assignment of all. On defense, he had to cover Hatchet Man No. 1, Bill Laimbeer, and on offense, he matched up against Hatchet Man No. 2, Dennis Rodman. Pippen got into some royal battles with Laimbeer, who was four inches taller and outweighed him by at least forty-five pounds. In the 1989 playoffs, Laimbeer elbowed Scottie in the head and gave him a concussion during a tussle over a rebound. The following year, in Game 5 of the playoffs, Scottie took Laimbeer down with a necktie tackle as he was driving to the basket. Afterwards, according to Jordan, Laimbeer threatened to break Michael's neck in retaliation.

I wasn't happy with what Scottie had done. It was foolhardy and

Phil Jackson and Hugh Delehanty

dangerous. But I understood only too well the line between playing hard and playing angry. When I played for the Knicks, I had a
reputation for being a tough defender and opponents consistently
read malevolence into the aggressive way I used my elbows. It was
during the 1971–72 playoffs that I learned once and for all that
mean-spirited aggression is never worth the price.

The man who taught me that lesson was Jack Marin, a tough,
no-nonsense forward for the Baltimore Bullets who liked to bait
Bill Bradley, calling him a "pinko liberal" to rattle him. Marin was
an emotional time bomb, and I knew if I could get him angry
enough, he would do something stupid. So before a key game I
devised a scheme to provoke him that I feel embarrassed about to
this day. Late in the fourth quarter, I gave him a little shove as he
dribbled toward the basket. Then I confronted him at midcourt
and shoved him again. That did it. He whipped around and threw
a punch. The next thing he knew, he was ejected—it was his sixth
foul—and we went on to win the game.

Marin held on to his anger until the next time we faced each
other, almost a year later. All of a sudden, as I was going for the
hoop, he took a shot at me and I went crashing to the floor. It was
a painful lesson, but what Marin showed me was that using anger to
defeat an opponent inevitably comes back to haunt you.

A Brief History of NBA Warfare

In those days, brawling was a common occurrence in the NBA.
Most teams had an enforcer—the Celtics' "Jungle Jim" Loscutoff
was the prototype—whose primary job was to protect his teammates
when the going got rough. The Knicks' enforcer during my first
two years was Walt Bellamy, a 6'10 ½", 245-pound center, but he

was missing in action when I had my baptism by fire. The game was against the Hawks, who had just moved to Atlanta from St. Louis and were playing temporarily in a stadium at Georgia Tech, where there was no soundproofing in the locker rooms. Before the game we could hear the Hawks' coach, Richie Guerin, inciting his players to wage war against us. Guerin wasn't my biggest fan. The year before I had cut open forward Bill Bridges' forehead with my elbow, and Guerin was so enraged he ordered another player, Paul Silas, to pay me back. Silas didn't get around to it in that game, but he hadn't forgotten Guerin's charge.

With about thirty seconds left in the first half, I got the ball near the basket and started making a move on Silas when he shoved me in the back and sent me sprawling across the floor. As I got up and handed the ball to the ref, Silas took a wayward swing at my head. I dodged the blow and walked to the free-throw line, trying, as best I could, to stay calm.

At halftime the tirade in the other locker room continued, and tensions escalated. Finally, late in the game, a brawl erupted when one of the Atlanta players threw a punch at Willis Reed. Ironically, the only player on either team who didn't participate in the fight was Bellamy, who had withdrawn psychically from the team because of a dispute with management.

Soon after that game, the NBA started taking steps to reduce violence on court. First, players were fined, and, in some cases, suspended, for coming off the bench and joining in a brawl. Next, the league clamped down on throwing punches: anyone who struck another player was immediately ejected and suspended for at least one game. Those changes didn't eliminate violence; they merely gave it a different face. Hall of Fame enforcer Wes Unseld argued that the no-punching rule gave the bullies in the league license to hammer away at players and get away with all kinds of treachery without having to worry about retribution. In the late 1980s, the era of the Detroit Bad Boys, the NBA instituted a new rule severely penalizing players for committing "flagrant" fouls, malicious acts away from the ball that could cause serious injury. That helped, but some teams, in particular, the New York Knicks, still found ways to intimidate their opponents with brute force. So the league changed the rules again in 1994–95, restricting hand-checking and double-teaming in certain situations.

But the problem of uncontrolled anger and brutality rages on. Writer Kevin Simpson offered this analysis in *The Sporting News*. "It's not so much that violence in the NBA has flown out of control, but that deliberate violence has become the next step in a progression of sports culture. While the league has reveled in the raw, physical prowess of its athletes and promoted the game accordingly, it has also presided—unwittingly—over a land of spiritual deterioration, one that has seen an attitude of intimidation become the preeminent force on the floor."

Further Along the Path of the Warrior

There *has* to be another way, an approach that honors the humanity of both sides while recognizing that only one victor can emerge. A blueprint for giving your all out of respect for the battle, never hatred of the enemy. And, most of all, a wide-angle view of competition that encompasses both opponents as partners in the dance.

Black Elk spoke of directing love and generosity of spirit toward the white man, even as his people's land was being taken away. And in *Shambhala: The Sacred Path of the Warrior*, Tibetan Buddhist teacher Chogyam Trungpa wrote, "The challenge of warriorship is to step out of the cocoon, to step out into space, by being brave and at the same time gentle."

This is the attitude I try to encourage. It's a direct extension of the Lakota ideal of teamwork we started experimenting with during my years as an assistant coach. In the beginning, though the players were interested, it wasn't easy to turn their minds around. They'd been conditioned since early adolescence to think that every confrontation was a personal test of manhood. Their first instinct was to use force to solve every problem. What I tried to do was get them to walk away from confrontations and not let themselves be distracted. If somebody fouled them hard, I suggested turning around, taking a deep breath, and staying as composed as possible so they could keep their minds fixed on the goal: victory.

The system reinforces this perspective. The strength of the triangle offense is that it's based on the Taoist principle of yielding to an opponent's force in order to render him powerless. The idea is not to wilt or act dishonorably in the face of overwhelming force, but to be savvy enough to use the enemy's own power against him. If you look hard enough, you'll find his weaknesses. Bottom line: there's no need to overpower when you can outsmart.

For the strategy to work, all five players have to be moving in sync so that they can take advantage of the openings that occur when the defense overextends itself. If one player gets caught in a tussle with his man, resisting the pressure rather than moving away from it, he can jam up the whole system. That lesson has to be constantly reinforced. Once in a game against the Miami Heat in 1991, I called a timeout when I saw Scottie Pippen get into a trash-talking war with the other side. Scottie knew what I was going to say, and got defensive as soon as I started talking. But Cliff Levingston, a cheerful, fun-loving forward whose nickname was Good News, defused the tension, saying, "Come on, Pip. You know Phil's right." Afterwards, we talked about the incident, as an example of how we had to grow as a team and not retaliate every time our opponents did something we didn't like.

Teaching the players to embrace a nonbelligerent way of thinking about competition required continuous reinforcement. One of the first steps I took was to institute a series of "silly" fines to discourage players from insulting the other team. Example: a big man will get fined $10 for taking three-point shots at the end of the game when we're ahead by 20 or more points. That kind of shot demeans your opponent and only builds rage that might be returned later on.

I also discourage players from turning a good move into a humiliating one. Example: in the 1994 playoffs against the Knicks, Scottie Pippen drove to the basket and sent Patrick Ewing sprawling to the floor. After dunking the ball, Scottie straddled Ewing and waved his finger in Ewing's face. What did that accomplish? Pippen got a little ego rush, but he also got called for a technical and planted a seed of anger in the Knicks', not to mention the refs', minds.

Sometimes I use our opponents' anger to try to motivate the team. There's a clip from a Bulls-Knicks game I often screen that shows Ewing pounding his chest and yelling, "Fuck those motherfuckers!" That feeling is what the players have to steel themselves against. They have to develop a certain grittiness and dogged determination to stand up to brutality without being lured into the fray.

Extending the Metaphor
The implications of using the warrior ideal as a way of redirecting aggressive energy reach far beyond the NBA. The need is painfully obvious. A couple of years ago I watched a New York City high

school championship game in Madison Square Garden that made my heart sink. It was a messy game, marred by a lot of in-your-face posturing and dirty tactics. When it was over, the winning team approached the losers and started taunting them until a fight broke out. That kind of confrontation, which often leads to tragic consequences, wouldn't be so prevalent if young people knew how to preserve their pride and dignity without blindly acting out their anger.

There are those who've already picked up the ball. Ellen Riley, one of the few women who attended the Beyond Basketball workshop at the Omega Institute, is using the warrior model in an educational training program for at-risk teenagers in Yonkers, New York. Although it's not a sports program, the students have embraced the warrior imagery and the ideals of dedication and commitment. "What we're trying to convey is that individual performance is important, but it has to be embedded in a much larger context," Riley explains. "Being a responsible member of a community, or team, is simply the most effective way to live."

Testing the Waters

My goal in 1990—91 was to win the conference title and the home-court advantage in the playoffs. We had proved that we could beat the Pistons at home, but we didn't have the poise yet to win consistently in their arena. Until that happened, we needed to capture the conference title so that we could benefit from the unnerving effect Chicago Stadium, the loudest arena in the NBA, had on visiting teams. That year we won 26 straight games at home, the longest streak in the history of the franchise. I cautioned the players not to get too excited about victories or too depressed about defeats. When we lost, I'd say, "Okay, let's flush that one down the drain when you shower. Let's not lose two in a row." That became our motto for the season, and after mid-December we lost two straight only once. I also warned the team about becoming complacent with a three-game winning streak. If they let the momentum build, they could extend a streak to eight, nine, ten games. Winning started to come naturally. Going into a tough road trip, I'd say it would be great if we won five of the next seven games. Michael would reply confidently, "We'll win 'em all."

The first big test came on February 7 in a game against the Pistons at the Palace in Auburn Hills, Michigan. We hadn't won a game in the Palace since Game 1 of the 1989 playoffs, but this time Isiah Thomas would be out of action with a wrist injury.

Studying Detroit game films that week, I uncovered a clue to the Palace mystique: the rim of the basket closest to the Pistons' bench was stiffer than the one on the other end. This meant that off-line shots would be less likely to get a good bounce and go in. We had rarely shot well at that basket, and I had always chalked it up to the players' lack of poise in front of the Detroit bench. But perhaps a subtle act of gamesmanship was also a contributing factor. (Adjusting the rigidity of the baskets is not uncommon in the NBA. Some teams also install fast nets to speed up the tempo of a game or deflate the balls to slow it down.) As the visiting coach, I got to pick which basket we would shoot at in the first half. I usually chose the basket in front of our bench, so we would be playing defense at our end of the court in the second half. But this time I reversed strategy: the last thing I wanted was to have the players shooting at a rigged basket in the closing minutes of the game.

More important to me, however, was how the players dealt with Detroit's intimidation tactics, and I began to see some promising signs. Even though Bill Cartwright was ejected in the first half for elbowing Bill Laimbeer (okay, so the gentle warrior image was not in evidence every second of every game), the team didn't collapse when Cartwright left the floor. The younger players, especially Scottie and Horace, managed to maintain their focus. At one point somebody knocked Horace's goggles off and I thought he might unravel. But he recovered gracefully and raced back on defense after assistant coach Jim Cleamons jumped up and screamed, "Just play through it!" B. J. Armstrong also seemed unfazed by the Bad Boys' ploys and scored clutch baskets in the fourth quarter, as the team held on to win, 95–93. After the game, Jordan announced triumphantly to the media, "A monkey is off our back."

That's when the team really started to gel. We went 11–1 in February, the Bull's most successful month ever, and began to put long winning streaks together. Around this time Bill Cartwright and John Paxson decided to give up alcohol for Lent. They did it, in part, to set an example for the young players, to show that they were willing to make sacrifices to win a championship. Three or four other players joined in, and they continued to abstain till the end of the season.

Righteous Anger

Not everything went smoothly, however. On April Fool's Day, Stacey King, who had been carping at reporters about not getting enough playing time, walked out of practice. This act of rebellion had been building for months. Stacey, a forward who had been one of the nation's leading scorers in college, was having a difficult time adjusting to his role as a bench player. I had been patient with him, but the selfishness of his remarks pushed me over the edge. I decided to fine him $250 and suspend him for the next game, which would cost him about $12,000 in salary. When he showed up for practice the following day, we got into a shouting match in my office. I lost control and called him a "fat ass" and a few other less flattering names.

I wasn't proud of my performance, but my tirade had a positive effect on Stacey. Before that episode he had a distorted view of his role on the team, and some of the veterans felt he needed a dose of reality therapy to bring him in line. They were right. After sitting out a game and thinking over what he had done, he dropped the attitude. He never gave me a problem again.

As a rule I try not to unleash my anger at players that way. When it happens, I say what I have to say then let it pass, so the bad feelings won't linger in the air and poison the team. Sometimes what my father called "righteous anger" is the most skillful means to shake up a team. But it has to be dispensed judiciously. And it's got to be genuine. If you're not really angry, the players will detect it immediately.

Most importantly, eruptions shouldn't be directed at one or two members of a group; they should encompass the whole pack. The first time I got visibly angry at the team, after a loss to the Orlando Magic during my first year as head coach, the players were speechless because they had never seen that side of me before. It was right after the All-Star Game, which had taken place in Orlando, and many of the players had been hanging out in Florida all week, chasing women and partying every night. I was angry because we had blown a 17-point lead, and it was clear that the players' extracurricular activities were sapping their energy. After the game I kicked a can of soda across the locker room and gave the players a fire-and-brimstone sermon on dedicating themselves to winning and doing everything possible, on *and* off the court, to become champions. The next day the flock of groupies that had gathered around the team was nowhere in sight.

. . .

One Instant Is Eternity

We ended the 1990–91 season on a romp, beating Detroit in the final game, and finished with the best record in the conference: 61–21. Then after beating New York, 3–0, and Philadelphia, 4–1, in the early rounds of the playoffs, we faced Detroit again. The Pistons were hobbling after a tough series against Boston and several of their players, including Isiah Thomas and Joe Dumars, were nursing injuries. But that didn't make them any less arrogant.

This time we didn't *have to use* Michael as much as we had in the past. He didn't have to score 35 to 40 points a game because Scottie Pippen, Horace Grant, and the bench had learned how to take advantage of the openings Michael created by acting as a decoy and drawing the Detroit defense in his direction. In Game 1 he went 6 for 15 and scored only 22 points, but the reserves—Will Perdue, Cliff Levingston, B. J. Armstrong, and Craig Hodges—went on a surge in the fourth quarter and put the team ahead to stay.

As we moved toward a four-game sweep, the Pistons got more and more desperate. Scottie, as usual, took much of the abuse. Forward Mark Aguirre was relentless. "You're dead, Pippen, you're dead," he jabbered, according to an account in *The Jordan Rules*. "I'm getting you in the parking lot after the game. Don't turn your head, because I'm going to kill you. You're fuckin' dead." Scottie just laughed it off. In Game 4, Dennis Rodman shoved Pippen into the stands so hard it took him a few seconds to stagger to his feet. As he got up, Horace rushed over and screamed, "You play, you play!" Scottie shrugged it off and kept playing. "They really weren't focusing on basketball," he told reporters afterwards. "Basically Rodman's been making those stupid plays for the last couple of years, but I've been retaliating and giving him the opportunity to let that work to his advantage. We put our main focus into basketball, as we have all season."

Scottie wasn't alone. Everybody on the team was slammed around. John Paxson was thrown into the stands by Laimbeer. Other players were tackled, tripped, elbowed, and smacked in the face. But they all laughed it off. The Pistons didn't know how to respond. We completely disarmed them by not striking back. At that moment, our players became true champions.

The Pistons, on the other hand, gave up being champions long before the final whistle blew. In the final minutes of Game 4, which we won 115–94, four of Detroit's starters, Thomas, Laimbeer, Rodman, and Aguirre, got up from the bench and walked out of the arena scowling. On their way out, they passed by our bench without even acknowledging our presence.

After that series, the finals against the Los Angeles Lakers were anticlimactic. The Lakers won the first game in Chicago, 93–91, on a late three-pointer by forward Sam Perkins, but that was their last shining moment. After that our defense took over, pressuring Magic Johnson, keeping the ball out of his hands and double-teaming their post-up players, James Worthy and Vlade Divac. We won in five games, taking the last three in L.A.

The emergence of John Paxson as a clutch shooter was another key. When Jordan was pressed, he often dished the ball to Paxson, who shot 65 percent from the field during the series and scored 20 points in the final game, including the shot that sealed the win. After Game 4, Magic summed up the situation beautifully: "It's not just Michael. He's going great, but so is the team. It's one thing if he's going great and the team isn't. Then you have a chance to win. They've got Horace playing well; Bill is playing solid; and their bench is playing outstanding. They've got the total game going."

Before the final game, the Disney organization asked Jordan if he would do one of their "What are you going to do now?" commercials. He said he'd do it only if the ad included his teammates. This was a sign of how far Michael, and the team, had come. It brought back memories of the 1973 Knicks. After we won the title that year, Vaseline wanted Bill Bradley to do a post-victory commercial, but he suggested the company use his teammates instead. As it turned out, Donnie May, Bill's stand-in, ended up playing the starring role.

Here I was again at another victory party in L.A. After we stopped for a moment to say the Lord's Prayer, the champagne started flowing. It was an emotional scene. Scottie Pippen popped the first bottle of bubbly and poured it over Horace Grant's head. Bill Cartwright took a sip of champagne and sighed, "Finally." Sam Smith reported that B. J. Armstrong, Dennis Hopson, Stacey King, and Cliff Levingston serenaded Tex Winter with an impromptu rap song: "Oh, we believe in the triangle, Tex. We believe, yeah, we believe in that triangle. It's the show for those in the know." His eyes filled with tears, Michael Jordan hugged the championship trophy as if it were a newborn baby.

Strangely, I was somewhat detached. This was the players' show, and I didn't feel the same euphoria they did. But there was one last point I wanted to make.

Midway through the festivities, I gave my last speech of the season. "You should know," I said, "that many championship teams don't come back. This is a business. I'd like to have all of you back, but it doesn't always happen. But this is something special you have shared and which you'll never forget. This will be yours forever and it will always be a bond that will keep you together. I want to thank you all personally for this season. Now, get back to the party."

grief

———◇———

from

NINE-HEADED DRAGON RIVER

by Peter Matthiessen

Peter Matthiessen (born 1927) writes fiction
(*At Play in the Fields of the Lord, Killing Mister
Watson*) and non-fiction (*The Snow Leopard,
In the Spirit of Crazy Horse*). Much of his work
draws upon his expeditions as a naturalist and
explorer to remote areas in places like Nepal,
New Guinea and the Sudan. Matthiessen
began his study of Zen in 1969. Two years
later, his wife and fellow Zen student, Deborah
Love, discovered that she had cancer.

---◇---

In mid-November of 1971, Deborah and I attended a weekend
sesshin at the New York Zendo. For two months Deborah had
been suffering from pains that seemed to resist all diagnosis,
and she decided to limit herself to the Sunday sittings. On Saturday evening, meeting me at the door of our apartment, she stood
there, smiling, in a new brown dress, but it was not the strange,
transparent beauty in her face that took my breath away. I had been
in *zazen* since before daybreak, and my mind was clear, and I saw
Death gazing out at me from those wide, dark eyes. There was no
mistaking it, and the certainty was so immediate and shocking that
I could not greet her. In what she took as observance of sesshin
silence, I pushed past quietly into the bathroom, to collect myself
in order that I might speak.

On Sunday, Deborah chanced to sit directly opposite my own
place in the two long lines of buddha figures that faced each other.

During morning service, still resisting what I had perceived the night before, and upset that this day might exhaust her, I chanted for her with such intensity that I "lost" myself, obliterated my *self*— a function of the ten-line *Kannon Sutra*, dedicated to the bodhisattva Avalokiteshvara, which is chanted hard, over and over, thirty-three times, with wood gong and bells, in mounting volume and intensity. At the end, the chanters give one mighty shout of *MU!*—a mantric word corresponding to *Om*, which symbolizes the Absolute, eternity—this followed instantly by a great hush of ringing silence, as if the universe had stopped to listen. But on this morning, in the near darkness—the altar candle was the only light in the long room—this immense hush swelled and kept on swelling, as if this "I" were opening into infinity, in eternal amplification of my buddha being. There was no hallucination, only awe, "I" had vanished and also "I" was everywhere.

Then I let my breath go, gave my self up to immersion in all things, to a joyous *belonging* so overwhelming that tears of relief poured from my eyes. For the first time since unremembered childhood, I was not alone, there was no separate "I." Wounds, anger, ragged edges, hollow places were all gone, all had been healed; my heart was the heart of all creation. *Nothing was needed,* nothing missing, all was already, always, and forever present and forever known. Even Deborah's dying, if that had to be, was perfectly in place. All that day I wept and laughed.

Two weeks later, describing to Tai-san what had happened, I astonished myself (though not my teacher, who merely made a small bow) by a spontaneous burst of tears and the tears falling light and free as rain in sunlight.

The state of grace that began that November morning in the New York Zendo prevailed throughout the winter of my wife's dying, an inner calm in which I knew at once what must be done, wasting no energy in indecision or regrets. When I told Tai-san about this readiness and strength, and confessed a kind of crazy exaltation, he said quietly, "You have transcended." I supposed he meant "transcended the ego," and with it all horror and remorse. As if awakened from a bad dream of the past, I found myself forgiven, not only by Deborah but by myself.

Rohatsu sesshin, commemorating the Buddha's enlightenment, took place in the first eight days of December. The day before sesshin, Deborah entered Roosevelt Hospital for medical tests, and a bone biopsy was performed on December 1; consequently I came and went during the sesshin. On the morning of December 4—the same day that Susuki-roshi died in San Francisco—I told Tai-san the good news that the biopsy report was negative. I also told him that two weeks earlier, on November 20, in a knowing way that was not the same as knowledge, I had perceived that Deborah was dying.

The day after sesshin, with cancer suspected but undiagnosed, I took Deborah home to Sagaponack, where she went straight to bed, exhausted. Within a few days, two small lumps developed under her skin, and on December 14 the local hospital reported metastatic cancer. On December 16, when I told Tai-san the bad news, we sat together a few minutes in dead silence. Then he said quietly, "Oh, Peter," and offered his beautiful red fan as a gift for Deborah. The fan calligraphy, done by Soen-roshi, meant "Going Home."

Deborah was teaching at the New School for Social Research, and brought books with her to Memorial Hospital in New York City. A fortnight later the books were still untouched. Meekly she sewed at a Christmas stocking provided the patients by the recreation staff, and seeing this, I realized for the first time how much the disease and its violent therapy had stunned her.

On Christmas Eve I drove home to Sagaponack to pull together some sort of Christmas for the children. Deborah was to be taken out on Christmas Day by our friend Milly Johnstone and their Cha No Yu (Japanese tea ceremony) master, Hisashi-san. But she felt too weak and sick to go, and the day after Christmas, with Zendo friends—Milly, Tai-san and his wife, Yasuko, and Sheila Curtis—we put together a champagne-and-oyster party in her room, the first good time she had had in weeks and the last celebration of her life. Tai-san honored her fierce sincerity as a Zen student, giving her the Buddhist precepts and a Dharma name. He had brought to the hospital a brown robe for zazen and the bib-like garment known as a *rakusu*, inscribed with the characters Ho Ko (Dharma Light). Sheila gave us a poem by the Japanese poet Chora:

> I fell in love with the wings of birds
> The light of spring on them!

Under the covers, Ho Ko was already an old woman, her hips and beautiful legs collapsed, black and blue from needles, but she was still lovely when propped up in bed, and she wore her rakusu like a proud child. I watched our friends' faces admiring the brave, calm, smiling woman in the bed. I admired her, too, putting out of my mind those other days when her dying was neither calm nor lovely, those days that no one knew about but the nurses and me.

With the turn of the year, she retreated swiftly, battered insensible by radiation and chemotherapy. I could not ease her pain or fear or loneliness, or enter the half world of shadows closing around her. On January 3 there were serious complications that almost killed her, and by the time her downward progress stabilized again, her mind was disintegrating in feverish mutterings

about going on a journey, and the raging paranoia of death fear
and too much pain.

Tai-san spoke to me about Soen-roshi's mother, who had died
of cancer at Ryutaku-ji without sedation rather than cut off awareness of life and death, but seeing Ho Ko on January 18 for the first
time since the Christmas party, he wept and said no more. Like a
mad old woman, recognizing no one, anticipating pain, she fought
away those who tried to help her. Most of the few people I permit-
ted into the room, remembering an entirely different person,
went red in the face or burst into tears at the first sight of her.

Zen students volunteered as nurses, and the presence of Zen
people always calmed her, even when she appeared to be lost in coma.
The head nurse, dealing with the tense, desperate confrontations
between living and dying in the hushed rooms rank with flowers up
and down the corridor, told me that in all her years in the cancer
ward, she had never known such an atmosphere of support and
love. "I don't know what you Zen people do," she said, "but you're
doing something right." Bending all rules, she taught me how to
use the mucus respirator to clear my wife's throat when she was
strangling, let me sleep in the room overnight and bathe her and
carry her on the last diminishing journeys to the toilet, where her
weight had to be held above the seat to keep her from crying out in
pain. Finally I put a stop to the doctors' obsessive tests and weighing, which were excruciating, humiliating, useless. Deborah's great
courage had worn out at last, and she cowered and whined whenever she was lifted. The last tubes were attached, and she never left
her bed again.

For the first time in two weeks, I went home to see our little boy.
After hours of driving that cold January night, I could not clear my
nostrils of the stink of flowers in the cancer ward, the floor shine
on that corridor of death. Then a rabbit ran across the frozen

country road, in the winter moon. In that instant my head cleared; I was back in life again and ready to deal with whatever I met with when I returned the next day.

Deborah was far away in what the doctors told me was her terminal coma. She would not come to again and would almost certainly be dead in the next few days. But early Wednesday morning, January 20, a nurse rang from the hospital; my wife wished to speak with me on the telephone! I said there must be some mistake, and she said the staff was just as astonished as I was. Then the voice of Deborah as a young child said, "Peter? I have something to tell you. Peter? I'm very very sick! Come right away!" In tears, I ran all the way to the hospital through the daybreak streets, but by the time I arrived she had sunk again into her nether world.

Two days later, at weekend sesshin, I was given a place close to the door so that I could come and go inobtrusively to the hospital. Ordinarily Tai-san remained silent in the first hours of sesshin, as people calmed themselves, but this day he spoke out suddenly, very slowly, in the middle of the first period of sitting. "A few streets away, our beloved sister Ho Ko lies *dying!* The pain of your knees is nothing like the pain of *cancer!* She is still teaching us, still helping us, and by sitting with great concentration—*Mu!*—we will help her to erase her evil karma." After dedicating the sesshin to Ho Ko, Tai-san paused for a long time, then resumed quietly. "Last month, during our Rohatsu sesshin, Susuki-roshi died of cancer. This month Debby Matthiessen dies of cancer!" Again he paused for long taut seconds. "Who among you . . . will be *next*? Now . . . *sit!*"

Tai-san shouted the words *next* and *sit*; they resounded in the zendo like two cuts of a whip, and the whole place stiffened. Later all present would agree that the sittings that afternoon and evening were the most powerful in memory. At dawn next morning, everyone chanted with furious intensity, ending with a mighty shout of

MU! Immediately afterward I went to the hospital, where the bewildered nurses said that my wife was conscious.

Deborah's face was clear and lovely; she smiled softly and said, "I love you," and actually found strength to put her arms around my neck. Tai-san brought Maurine Freedgood, Ruth Lilienthal, and other senior students, still in their robes. Deborah recognized and embraced them all. Happy and radiant in her awakening after three days and nights of torment and delirium, of raving about death and journeys, she blessed everyone with a smile of childlike sweetness, murmuring, "Oh, I love you so!" Later she asked me shyly, "Will I die?," and when I repeated the question—"Will you die?"—to make sure she wished to hear the answer, she nodded without fear and moved gently away from the whole matter, as if to spare me. Next day she was still calm and happy, though less clear, and on Monday morning she smiled at me, whispering, "Peter." Deborah never spoke again, but neither did she return to the wild fear and distress of earlier days. She seemed to be in a blessed state, and Tai-san wondered if she had not had a spontaneous *kensho*. That afternoon she returned into the coma, and she died peacefully three nights later, with Tai-san and I holding her cooling hands. After three suspended pauses between breaths, my beautiful wife—how incredible!—made no effort to inhale again. We sat with her for two more hours until her body was removed for autopsy.

To the great annoyance of the mortuary and crematorium attendants, who hurried and chivied us from start to finish, Tai-san and I accompanied Ho Ko right to the oven door of a strange, windowless temple far out in the winter wastes of the huge gray cemetery in Queens. She wore her beads, brown linen robe, and rakusu for the great occasion. Years ago in Paris I said goodbye to my infant son by touching kissed fingers to his forehead, at a small service in the hospital yard conducted by a wine-spotted cleric and two conscripted witnesses, still clutching brooms. But New York law forbids the touching of the deceased by the unlicensed; two gay attendants in tight, broad-shouldered suits hissed like cobras as I put forth my hand. Under their disdainful gaze, as the stretcher slid into the oven, we chanted the Four Vows, as we had done at the moment of her death. Then the iron door rang to on the regal, gray-faced form, reassembled so skillfully after an autopsy that had traced her cancer even to the brain.

We bowed to Ho Ko and departed under a full moon in the old gray sky of New York winter afternoon. By now the foul-mouthed mortuary driver had divined that something not so ordinary was in the wind, and was circumspect, asking shy questions, all the way back into the city.

To tell six-year-old Alex that his mother had died, I took him for a walk on the winter beach. Alex assured me she could not be dead. "If she was dead," he explained, hoping to comfort us, "I would be crying."

In the grayest part of the empty months that followed, my heart was calm and clear, as if all the bad karma of our past together had been dissolved on that early morning of November. Toward that experience that prepared me for my wife's death I was filled with gratitude, which had nothing to do with the thankfulness I felt toward Tai-san and our Zen community, toward kind family and friends and children. I could scarcely feel grateful to *myself*, yet there it was: where could that Buddha-self reside if not in my own being? Chanting the *Kannon Sutra* with such fury, I had invoked Avalokiteshvara Bodhisattva, but I paid no attention to the words. All energy was concentrated upon Deborah, who sat in the line of buddha forms across the way. Avalokiteshvara was also Deborah, also myself—in short, what Meister Eckhart meant: "The eye with which I see God is the Eye with which God sees me." Or Jesus Christ: "I and my Father are one." Surely those Christian mystics spoke of the Lord Who Is Seen Within.

Almost another year had passed before something said by an older student made me realize what must have happened. At dokusan, Tai-san confirmed it. But an opening or kensho is no measure of enlightenment, since an insight into one's "true nature" varies widely in its depth and permanence. Some may overturn existence, while others are mere fragmentary glimpses that "like a mist will surely disappear." To poke a finger through the wall is not enough— the whole wall must be brought down with a crash! The opening had been premature, and it seeped away, month after month. This saddened me, although I understood that I had scarcely started on the path; that but for Deb's crisis, which had cut through forty years of cynicism and defensive encrustations, I might never have had such an experience; that that small opening was very far from great enlightenment, *dai kensho,* in which the self dissolves without a trace into the One.

February sesshin, a few weeks later, was dedicated to Ho Ko, whose bones and photograph shared the altar with fat white carnations. At morning service on the second day, Tai-san repeated the dedication to Deborah, after which the *sangha*—the community of Buddhist followers—chanted the *Kannon Sutra* thirty-three times with mounting intensity, followed by the shouted *MU!* Because this was dawn of a Sunday morning, great care had been taken to shut all doors so as not to rouse the neighborhood against weird Zen practices. There was no draft whatever in the windowless room, where the service candle always burned without a tremor. But this morning, in the ringing hush that falls after such chanting, the candle suddenly flared wild and bright, remaining that way for at least ten seconds before diminishing once more to its normal state.

Don Scanlon, sitting near the altar, had always been incorrigibly curious and missed nothing, but later, when I whispered to him about the candle, he assured me that I was going nuts. Discovering that no one else had seen that flaring, I realized that Don must be right. But at dokusan, when I said I was disturbed by something that occurred after the shouted Mu, Tai-san nodded and smiled before I could finish. "The candle," he murmured. We gazed at each other and said nothing more.

In March, 1972, the first Dai Bosatsu sesshin was held in the old lodge on Beecher Lake. In the small upstairs zendo, the Buddha silhouette was black against the brilliant winter pane; the woods sparkled with snow blossoms of ice and sun. During this week, using a pick-axe, I dug a hole at the foot of a lichened boulder in the wild meadow, and on the last day of sesshin, in a ceremony that consecrated the new graveyard, a lovely urn containing half of Ho Ko's bones became the first ever interred in what is now the "sangha meadow" at Dai Bosatsu. (Marsha Feinhandler, who had made the urn, said she had felt the clay breathing in her hands—a nice experience!) I covered the hole with a small capstone, then a large flat stone, and scattered pine boughs over the fresh earth. By the time those boughs rotted, there would be no trace of Deborah Love's return into the earth.

The remaining bones went home to Sagaponack, where on May 4, with Alex, I dug a grave in the old cemetery, choosing a spot where a robin had left a wild blue egg in the spring grass. Together we planted the grave with heath and marigold. All day it had been very dark, but as we finished, a bright storm light illumined the pale chickweed blossoms scattered like light snow in the cemetery.

On the spring wind, the winter geese were restless; an indigo bunting came to the copper leaves of an old cherry. I went for a long walk along the dunes.

On May 6, Tai-san arived with his Dharma brothers Do-san and Dokyu-san (now Kyudo-roshi) and a few Zen students. My four children participated in the simple service, taking turns tossing earth into the hole. (Alex said, "I liked the shoveling the best! It made me feel just like a workman!" He was later observed showing his mother's grave to friends, his arm companionably around the headstone.) In the afternoon we went clamming in Northwest Harbor. On no occasion before or since have I seen Tai-san so relaxed and joyful as he was that day, digging clams with his brother monks from Ryutaku-ji. Later that year he would receive from his teacher *inka*, or "seal of approval," and already Soen referred to him as Eido-shi, which is short for Eido-roshi.

We celebrated something at our seafood supper. Tai-san said to me quietly, "So . . . it's over now," but of course it wasn't. Still clinging, I had saved out a brown bit of bone, which I taped to Ho Ko's small memorial plaque in our small zendo. The following week, grief took me by surprise during Ozu's great film, *Tokyo Story*, when the old country people, packed off to a garish and noisy modern seashore hotel for their vacation when they attempt to visit their married children in Tokyo, agree shyly that they are homesick for their country village.

Here I am in Sagaponack,
Yet my heart longs for Sagaponack.

writing

—◇—

from
LONG QUIET HIGHWAY
by Natalie Goldberg

Natalie Goldberg (born 1948) is best known for *Writing Down the Bones* (1986), which proposes that writing—like meditation—is a spiritual practice. This excerpt from Goldberg's 1993 memoir finds her moving more deeply into her own writing practice after years of intensive Zen study.

—◇—

After six years of living six blocks from the Minnesota Zen Meditation Center, I left. The original reason I had moved to Minneapolis—to be married—no longer existed. I wanted to leave the deep north, I was finished there. And Zen Center? I barely said good-bye. It seemed as though I left the zendo, almost the way water mixes with Kool-Aid. The water becomes red from the cherry flavor. I left colored for life. But red water doesn't know it's red. It has not met itself yet. I left not knowing what I had learned, but I knew I would never leave Zen. Though my personal life took a different direction, I carried Zen with me. I knew the dharma was bigger than the Minnesota Zen Center. Roshi had taught me that.

We have an illusion that a certain time, a certain place, a certain person is the only way. Without it or them, we are lost. It is not true. Impermanence teaches us this. There is no one thing to hold on to. Once, a few years earlier, I told Roshi in anger, "I'm never coming back here." He laughed and said, "The gate swings both ways. I cannot hold anyone." Yet, when I returned two months later, I could tell he was happy to see me, but he had to go beyond his personal likes and dislikes. He could not say to me, "Please, Natalie, don't go. I like you." He was my teacher. As a teacher, he had the responsibility to teach me, to put forth the depth of human existence, whether he or I liked it or not. "Meetings end in departures" is a quote from the early sutras of Shakyamuni. No matter how long the meeting or what the relationship, we depart from each other. Even marriage or monkhood, those lifelong commitments, end in death. In the face of that truth, he said, "You can go or come." He was not tossed away by personal preferences; it was his practice to stand on something larger, regardless of his subjective feelings. And if I returned, the choice had to be mine. I was responsible for myself.

So I left Minnesota. I returned to New Mexico, but Roshi came with me. I carried his teachings south down Interstate 35, then out 90, past the exit to Blue Earth and Worthington, into the tip of South Dakota, stopping at Costa's Café and eating at the salad bar full of marshmallows, canned fruit salads, and small cellophane packages of saltines. I carried his words, his friendship, down highway 81 into Nebraska, lingering in Norfolk among fertile fields and cows, with friends, Bob and Barbara, who lived in a big white house, then along Interstate 80, going west, past Kearney and North Platte, and then south through Colorado, opening into my beloved big sage space of northern New Mexico.

I never said good-bye formally to Roshi and I am sorry for that. Though I carried him with me, our formal time of teacher and student in Minnesota was over and I wish I had expressed my gratitude. But I was ignorant. I didn't know it was over. It seems to me now that I still didn't know anything. Gratitude is a mature emotion. Only in the last year or two in Minneapolis, with the divorce, did I start to digest the teachings on a quieter, deeper level inside me. And at that time of my departure, I was in too much pain to understand my relationship with Roshi and what he had given me. I knew Roshi meant a lot to me, but I thought he would always be around, the way you think as a young child that your mother will be there, or a house, a street you live on. We are naive, innocent when we are children. I was still ignorant as an adult and as a Zen student. Six years I had been there and still ignorant! We take a long time to learn some things.

Roshi once told us that there were three different kinds of horses: with one, just a tug at the reins made them start moving; the second, a kick in the flanks and they were off; and then there were those that had to be beaten to the bone with a whip before they started to move. "Unfortunately," he said, "most human beings are the third kind." He told us we act as though we were going to live forever. "Wake up," he said.

I drove my thick carcass out of Minnesota. I regret I did not thank him for his great effort, did not bow in front of him, present him with a little spice cake, an orchid, a wool cap to keep his shaved priest's head warm. I know he understood. He did not teach in order to receive anything, but gratitude may be the final blessing for a student. Thank you, thank you, thank you. I know what I have received. Knowing that, the duality of teacher and student dissolves. The teacher can pour forth the teachings; the student absorbs them. No resistance, no fight. It is a moment of grace.

Instead, most of us want more and more. We want to be recognized. We want our egos fed. To feel gratitude is to recognize the other, to lay down our own greed and aggression. What a relief! What joy!

But a teacher does not teach to receive presents. That is the work of a teacher, not to get caught in the likes or dislikes of a student, but to come forth always with the deepest teachings. Often the student does not like this, thinks the teacher is mean, unfeeling, but a good teacher knows that if he or she plants a real seed, someday, maybe years later, even in the most ignorant of students the seed may sprout. So the teacher's job is to close the gap between the student's ignorance and the teachings, but often the student does not understand any of this. That is why the student is a student. The teacher understands this. That is why the teacher can have abundant patience.

But if the student doesn't know about the gap, how can she learn? There is something in us, an urgency to meet the teachings on the other side, that gnaws at our ignorance, that desires to meet our own true face, however lazy and comfort-loving we may seem to be. This something was working in me, albeit slowly, and often underground.

When I arrived in Taos, I stayed for a month in a silver school bus out on the mesa with my friends Gini and Michael. It was wonderful to be back up in Taos, but I walked around there like a ghost. I'd see a new restaurant and remember when it was The House of Taos, a place where Neil and I hung out that served the best green chili pizza, and where Ron, the owner, stood in the back, tall and bearded, over the ovens. I'd see Taos Valley School, now a private elementary school, and remember when it was DaNahazli, the old hippie school where I taught writing to barefoot kids wearing cantaloupe-seed necklaces, and where Ram Dass would stop in when he was visiting Lama Foundation, and where we did Sufi dancing every Friday afternoon in the playground. Taos wasn't the same, it was becoming gentrified—no, that wasn't it. It was that almost everyone I knew had left. I carried an old dream of it in my body, but most of my friends had moved on to meditation centers in Boulder, San Francisco, Los Angeles.

And Taos was also the same: There was the land, the golden light, the ecstatic experience of being brought into the moment with that huge sky behind you, the sacred mountain of Taos ever present on the landscape. There was absolutely no place else to be but where you were, watching that hummingbird feed on the pink hollyhock in front of you. Yes, this was still the best place. But I had left. I had met Katagiri Roshi, and now I was back, alone, carrying his practice with me.

I moved on after a month to stay with my friend Rob in Albuquerque, and while I was there I worked on *Writing Down the Bones,* which I had started a few months earlier in Minnesota. Each morning before I began to write, I walked along the irrigation ditch in the south valley of Albuquerque. The Sandias were in the distance to my left, in a blue-purple haze, and close up all around me were snarling, black dogs behind fences that also held old pickups, rundown adobe houses, chickens pecking at nails and pigweed, horses, goats, tires, and old bottles. I loved those walks, the pale soft yellow earth, the surprising rush of water, the delicate green of willows. I thought of that mile stretch along the ditch as one of my angel places. I felt good there, glad to be in New Mexico again near Twitty's Rib Hut and Consuelo's Chiles Rellenos.

After that month in Albuquerque, I settled in Santa Fe. It was the place I had the least attachment or connection with and so it seemed the least haunted by the past. I rented an adobe on Don Cubero Street.

"Make writing your practice," Roshi had told me.

"Oh, no, I can't. My brain," I pointed to my head, "I can't shut it up."

"If you commit to it, writing will take you as deep as Zen," he told me.

I settled into writing in Santa Fe. Sitting meditation seemed to fade away. Everything about my years in Minnesota fell away, except my relationship with Roshi. I hardly remembered the cold, the gray sky, the thunderous Mississippi, not because Minnesota hadn't been a deep time for me, but because I was so happy to be back in New Mexico, where I belonged. I do remember one day after being back several months, I suddenly ached for a white clapboard house on the corner of Emerson and Thirty-second. I'd never been in that house; I'd hardly noticed it, but it was on my route to the food coop and the zendo and it was catty-corner to the mailbox. I must have taken it in on a body level, and later after I left Minneapolis I spent a whole afternoon oddly aching for it, a symbol to me of the Midwest, plain clean lines, a second story, on a block with a square lawn, a wooden porch—different from the sage and rambling adobe of the Southwest.

I had never spoken about New Mexico in Minnesota, and now I didn't know how to explain my experience in the zendo—all that formal sitting—to my old friends in New Mexico. What could I say? I sat a lot. Yeah, so what did you learn? my friend would ask. We would be walking in an arroyo behind St. John's. The sky was turquoise; the earth, shades of pink; and there was red rock dotted with piñons. I don't know, I'd say. And I'd shake my head. It was all in me. It was nothing I could tell about. I did not learn computer programming or aerodynamics in the zendo. I wasn't sure yet how to apply it to my world. I was still working to digest it.

The only place in Santa Fe I felt comfortable writing in was The Haven, on Canyon Road. That was odd for me. Usually I could write any place, and The Haven was a bit high-priced, not a café, really, where you could just order tea, but more a full-meal restaurant with linen napkins. Yet, when I opened my notebook there, I was content to write *Bones,* to tell about writing practice, to share what Roshi had taught me. I was afraid to write the book, afraid that after divulging the deepest ways I saw writing and the world, everyone would laugh at me, so if I felt good at The Haven, I didn't question it. I went there often, ordered their cheapest lunch, and sat at the table near the window. I'd think to myself as I wrote, no one in Santa Fe knows Roshi. I'm alone here in this writing.

After I'd been going to The Haven for several weeks, the owner came up to me.

"Hi. I see you write here often. What are you writing?"

"Oh, a book about using writing as a practice, like Zen practice," I said.

"Oh, yeah, I'm a Zen student. I study with Baker Roshi at the Cerro Gordo zendo," she said.

"You do?" I asked, incredulous. "You must know Katagiri then. He's my teacher."

"Of course I do." She sat down at my table. She'd sat sesshin with Katagiri many times when he was in San Francisco. She then proceeded to tell me about her recent trip to Japan and how she had visited Dogen's ashes at his monastery, Eiheiji. She turned her head. "You know, most of the cooks and waiters here are Zen students."

"You're kidding."

She nodded her head. "Hey, Robert, come over." She pointed to me. "She studied with Katagiri." Then she turned back to me. "Oh, come and write any time. You're welcome here."

I was delighted. No wonder I felt good about writing my book here. My instincts were strong. I had found a safe place.

In the spring, I began working at The Haven as a part-time cook. I needed the money and I was having a hard time with the writing of *Bones*. I had suddenly become very afraid of failure—and just as afraid of success. I watched myself avoid the notebook as if it were a plague. Getting a job will be a good thing, I thought to myself. I became the dessert cook. I marveled over my chocolate mousses, chocolate cakes. I licked my fingers often. Chocolate became the basic ingredient in all the desserts except the flan. For two months, I enjoyed the job, my coworkers, the new activity. Then I became tired of it. What am I doing with my life? I'd ask. What about the book?

I'd just broken up with a boyfriend I dated for six months. After only two weeks, he'd already found someone else. It made me mad.

"But you didn't want to be with him," my friends kept saying.

"I know," I said, "but it doesn't matter. How could he find someone so quickly?"

One night at my most depressed the phone rang as I iced a cake. I picked it up. "The Haven—can I help you?"

It was my friend Janet in Albuquerque. I was surprised. "Listen, Nat, a bunch of us are going down to the jazz festival in New Orleans. We have an extra ticket. Why don't you come? It will cheer you up. You've been so down."

"I can't afford it," I said. "I have a book to write." Meanwhile, I wasn't writing. It felt like a term paper due in school that I had hanging over my head. It wasn't that the writing was hard. I was afraid to complete it, to finish it.

Janet insisted. "Oh, come on, Nat. We'll have a great time. "

"Okay, I'll do it," I said and hung up, looking for people in the kitchen who would substitute for me for that week.

I drove down to Albuquerque that Thursday. We were all going to meet at Rob's—there were six of us. I was an hour early. I decided I'd take a walk along the ditch where I'd been a year earlier. I walked for ten minutes, felt the soft earth beneath my shoes. Suddenly I began to shake and fell down crying, my face right down there in the dirt. "You've got to finish that book. You've got to finish that book," an inner voice cried. I pounded my fist on the ground. "You've got to do it for Roshi, for all he gave you. I don't care if you're afraid. Finish it." I wept and wept as those fierce black dogs behind their fences growled and barked.

When I got up, I brushed myself off. There was resolve in my body as I walked back to Rob's.

We flew to Louisiana, and during the whole music festival I sat in the gospel tent, right up close to the stage. I couldn't believe the sound coming out of those Christian women, how a chest could be that big and open, and how huge a voice it could produce.

When I returned home, I quit cooking at The Haven; I quit everything else I was doing. I wrote seven days a week for seven weeks, rarely leaving that little adobe on Don Cubero. I moved through the book. No resistance, no thought; I just kept writing. I pulled the last page from my typewriter on a Sunday evening and knew it was finished.

During the time I was struggling with *Bones*, I taught writing work-shops in my living room. I knew most people in Santa Fe hadn't known anyone like Roshi and I was surprised, though the town was a New Age mecca, how few people had sat meditation. I realized zazen was an old-fashioned kind of thing and hard. Simple things my students in my writing classes did not know. I told them to ground themselves in detail. They argued with me. They wanted to write about the cosmic world. I said, "Give me the details of drink-ing a cup of mint tea. That's cosmic enough." I told them to con-tinue whether it was hard or easy. Often they said no and drifted to other things. I made up a motto for them—"With your feet in the clouds and your head on the ground."

I took a so-called New Age workshop in my first year back. Its advertisement said, "You want to go fast. You're unlimited." Well, it sounded good, but then I stopped to think: We're all exhausted from going fast. Who's unlimited? I'm not. I'll die someday. I'm in a human body. When I stopped to argue this with a group member, she said, "Well, the psyche grows fast." No, it doesn't, I thought. Look at history. We are dumb and slow; the sins of the fathers and mothers are carried on by the children, and only through our willingness to slow down and examine can we feel the effects of alcoholism, incest, rage, hatred, greed, and lumberingly change our behavior.

That statement that the psyche grows fast was unrooted, wasn't connected with the earth. A tree has a growth spurt, but it is grounded by the depth of its roots. That New Age workshop borrowed from Zen, from religion; I heard watered-down statements that were directly out of Buddhism, but they were empty of the spiritual connection. Something smart from religion was taken for the sake of self-aggrandizement and pleasure. I worried about my Santa Fe writing students, thinking that one moment they'd take a writing workshop and the next moment they'd go on to Rolfing as a way to save themselves. No practice was taught at that workshop. By the end of the weekend, everyone was salivating, drooling with their own ecstasy, but by Monday or Tuesday morning they were flat out, deflated, depressed. They had no way of integrating what they had learned and no way of maintaining it—except, of course, by signing up for another high-cost weekend.

I told my writing students that practice is something done under all circumstances, whether you're happy or sad. You don't become tossed away by a high weekend or a blue Monday. It is something close to you, not dependent on high-tech gyrations or smooth workshop-leader talk. Writing is something you do quietly, regularly, and in doing it, you face your life; everything comes up to fight, resist, deny, cajole you. Practice is old-fashioned, not hip or glamorous, but it gets you through Monday, and it lets you see the ungroundedness of hyped-up New Age workshops or quick ways to write a best-selling novel that you end up never writing.

After I had been in Santa Fe a year, I went back to visit Minneapolis and I made an appointment to see Roshi. I brought him an Acoma Pueblo pot. I wanted him to have something of New Mexico. It was hand-done, smooth, brown and white, with a black line design on it. I loved Acoma. The old pueblo was built on top of a mesa and was called Sky City.

I walked into Roshi's study. There he was, softer, kinder than I remembered him. It was summer. He wore a white T-shirt, and I noticed the skin at the base of his neck had gathered a little. He was growing older.

"Roshi, they're crazy in Santa Fe. I need a teacher again." I was afraid I'd soon be gobbled up by Santa Fe, seduced into a hundred different things: aura balancing, shamanic journeys, crystal readings, rebirthings, past-life regressions. I needed a teacher to keep me on the path.

"Don't be so greedy," he said when I told him I wanted a teacher. "Writing is taking you deep." He tapped the *Bones* manuscript I brought to show him. "Keep writing. You can write or visit me, if you need to."

No teacher? That was too lonely. Out there alone with my writing? Then he told me, "Anything you do deeply is lonely. Even the Zen students here," he said, "the ones who are going deep are very lonely."

I nodded. I understood, though I didn't want to. It was up to me now, and it was true that the writing of *Bones* had taken me deep. In the act of writing, alone at my old oak dining room table on Don Cubero Street, I had begun to close the gap between what Roshi was saying all those years and my own understanding of it. Writing was the vehicle for making the teachings mine, for knitting them close to me.

When *Bones* was published a year later, a Zen monk, Steve Hagen, who knew me all those years in Minnesota and who read it, asked me in amazement, "Did you know all this stuff when you were practicing here?"

I smiled. I knew I had been quite a misbehaved student. "No," I said. "Writing taught it to me."

When I returned to Santa Fe after visiting Roshi, an acquaintance asked, "What did you do up there?"

"I gave a reading," I said.

"Astrological?" she inquired.

"No, poetry," I answered.

Once I went to Roshi when I lived in Minnesota and told him, "When I'm at Zen Center, I feel like a writer. When I'm with writers, I feel like a Zen student."

"Someday you will have to choose. You're not ready yet, but someday you will be. Writing and Zen are parallel paths, but not the same."

We never spoke about it again. I continued to write; I continued to sit.

Three months after I finished *Bones,* I went camping alone one weekend in August by the Chama River. I wondered why I insisted on going alone, since I'd just met a man I really liked in Santa Fe. The whole weekend I anticipated some vision or epiphany I was supposed to have. I woke Sunday morning to the loud gallop of deer hooves inches from my head. I'd slept out in a sleeping bag on the ground, no tent, and the deer were heading for the river. There must have been fourteen of them. I'd never seen them from that angle before: black hooves, beige bodies. Mostly I was panicked. By the time I sat up, I saw the last of them crashing through the willows at the Chama's edge.

I thought, this must be it, the epiphany: I was almost trampled to death. I can leave now. I made a breakfast of brown rice and roasted nuts over a fire and then packed up. I had to drive eleven miles on winding, rutted dirt roads before I hit the blacktop. Pink cliffs shot up from the dry desert to my left and the Chama River and its valley spread out to my right.

I'd gone about three miles when suddenly I burst out crying. At the same instant, my blue Rabbit, which had never done this before, overheated, and steam shot up with great force from the hood of the car. I cried; it steamed. I repeated over and over: "I chose being a writer. I chose being a writer," and sobbed and sobbed. Before that moment I had no idea that that question had been working in me so deeply. Though I had written a book and talked about writing practice, I still never consciously considered myself a writer rather than a Zen student.

That talk with Roshi had occurred maybe six years earlier. I had forgotten it, but beings seen and unseen and our wild minds continue to work while we are busy apparently only shaking salt on our french fries. I felt a great relief after that morning by the Chama. I drove back to Santa Fe, stopping in Tesuque for a wonderful meal all by myself at El Nido's.

Why did I have to choose? I don't know if we do really choose. Eventually, I think, something chooses us and we shut up, surrender, and go with it. And the difference between Zen and writing? In writing you bring everything you know into writing. In Zen you bring everything you know into nothing, into the present moment where you can't hold on to anything.

• • •

It's a great challenge to write about a place you lived in while you are still living in it, to have perspective on it. It's not impossible. It's been done and done beautifully. After all, it is only in the last century that we've had such freedom of travel and movement. And I imagine if we don't change place, time is always changing anyway, so we are always looking back over our shoulder at the past, something that is no longer here, as we write.

But not being in the close physical vicinity of Roshi, not meeting my own resistances head on, having the distance and time, my appreciation for Roshi deepened, flowered. I was no longer doing *my* work, *my* books, *my* writing workshops; I was doing his work, our books; I was teaching writing to help all sentient beings. I was teaching it the way he taught me Zen. He inspired me, gave me a vision of a way to be.

Sometimes at the beginning of a writing workshop, I'd look out at my students and think, Oh, no, I don't want to start again, all over, another group. I've been doing this for years. Then I'd think, did Roshi not put up with you, no, not "put up with," treat you like a Buddha consistently under all circumstances? Yes, I'd nod. Well, get out there, I'd say, and I'd begin my class with gratitude.

Once over tea with a friend in Santa Fe—it was November, the month was important, the branches were bare, a few birds darted past the window, I wore sweaters one over another, and the wood stove was crackling—I held the teacup in both my hands, and I remembered something. I began to tell my friend who was sitting there with me:

"You know, in Minnesota sometimes it can be this cold in early October." I paused. "Once I was on the Zen center's land in southeastern Minnesota, near New Albin, Iowa. We planned to build a permanent monastery there eventually, but at the time we sat a weekend sesshin in a big army tent. It was after lunch, we had work period and we all lined up and the work leader announced who would be doing what job. He said, 'Natalie and—I don't remember who the other person was—go over and carry the wood from up the hill down to the creek.' We were in silence. You didn't say, 'Oh, I don't want to do that,' you just did it. It was part of the training. So we went up and there were these huge tree trunks that had been cut down." I stood up in the kitchen and showed her how long the trunks were. "From here"—I paced the distance from the side cupboard door to the living room—"to here. And they were this big around." I showed her with my arms two and a half feet.

"My work partner motioned me in silence to get to the back end of a trunk and together we'd lift it up on our shoulders and carry it down. Well, I knew that it was impossible for me to do it. I can't remember who I was with, but he was huge—probably was a football player in college. I couldn't think 'impossible'—I couldn't think. I'd freak out. So I just did it. I walked across this long field with that huge trunk. If I thought, I would panic and the trunk would come crashing on top of me. At one point we passed Neil. He was raking. I saw him out of the corner of my eye. I think he stopped dead and was staring with his mouth open." My friend and I laughed. "But I didn't dare look at him. No thought. No thought. I just had to keep walking with that trunk."

Later my friend and I took a walk. When we got to the top of a hill, she turned to me. "You know, I realize you did something in Minnesota. You were gone and now you're back, so I forget those years, but something happened."

I nodded. It was true. And I remembered more about that weekend. I had seen wild turkeys up the hill in the afternoon, and the full moon crested the bluff near the Mississippi just as we stepped out from evening zazen.

The next morning had been very cold. There was frost on the

bell. We hadn't expected it to get that cold that early in the year. After all, we slept and sat in tents. After the two periods of zazen beginning at five A.M., I was signed up to be the breakfast server. Servers never wore socks or gloves. I had to bow, barefoot, with my big pot of steaming rice in front of each student, then kneel on the ground and serve them—they were all sitting on the floor on cushions—then lug up the pot and go to the next person. I was cold. Roshi was the last person to be served. I couldn't wait to get it over with, to run out of the tent and put on my socks and gloves. As I knelt in front of Roshi, about to scoop a ladle of rice into his bowl, he sharply, clearly said to me, "Eat the cold." I took a deep breath, slowed down, and tried to open to weather. This man wasn't kidding around. Don't run away, not even from cold—digest it, he was saying. And he meant this for all my life, not just the moment I was there.

Now I was a thousand miles away from him. My deep love for him bound me to the teachings, kept me in them when I forgot them, now that I was back in New Mexico, far from the Minnesota zendo.

That is one of the things a teacher does for a student. She gives the student a personal connection to the teachings. They are no longer abstract high ideals. They are real. The Buddha dharma became a reality for me, because I saw Katagiri Roshi living it.

This is no different from an English teacher sharing a poet with you. Mr. Clemente read Dylan Thomas and Brother Antonius aloud to us at the beginning of class and said, "I like this." I liked Mr. Clemente and I wanted to hear what he liked. It is much harder—almost impossible—to enter the teachings, even of poetry, on our own. Somewhere along the way someone showed us the beauty of one poem, so then we could enter other poems.

Jack Kerouac, the famous Beat author who wrote *On the Road,* read the Buddhist sutras and tried to sit meditation alone without a teacher. It was too hard. He did not succeed in any regular practice. He died an alcoholic, choking on his own vomit in Florida, living with his mother.

But, of course, being on the Buddhist path is no guarantee. We each have to eat the teachings ourselves. I remember Roshi telling me that there were ten monks ordained when he was ordained. One was now in jail; one went crazy and now was in a mental hospital; one physically attacked his teacher; and one committed suicide. He didn't know what had happened to the others. "Life is no guarantee," he said often. "You must make effort."

I finished *Writing Down the Bones* and began a novel, *Banana Rose.* I left Santa Fe, moved back to Taos, and had a solar one-room house built on the mesa next to my friends Gini and Michael. I went up to Minnesota about once a year, and when I was there, I'd visit Roshi. There he is, I'd think to myself when I saw him. Still here. Still studying the sutras, still sitting.

I asked him a question. "You know, Roshi, I'm writing a novel. Some of it's about me and Neil. I think I'm still protecting him. My friends say, 'You have to tell the truth.' I don't want to hurt him. I'm not writing the book to be mean."

Roshi didn't hesitate. He nodded. "Yes, you have to tell the truth."

Then his face lit up. "Don't worry. You won't hurt Neil, you'll help him. He'll read the book and know you better. He'll read the book and know what a woman is."

I smiled. My face lit up. He gave me tremendous permission. "Thank you," I said and that one short interview carried me easily for a year. I brought it home to Taos, chewed at it, shared it with my students: "If you write the truth, it doesn't hurt people, it helps them. They know you better."

from Long Quiet Highway

. . .

Roshi went on sabbatical for a year to Japan. I was deep in *Banana Rose*, drinking mint tea at the Garden Restaurant every morning, while I kept my hand moving across the page, parking my car at an angle through the snow slush on the Taos plaza, walking out into the open sunlight at one o'clock after I was done writing. It sounds simple now. It was hard. Writing that novel, staying with it, was one of the hardest things I'd ever done. Knowing that it was a practice, that a practice was something you continued under all circumstances— Roshi had trained me in this—was what kept me going. I was making the teachings mine.

I finished the second draft of *Banana Rose* in January 1989. For several months, Roshi had been back in Minnesota from his sabbatical, and I heard he wasn't feeling well. He was in and out of the hospital. Pneumonia? Tuberculosis? There were many rumors. When I called Zen Center, everything was vague. This vagueness protected me.

Right before I flew to Baja in Mexico to hop a boat to follow the blue whales as a celebration for finishing my novel, I heard the word "cancer" on the long distance telephone wire that stretched from Minnesota to New Mexico. Cancer. My mind stopped. Cancer. It stunned me. The word echoed in my hollow skull. Cancer. Cancer. No mention of anything fatal. Chemotherapy. Radiation. "Roshi's in good spirits," the long-distance voice said. "He'll be all right." Cancer. I hung up the phone. Cancer. My whole bone structure dissolved and anything else that held me up on two feet. I don't remember if I cried then or not. At that moment it was deeper than crying.

Several times we caught sight of the blue whales. Their tails, their enormous backs. I was the only one aboard who did not bring a camera, who viewed those animals with her naked eye. The rest of the passengers snapped picture after picture, never taking their face from the lens. I planned to buy a few postcards once we hit land. I was sure a professional photographer had snapped a good one.

At night, when eveyone was asleep below, I climbed on the upper deck, squatted by the rail, looked out at the sea, the amazing star-studded night sky, and I cried. I repeated over and over, "Please don't die. Please don't die."

At the same time I felt that this was the destiny of my teacher, the man who worked so hard to bring the dharma to America. He was only sixty-one years old. I had lived as though I had years left with this man. I'd never said it to myself before, but crying those nights on the deck I knew I loved this person more than anyone I had ever loved, and the love was full, clean, not broken by resentment, no holding back—this teacher had been able to pull that kind of love out of me. My heart poured forth with gratitude. If he was dying, I didn't know what I would do without him. Though I hadn't lived in Minnesota for four and a half years, Roshi was still my guiding light. I had no other model but him, though I think I never thought it possible to be like him.

In interviews and classes and among friends, people have asked me over the years, "So whom do you admire? Who are your models?" My response was singular, "Katagiri Roshi." Katagiri Roshi? What about women—Rosa Luxemburg? Gloria Steinem? No, Katagiri Roshi. What about writers? Eudora Welty? Willa Cather? Colette? Yes, I like them; they're fine, too, but for me everything paled next to Roshi, a small Japanese man who spoke broken English. I could go into dokusan, speak to him straight, and be answered straight. And never for a moment did I have to be concerned about him crossing a sexual boundary. I did not have to close down or protect myself. This is no small feat given the sexual transgressions of many spiritual teachers today. I needed that freedom to find myself, a place to step out whole, to be treated whole. I was in the presence of someone who was paying attention. Paying large attention. As though you suddenly planted the sun into a seat in a busy café and it beamed there. Think of that power, to work like the sun. The café would get quiet; everyone would turn toward it. And this power is in all of us: to shine in our heavens.

But I wasn't idealistic. My feelings were grounded in reality: I knew Roshi had trouble expressing his emotions; he clashed with some of the students; some thought he was too rigid, old-fashioned; the sangha was sometimes narrow, slow, did not reflect his magnanimity. Finally, he was disappointed in the midwestern students' commitment and in their inability to raise the money to realize his dream of a permanent monastery near New Albin, Iowa:

> I wish to build a place and an environment to pro-
> mote the quiet sangha life in unity. We have some
> land, and I want to construct a building there to
> practice the Way revering the old ways. I think that
> the mode of old ways reveals the modern one from a
> different aspect. Modern life is artificially protected.
> When the artificial environment collapses, for
> instance in a natural disaster or an economic
> calamity, people suffer severely. Modern people,
> therefore, need to live in direct contact with nature
> and find a practice method in tune with nature's
> rhythm. Old ways of life fit this purpose. Such a life
> will put the modern life in a different perspective
> and teach us how we should live. Therefore, I am
> convinced we must build such a practice place in
> America.

• • •

But he was patient, he continued.

And now he had cancer. Finally, in May, it dawned on me that I should visit. I think I wanted everything to get better long distance, for him to be healed, and then I could forget his mortality. I was in denial, scared. He was getting out of the hospital after a long series of chemotherapy treatments and complications. I called ahead of time to let him know I was coming. He asked Tomoe, his wife, to request that I give a poetry reading at Zen Center while I was there, to lift people's spirits. I said, "Of course," but all I really wanted to do was see him. I would be happy just to have tea with him for ten minutes. I knew he wasn't well. I braced myself for seeing him. I knew he might look very different; old, thin, tired.

I brought his favorite shortbread cookies and small purple flowers—he loved any kind. We sat in his living room. We joked. He looked beautiful. It was hard to believe that he was so ill. I told him I loved him. He nodded. I told him, "When you were well, I didn't miss you. It was okay that I was so far away, but now I miss you all the time." He nodded.

That night, I read in the zendo. He didn't come down; I didn't expect him to, but a long time later Tomoe told me he lay down on a blanket on their living room floor, which was above the zendo, so he could hear me. He hoped I would sing a funny song I'd written many years earlier that he liked, about being on the Zen center's land. It was called "Boodie Land." I was surprised. I didn't even remember the song anymore. I never knew it meant so much to him. I remember thinking at the time I wrote it that it might be a bit disrespectful or sacrilegious.

Two days after that reading, I returned to New Mexico, but now even my darling state couldn't hold me. It was as though all my cells turned toward that one northern midwestern city that held my teacher. I sent presents each week: wooden birds from Mexico, a

turquoise and gray Pendleton blanket, a Zuni amber coyote fetish
with a turquoise arrow at its heart indicating healing. Still, when I
called Zen Center, it was hard to figure out what was going on. He
completed chemotherapy and radiation treatments. They were waiting
to see if his cancer went into remission. Tomoe called me early one
morning, ecstatic, "The tests show no more cancer."

I went into a cautious relief. I dreamed that night that I was
walking round and round Zen Center, that I was keeping guard.
That morning, I decided that after I finished *Wild Mind*, the new
book I was working on, I'd go up there for a few months and help
out. If he was healing, I'd help him heal, and if he was dying—
please, no—I'd help him do that. There was no place else I wanted
to be, but near him.

Two or three weeks after Tomoe's call, I received another one.
"They found cancer again." More chemotherapy, but the Zen
students were optimistic. Roshi was on a pure diet; he was doing
visualizations, receiving special acupuncture treatments.

At the end of September—I had one more month until I could
move up there—the word "dying" was mentioned on the long distance wire. I hung up. The word I knew to be behind every thought
but was not said, now was said. I sat down on the couch and I cried
as though the earth poured out of me. That afternoon I was supposed to take a small Mesa Airlines plane to Albuquerque from the
Taos airport seven miles from my home. Then I was to take a cab
to the Pyramid Hotel and give a talk the next morning to a conference of English teachers. I had two hours until the plane left. I was
crying so hard I left logic—I couldn't calculate how long I needed
to get to the plane and coordinate that with the hands on the clock
over my refrigerator. I drove those seven miles as though my car
were Jell-O and I was sliding across a vista of sage brush. I pulled
into the Taos airport just as they were closing the door on the

plane. I ran down the runway and they let me on. We flew over the Rio Grande gorge and over country I knew well, but I'd never seen it from this angle: There were Dixon, Velarde, the apple orchards. Roshi wasn't dead yet, not yet, not yet. There was time.

I checked in at the Pyramid and went straight to my room. I was on the sixth floor, overlooking a golf course. It was early evening. I sat and stared out the big window that did not open and watched night descend over my sky. I did not leave the room. I did not sleep. I cried through most of the night. I didn't prepare a talk. The next morning I wore sunglasses to the lectern—my eyes were swollen. I took a deep breath, removed the dark glasses and looked at three hundred teachers. I hoped something would come. To my surprise, I talked about pleasure, about teaching out of pleasure, of teaching what you love. The audience was pleased. I put the sunglasses back on and headed for the back of the room and out to a cab at the front of the hotel. I flew back to Taos and though I was driving up to Minnesota in a month for a long stay, I made plane reservations for the coming weekend. I wanted to go up there and I didn't want to wait.

Unbeknownst to me, a group of twelve, the monks whom Roshi had ordained and Yvonne Rand, who had also studied with him, were called into Minneapolis that weekend. Plans for dharma transmission, the carrying on of the lineage, were being made. Roshi wasn't strong enough to do the whole ten-day ceremony, so his close friend Tsugen Narasaki Roshi was going to come in from Japan in December to perform it. This weekend, before he might become too weak, Roshi was to perform the part of the ceremony— eye-to-eye with the teacher—that was essential to take place with him in order for the transmission to be legitimate.

Shoken and Nonin, two American monks, flew in from Japan. Someone flew in from Milwaukee; another person from St. Louis; Yvonne Rand, from California. Most of the monks I had known before their ordinations, when they were Floyd and Mike, Janet and Roberta, before they took on their dharma names, Shoken, Dosho, Joen, Teijo.

I don't even remember getting to see Roshi that weekend—he was too sick, conserving his strength for the ceremony, but I was so happy to be there, near him, among my old friends. I felt like the thirteenth monk. I joined them for dinner; they invited me into the Buddha hall to chant with them. They thought Roshi would do the ceremony from his bed, but Roshi insisted on dressing in full regalia, in his special silk monk robes, and they told me he sat in full lotus as he performed the ceremony for each monk individually.

Some of the monks had drifted from Zen Center over the years, had gotten involved with family life and children. Suddenly everyone was called together, called out of their homes and jobs to receive this dharma transmission, probably too early, too young in their practice, but Roshi might be dying—still the word was hardly mentioned. Roshi said he did it this way so things would not become political, so the transmission would be spread out among several people. He said no one was ready; over time, someone might emerge as a teacher.

It was during that weekend that Nonin remembered he was the one carrying those big logs with me on the Zen land that weekend. He was Don Chowaney then. "I wondered why you were so scared." He laughed. "Of course, look how much smaller you are than me." It was that weekend that I began to regret not having been ordained as a monk, only so I, too, could have eye-to-eye with my dearest teacher.

On Monday, I flew back to New Mexico and worked hard to finish *Wild Mind*. Those few weeks were a blur for me. I was racing against time, against the heartbeat and breath of my teacher. I sent the manuscript to my editor, locked up my house, packed up my car and drove north through Colorado and Nebraska. I remember staying in a hotel in Nebraska, near Kearney, that had free videos. I watched *Gone with the Wind* late into the night, and the next morning sped on to Minnesota.

I settled into my friends', Joni and Cary's, house on York Avenue—they had an extra bedroom—and I made a vow to go to Zen Center each day, whether anyone else was there or not, and to make myself useful. I was assured I couldn't see Roshi: he was too sick. I didn't expect to see him; I wanted to help.

The first day on my way to Zen Center I stopped and picked up some purple violets at a florist's and brought them over.

"Go ahead up and put them in Roshi's apartment. He's at radiation treatment. He'll be back in an hour," one of the Zen students told me.

I filled a vase in the kitchen and placed the flowers on the coffee table. I looked around. Flowers that people had sent or dropped off were everywhere, on the kitchen table, near the sink, on a dish cabinet, on two window sills. I went downstairs to the basement to help collate newsletters.

An hour later someone came downstairs. "Natalie, Roshi's back. He lay down on the couch, pointed at those flowers you brought, and asked, 'Who brought those?' When we told him you were here, he told us to send you up."

I went up. There he was, on the couch. I knelt next to him. He still looked so beautiful, his face radiated. He took my hands.

I said, "I'm here to help *you* now. I'll be here a while."

He nodded. "Dress warm. It's cold in Minnesota. You can catch a cold. Be careful."

"Yes," I said. I nodded. "Rest now," and he closed his eyes. I left him and went downstairs.

On the bulletin board in the basement a small sign was pinned up:

Just
to be
is a
blessing.
Just
to
live
is
holy.

—Abraham Joshua Heschel

I read it every day I was there.

dying

—◇—

from

THE TIBETAN BOOK OF
LIVING AND DYING

by Sogyal Rinpoche

Sogyal Rinpoche as a child studied under some of Tibet's greatest lamas. He began teaching Buddhism in the West in 1974. His 1992 book offers Westerners down-to-earth and mystical perspectives on death and dying.

—◇—

M y students and friends in the West have told me many inspiring accounts of people they knew who were helped, as they died, by the teachings of Buddha. Let me tell you here the stories of two of my students, and of the way they have faced death.

Dorothy

Dorothy was a student of mine who died from cancer at St. Christopher's Hospice in London in England. She had been a talented artist and embroiderer, art historian, and tour guide, as well as a color therapist and healer. Her father was a well-known healer, and she had a great respect for all religions and spiritual traditions. It was late in her life when she discovered Buddhism, and became, as she said "hooked"; she said she found its teachings gave her the most compelling and complete view of the nature of reality. Let some of her spiritual friends, who cared for her while she died, tell you in their own words how Dorothy let the teachings help her when she came to die:

Dorothy's death was an inspiration to us all. She died with such grace and dignity, and everyone who came in contact with her felt her strength—doctors, nurses, auxiliary helpers, other patients, and not least her spiritual friends, who were fortunate enough to be around her during the last weeks of her life.

When we visited Dorothy at home before she went into the hospice, it was dear that the cancer was in a very aggressive phase, and her organs were beginning to fail. She had been on morphine for over a year and now she could hardly eat or drink; yet she never complained, and you would never have known that she was in fact in considerable pain. She had grown terribly thin, and there were moments when she was obviously exhausted. But whenever people came to visit her, she would greet them and entertain them, radiating a remarkable energy and joy, unfailingly serene and considerate. One of her favorite things was to lie on her couch, and listen to tapes of Sogyal Rinpoche's teachings, and she was delighted when he sent her some tapes from Paris, which he said would have a special meaning for her.

Dorothy prepared and planned for her death right down to the last detail. She wanted there to be no unfinished business for others to sort out, and spent months working on all the practical arrangements. She didn't seem to have any fear of dying, but wanted to feel that there was nothing left undone, and that she could then approach death without distraction. She derived a lot of comfort from the knowledge that she had done no real harm to others in her life, and that she had received and followed the teachings; as she said "I've done my homework."

When the time came for Dorothy to go into the hospice, and leave her flat for the last time—a flat once full of beautiful treasures collected over the years—she left with just a small holdall and without even a backward glance. She had already given most of her personal possessions away, but she took a small picture of Rinpoche that she always kept with her, and his small book on meditation. She had essentialized her life into that one small bag: "traveling light," she called it. She was very matter-of-fact about leaving, almost as though she were only going as far as the shops; she simply said "Bye bye, flat," waved her hand and walked out of the door.

Her room in the hospice became a very special place. There was always a candle lit on her bedside table in front of Rinpoche's picture, and once, when someone asked if she would like to talk to him, she smiled, looked at the photograph, and said: "No, there's no need, he's always here!" She often referred to Rinpoche's advice on creating the "right environment," and had a beautiful painting of a rainbow put on the wall directly in front of her; there were flowers everywhere, brought by her visitors.

Dorothy remained in command of the situation, right up to the end, and her trust in the teachings seemed never to waver, even for a second. It felt as though she was helping us, rather than the other way round! She was consistently cheerful, confident, and humorous, and had a dignity about her, which we saw sprung from her courage and self-reliance. The joy with which she always welcomed us secretly helped us to understand that death is by no means somber or terrifying. This was her gift to us, and it made us feel honored and privileged to be with her.

We had almost come to depend on Dorothy's strength, so it was humbling for us when we realized that she needed our strength and support. She was going through some final details about her funeral, when suddenly we saw that, after having been so concerned about others, what she needed now was to let go of all these details and turn her attention toward herself. And she needed us to give her our permission to do so.

It was a difficult, painful death and Dorothy was like a warrior. She tried to do as much as possible for herself, so as not to make work for the nurses, until the moment when her body would no longer support her. On one occasion, when she was still able to get out of bed, a nurse asked her very discreetly if she would like to sit on the commode. Dorothy struggled up, then laughed and said, "Just look at this body!" as she showed us her body, reduced almost to a skeleton. Yet because her body was falling apart, her spirit seemed to radiate and soar. It was as though she were acknowledging that her body had done its job: It was no longer really "her" but something she had inhabited and was now ready to let go of.

For all the light and joy that surrounded Dorothy, it was clear that dying was by no means easy; in fact it was very hard work. There were bleak and harrowing moments, but she went through them with tremendous grace and fortitude. After one particularly painful night when she had fallen over, she became afraid that she might die at any moment, all alone, and so she asked for one of us to stay with her all the time. It was then that we began the 24-hour rotation.

Dorothy practiced every day, and the purification practice of Vajrasattva was her favorite practice. Rinpoche recommended teachings on death for her to read, which included an essential practice of phowa. Sometimes we would sit together reading passages out loud to her; sometimes we would chant Padmasambhava's mantra; sometimes we would simply rest in silence for a while. So we developed a gentle, relaxed rhythm of practice and rest. There were times when she would doze, and wake up to say: "Oh, isn't this lovely!" When she appeared more energetic and alive, and if she felt like it, we would read passages from the bardo teachings, so that she could identify the stages she would go through. We were all astonished at how bright and alert she was, but she wanted to keep her practice very simple—just the essence. When we arrived to change "shifts" we would always be struck by the peaceful atmosphere in the room, Dorothy lying there, her eyes wide open, gazing into space, even while she was sleeping, and her attendant sitting or quietly reciting mantras.

Rinpoche would often telephone to find out how she was getting on, and they talked freely about how near she was to death. Dorothy would speak in a down-to-earth way, and say things like, "Just a few more days to go, Rinpoche." One day the nurses wheeled in the telephone trolley saying, "Telephone call from Amsterdam." Dorothy brightened up immediately, and glowed with pleasure as she took the call from Rinpoche. After she hung up she beamed at us and said he had told her that she should no longer concentrate on reading texts, and that now was the time simply to "rest in the nature of mind, rest in the luminosity." When she was very close to death, and Rinpoche called her for the last time, she told us he had said, "Don't forget us; look us up some time!"

Once when the doctor came round to check on how she was and adjust her medication, Dorothy explained, in a disarmingly simple and straightforward way, "You see, I am a student of Buddhism, and we believe that when you die you see lots of light. I think I'm beginning to see a few flashes of light, but I don't think I've really quite seen it yet." The doctors were astounded by her clarity and her liveliness, particularly, they told us, in her advanced stage of illness, when they would normally have expected her to have been unconscious.

As death came closer, the distinction between day and night seemed to blur, and Dorothy went deeper and deeper into herself.

The color in her face changed and her moments of consciousness became fewer. We thought we could detect the signs of the elements dissolving. Dorothy was ready to die, but her body was not ready to let go, because her heart was strong. So each night turned into an ordeal for her, and she would be surprised in the morning that she had made it through to another day. She never complained, but we could see how she was suffering; we did everything we could to make her more comfortable, and when she could no longer take fluids, we would moisten her lips. Right up until the last thirty-six hours, she politely refused any drugs that would interfere with her awareness.

Not long before Dorothy died, the nurses moved her. She lay curled up in a fetal position, and even though her body had now wasted away to almost nothing, and she could neither move nor speak, her eyes were still open and alive, looking directly ahead, through the window in front of her, out into the sky. In the moment just before she died, she moved, almost imperceptibly, looked Debbie straight in the eye, and communicated something strongly; it was a look of recognition, as if to say, "This is it," with a hint of a smile. Then she gazed back out at the sky, breathed once or twice, and passed away. Debbie gently let go of Dorothy's hand, so that she could continue, undisturbed, through the inner dissolution.

The staff at the hospice said that they had never seen anyone so well prepared for death as Dorothy, and her presence and inspiration were still remembered by many people at the hospice even a year after her death.

Rick

Rick lived in Oregon and had AIDS. He had worked as a computer operator, and was forty-five when, a few years ago, he came to the

annual summer retreat I lead in the United States, and spoke to
us about what death, and life, and his illness meant to him. I was
amazed by how Rick, who had only studied the Buddhist teachings
with me for two years, had taken them to heart. In this brief
period he had, in his own way, captured the essence of the teachings: devotion, compassion, and the View of the nature of mind,
and made them a part of his life. Rick sat in his chair and faced us
all and told us how he felt about dying. I hope that these excerpts
will give you some flavor of this moving occasion:

When I thought I was dying, two years ago, I did what was natural:
I cried out, and I was answered. And it took me through several
weeks of horrible fevers, where I thought I was going to go in the
middle of the night . . . This devotion, this crying out . . . When
this is all you can do, we have that promise from Padmasambhava
that he is there. And he doesn't lie: he has proved himself to me
many times.

If it were not for Padmasambhava, whom Rinpoche teaches us is
the nature of our own mind, our own Buddha nature, if it were not
for that glorious shining presence, I couldn't go through what I'm
going through. I just know I couldn't.

The first thing I realized was that you must take personal responsibility for yourself. The reason I am dying is that I have AIDS. That
is my responsibility; no one else is to blame. In fact there is no one
to blame, not even myself. But I take responsibility for that.

I made a vow to myself and to whatever gods there may be,
before I came into Buddhism, that I just wanted to be happy. When
. . . I made that decision, I stuck to it. And this is very important
in doing any kind of training of the mind. You must make the
decision that you really want to change. If you don't want to
change, no one is going to do the work for you.

Our part . . . is to work with the daily aspects of our situation. First is to be grateful that you are in this body, and on this planet. That was the beginning for me—realizing gratitude for the earth, for living beings. Now that I feel things slowly slipping out, I am becoming so much more grateful for everyone and everything. So my practice now centers on this gratitude, simply a constant offering of praise to life, to Padmasambhava, who is living all of these multitudinous forms.

Don't make the mistake I did for so many years, that "practice" means sitting straight and saying mantras, thinking, "I'll be glad when this is over!" Practice is much bigger than that. Practice is every person you meet; practice is every unkind word you hear or that may even be directed at you.

When you stand up from your practice seat, that's when practice really begins. We have to be very artful and creative in how we apply the practice to life. There is always something in our environment we can connect with, to do the practice. So if I'm too dizzy to visualize Vajrasattva above my head, I stand up, and I go and wash my morning dishes, and the plate I'm holding in my hand is the world and all its suffering beings. Then I say the mantra . . . OM VAJRA SATTVA HUM . . . and I'm washing away the suffering of beings. When I take a shower, it's not a shower; that's Vajrasama above my head. When I go out in the sunshine, it is the light, like a hundred thousand suns, shining from Vajrasattva's body and entering me, and I just take it in. When I see a beautiful person walking down the street, I might in the beginning think, "What a nice-looking person," but the next instant I am offering that up to Padmasambhava with my full heart, and letting it go. You have to take real life situations and make them your practice. Otherwise you will have only an empty belief that gives you no solace, no strength, when hard times start. It's just a belief: "Oh, some day, I'll go to heaven.

Some day I'll be a Buddha." Well, some day you won't be a Buddha. You are a Buddha, now. And when you practice, you are practicing at being who you are. . . .

It's very important to take situations that are occurring in your life and use them. As Rinpoche keeps saying, if you have practiced calling out and asking for help, then in the bardos it will be natural to do the same . . . I made a mantra out of this line by Dudjom Rinpoche: "Lama of unrepayable kindness. I only remember you." Some days, it is all I can manage to think; is is the only practice I can get out. But it works great.

So . . . happiness, self-responsibility, gratitude . . . don't confuse a dead, ritualistic practice for a living, ongoing, changing, fluid, opening, glorious practice. Because, and it's my experience right now—and I know it sounds like words perhaps, but I know in my heart it's not—I see Padmasambhava everywhere. That's just my practice. Every person, especially the difficult ones, who make life difficult for others, encountering them is the blessing of the master. To me this illness is the blessing of the master. It is grace. So much grace I could chew on it.

But this has happened because I have gained my mind . . . When I started, I used to judge things constantly in my mind. I would judge this person; I would judge that one. I would judge the way he looked; I would judge the way she sat; I would judge, "I don't like today, it's too rainy, too gray. Oh, poor me . . . Oh love me . . . Oh help!" So I started with that. It was just a constant commentary in my mind. But I made a start. I would write myself little notes and stick them on my refrigerator. "Don't judge!"

When you live in your mind—that is choosing between this and that, "This is good . . . this is bad, I don't want it," between hope and fear, between hate and love, between joy and sorrow, when you are actually grasping for one of those extremes—the essential peace of your mind is disturbed. A Zen patriarch says: "The Great Way is not difficult for those who have no preferences." Because your Buddha nature is there. Happiness is everywhere.

So I began to work with my conceptual mind. At first it seemed like an impossible thing to do. But the more I practiced at it . . . I found out: If you leave the risings in their own place, they are perfectly fine, where they are. Just be with them, and be happy, because you know you have the Buddha nature.

You don't have to *feel* like you have the Buddha nature. That's not the point. The point is trust, which is faith. The point is devotion, which is surrender. That, for me, is the essence. If you can trust what the master is saying, and study and try to bring the teaching back to yourself in difficult times, and train your mind not to fall into its habitual patterns, if you can just be with what is happening, with bare attention, after a while you notice that nothing stays around very long. Not even negative thoughts. Especially not our bodies. Everything changes. If you leave it in its place, it will liberate itself.

In a situation like mine, when fear becomes so obvious to you, and so predominant, and you feel like you are being swallowed by the fear, you must take your mind in hand. I have realized that fear is not going to kill me. This is just something that is passing through my mind. This is a thought and I know that thoughts will liberate themselves if I just keep my hands off. I also realize that's what happens in the bardos, when and if you see a vision coming at you that might be frightening; it's not coming anywhere other than from you! All those energies we have kept damped down into our bodies are being released.

I also discovered, early on, when I was training my mind, there is a certain point, a certain line you must draw, and beyond that point you cannot let your mind go. If you do, you risk mental problems, you risk moroseness, you risk being a real downer for everybody around you: that would be the least. But you could flip out. People do flip out, get unbalanced by believing what their minds are telling them about reality. We all do it, but there is a certain line beyond which you cannot go . . . I used to have panic attacks. I thought there was a big black hole in the ground in front of me. Since I have allowed myself the privilege, and the grace of being happy, all the time, I don't see black holes any more.

Some of you have been dearer to me than my family. Because you allow Padmasambhava to come to me in just another way, through your care and your concern and your love. You don't seem to care that I have AIDS. No one has ever asked me: "Well, how did you get it?" No one has ever intimated that this might be a curse on me; except one old friend of mine who called me a week or so ago and said, "Aren't you afraid that this is God's curse on you?" After I stopped laughing, I said, "You believe that God has cursed the earth and the human body is impure. I, on the other hand, believe that blessing is the original starting point, not a curse." From beginningless time, everything has already been accomplished, pure and perfect.

So what I do now is just rest in the radiance. It's everywhere. You can't get away from it. It is so intoxicating that sometimes I feel like I am just floating in the radiance. I am letting Padmasambhava, as he flies through the sky of the mind, just let me tag along.

Now if I were sitting out there listening to this, I would say, "OK then, why aren't you healed?" People have asked me that. It's not that I haven't tried: I bought a whole suitcase full of pills. But I stopped that question quite a while ago. I guess the reason I did was because it seemed it would be manipulating and interfering with the process that has started. This process is very cleansing for me. I know there is a lot of karma being burned up. It's cleansing perhaps for my mother, because I offer this for her. She suffers quite a bit. Then there are spiritual friends in this group whom I love like brothers and sisters; they suffer too. I have made this covenant with Padmasambhava: If I have to stay around and suffer so that some of it could help cleanse and purify you as well as me, what a blessing that would be! This is my prayer. And I'm not a person who likes to suffer, I can guarantee you that! But I feel that grace, that blessing, pushing me gently into that suffering.

And at this point, from studying what I have studied of Rinpoche's teachings on the bardos, death is not an enemy. Just like our thoughts are not to be seen as enemies. . . . And life is not an enemy. Life is something glorious, because in this life we can awaken to who we truly are.

So I beg you—from the bottom of my heart—not to waste the opportunity you have, while you are still relatively healthy, to work with what Rinpoche is offering you . . . He knows how to get to the point in speaking and teaching about what Dzogchen is, and he knows how to take you there in the heart. That is so important: and especially when you are getting ready to die.

So I'm here to say goodbye. At least for this time around . . . I want to say goodbye to all those of you who have become my brothers and sisters, those of you whom I know but have not had the privilege of getting to know better, those of you I have not even met . . . I have a feeling that within the next six months I may die. It could be within the next three months. So I hold you all in my heart, and I see you all bright and shining. There is no darkness. It is just light from Padmasambhava's heart, pervading all of us. Thanks to the master's blessing.

simplicity

—◇—

from

VOLUNTARY SIMPLICITY

by Duane Elgin

Voluntary Simplicity's 1981 publication helped to inspire a movement toward living more simply. It also is a book about living more consciously and thus more freely. Duane Elgin (born 1943) suggests that such behavior can change the world in fundamental ways.

—◇—

To live voluntarily requires not only that we be conscious of the choices before us (the outer world) but also that we be conscious of ourselves as we select among those choices (the inner world). We must be conscious of both the choices and the chooser if we are to act voluntarily. Put differently, to act voluntarily is to act in a self-determining manner. But who is the "self" making the decisions? If that "self" is both socially and psychologically conditioned into habitual patterns of thought and action, then behavior can hardly be considered voluntary. Therefore, self-realization—the process of realizing who the "self" really is—is crucial to self-determination and voluntary action.

The point is that the more precise and sustained is our conscious knowing of ourselves, the more voluntary or choiceful can be our participation in life. If we are inattentive in noticing ourselves going through life, then the choicefulness with which we live will be commensurately diminished. The more conscious we are of our passage through life, the more skillfully we can act and the more harmonious can be the relationship between our inner experience and our outer expression.

Running on Automatic

To fully appreciate what it means to act voluntarily, we must acknowledge to ourselves the extent to which we tend to act involuntarily. We tend to "run on automatic"—act in habitual and preprogrammed ways—to a much greater extent than we commonly recognize.

Consider, for example, how we learned to walk as children. At first walking was an enormous struggle that required all our energy and attention. Within a few months the period of intense struggle passed. As the ability to walk became increasingly automated, we began to focus our attention on other things—reaching, touching, climbing. In the same manner we have learned and largely automated virtually every facet of our daily lives: walking, driving, reading, working, relating to others, and so on. This habitual patterning of behavior extends into the most intimate details of our lives: the knot we make in tying our shoes, the manner in which we brush our teeth, which leg we put first into a pair of pants, and so on. Not only do automatic patterns of behavior pervade nearly every aspect of our physical existence, they also condition how we think and feel. To be sure, there is a degree of variety in our thinking, feeling, and behaving; yet the variety tends to be predictable since it is derived largely from preprogrammed and habituated patterns of response to the world. If we do not become conscious of these automated patterns of thinking, feeling, and behaving, then we become, by default, human automatons.

We tend not to notice or appreciate the degree to which we run on automatic—largely because we live in an almost constant state of mental distraction. Our minds are constantly moving about at a lightning-fast pace, thinking about the future, replaying conversations from the past, engaging in inner role-playing, and so on. Without sustained attention it is difficult to appreciate the extent to which we live ensnared in an automated, reflexive, and dream-like reality that is a subtle and continuously changing blend of fantasy, inner dialogue, memory, planning, and so on. The fact that we spend years acquiring vast amounts of *mental content* does not mean that we are thereby either substantially aware of or in control of our *mental process*. This fact is clearly described by Roger Walsh—a physician, psychiatrist, and brain researcher. His vivid description of the nature of thought processes (as revealed in the early stages of meditative practice) is so useful to our discussion that I quote his comments at length:

> I was forced to recognize that what I had formerly
> believed to be my rational mind preoccupied with
> cognition, planning, problem solving, etc., actually
> comprised a frantic torrent of forceful, demanding,
> loud, and often unrelated thoughts and fantasies
> which filled an unbelievable proportion of con-
> sciousness even during purposive behavior. The
> incredible proportion of consciousness which this
> fantasy world occupied, my powerlessness to remove
> it for more than a few seconds, and my former state
> of mindlessness or ignorance of its existence, stag-
> gered me. . . . Foremost among the implicit beliefs
> of orthodox Western psychology is the assumption
> that man spends most of his time reasoning and

problem solving, and that only neurotics and other
abnormals spend much time, outside of leisure, in
fantasy. However, it is my impression that prolonged
self-observation will show that at most times we are
living almost in a dream world in which we skillfully
and automatically yet unknowingly blend inputs
from reality and fantasy in accordance with our
needs and defenses. . . . The subtlety, complexity,
infinite range and number, and entrapping power of
the fantasies which the mind creates seem impossible
to comprehend, to differentiate from reality while in
them, and even more so to describe to one who has
not experienced them.

The crucial importance of penetrating behind our continuous
stream of thought (as largely unconscious and lightning-fast flows of
inner fantasy-dialogue) is stressed by every major consciousness tradition in the world: Buddhist, Taoist, Hindu, Sufi, Zen, and so on.
Western cultures, however, have fostered the understanding that a state
of continual mental distraction is in the natural order of things.
Consequently, by virtue of a largely unconscious social agreement
about the nature of our inner thought processes, we live individually
and collectively almost totally embedded within our mentally constructed reality. We are so busy creating ever more appealing images
or social facades for others to see, and so distracted from the simplicity of our spontaneously arising self, that we do not truly
encounter either ourselves or one another. In the process we lose a
large measure of our innate capacity for voluntary, deliberate, intentional action.

Bringing more conscious attention to our thought processes
and behavior has profound social as well as personal implications.

The late E. F. Schumacher expressed this forthrightly in his book, *A Guide for the Perplexed*: "It is a grave error to accuse a man who pursues self-knowledge of 'turning his back on society.' The opposite would be more nearly true: that a man who fails to pursue self-knowledge is and remains a danger to society, for he will tend to misunderstand everything that other people say or do, and remain blissfully unaware of the significance of many of the things he does himself."

How are we to penetrate behind our automated and habitual patterns of thinking and behaving?

Living More Consciously

The word *consciousness* literally means "that with which we know." It has also been termed the knowing faculty. To live more consciously means to be more consciously aware, moment by moment, that we are present in all that we do. When we stand and talk, we know that we are standing and talking. When we sit and eat, we know that we are sitting and eating. When we do the countless things that make up our daily lives, we remember the being that is involved in those activities. We remember ourselves (and to "re-member" is to make whole; it is the opposite of dis-memberment). To live consciously is to move through life with conscious self-remembering.

We are not bound to habitual and preprogrammed ways of perceiving and responding when we are consciously watchful of ourselves in the process of living. Consider several examples. It is difficult to relate to another person solely as the embodiment of a social position or job title when, moment by moment, we are consciously aware of the utter humanness that we both possess—a humanness whose magnificence and mystery dwarfs the seeming importance of status and titles as a basis of relationship. It is difficult to deceive another person when, moment by moment, we are consciously aware of our unfolding experience of deception. It is difficult to sustain the experience of sexual desire by projecting a sexual fantasy when, moment by moment, we are conscious that we are creating and relating to a fantasy rather than the authentic individual we are with. In short, when we begin to consciously watch ourselves, in the activities of daily life, we begin to cut through confining self-images, social pretenses, and psychological barriers. We begin to live more voluntarily.

We all have the ability to consciously know ourselves as we move through life. The capacity to "witness" the unfolding of our lives is not an ability that is remote or hidden from us. To the contrary, this is an experience that is so close, so intimate, and so ordinary, that we easily overlook its presence and significance. An old adage states, It's a rare fish that knows it swims in water. Analogously the challenge of living voluntarily is not in gaining access to the conscious experiencing of ourselves but rather in consciously recognizing the witnessing experience and then learning the skills of sustaining our opening to that experience.

To clarify the nature of conscious watchfulness, I would like to ask you several questions. Have you been conscious of the fact that you have been sitting here reading this book? Have you been conscious of changes in your bodily sensations, frame of mind, and emotions? Were you totally absorbed in the book until I asked? Or had you unintentionally allowed your thoughts to wander to other concerns? Did you just experience a slight shock of self-recognition when I inquired? What does it feel like to notice yourself reading while you read; to observe yourself eating while you eat; to see yourself watching television while you watch television; to notice yourself driving while you drive; to experience yourself talking while you talk?

Despite the utter simplicity of being consciously watchful of our lives, this is a demanding activity. At first it is a struggle to just occasionally remember ourselves moving through the daily routine. A brief moment of self-remembering is followed by an extended period where we are lost in the flow of thought and the demands of the exterior world. Yet with practice we find that we can more easily remember ourselves—while walking down the street or while we are at home, at work, at play. We come to recognize, as direct experience, the nature of "knowing that we know." As our familiarity with this mode of perception increases, we get lost in thought and worldly activities less and less frequently. In turn, we experience our behavior in the world as more and more choiceful, or voluntary.

Bringing conscious attention into our daily lives may lack the mystery of searching for enlightenment with an Indian sorcerer and the spiritual glamour of sitting for long months in an Eastern monastic setting, but consciously attending to our daily-life activities is an eminently useful, readily accessible, and powerful tool for enhancing our capacity for voluntary action.

Embedded and Self-Reflective Consciousness

Because these two modes of consciousness are so crucial to our discussion, I want to define them more carefully. What follows is not an original distinction but an ancient one that has been variously labeled, but similarly described, by many others.

The first mode of consciousness I will call embedded consciousness. Embedded consciousness is our so-called normal or waking consciousness and it is characterized by our being so embedded within the stream of inner-fantasy dialogue that little conscious attention can be given to the moment-to-moment experiencing of ourselves. In forgetting ourselves we tend to run on automatic and thereby forfeit our capacity for voluntary action. In the distracted state of embedded consciousness we tend to identify who we are with habitual patterns of behavior, thought, and feeling. We assume this social mask is the sum total of who we really are. Consequently we feel the need to protect and defend our social facade. Having identified ourselves with this limited and shallow rendering of who we are, we find it difficult to pull away from our masks and freshly experience our identity.

The next step beyond embedded consciousness I will term self-reflective consciousness. Where the distinctive quality of embedded satisfaction is self-forgetting (running on automatic), the distinctive quality of self-reflective consciousness is self-remembering (acting in the world intentionally, deliberately, voluntarily). Self-reflective consciousness provides us with a mirror that reveals or reflects who we are as we move through our daily lives. This is not a mechanical watchfulness but a living awareness that changes moment by moment. It means that to varying degrees we are continuously and consciously "tasting" our experience of ourselves. Overall, the opening to self-reflective consciousness is marked by the progressive and balanced development of the ability to be simultaneously concentrated (with a precise and delicate attention to the details of life) and mindful (with a panoramic appreciation of the totality of life). Nothing is left out of our experience, as both the minute details and larger life circumstances are simultaneously embraced in our awareness.

To make friends with ourselves in this way requires that we be willing to accept the totality of ourselves—including our sensual desires, self-doubts, anger, laziness, restlessness, fears, and so on. We cannot move beyond the habitual pushes and pulls of these forces until we are conscious of their presence in our lives. In turn, to see ourselves in this manner calls for much patience, gentleness, and self-forgiveness, as we will notice ourselves thinking and acting in ways that we would like to think we are above or beyond. To the extent that we are able to see or know our automated patterns, we are then no longer bound by them. We are enabled to act and live voluntarily.

Beyond Self-Reflective Consciousness
The conscious evolution of consciousness does not end with becoming knowingly attentive to our everyday life experience. This is but a beginning of a much larger journey. Self-remembering is the immediately accessible doorway that gradually opens into the farther reaches of conscious knowing. By our being knowingly attentive to the "self" moving through our ordinary, day-to-day life experience, the entire spectrum of conscious evolution unfolds. Just as a giant tree grows from the smallest seedling, so, too, does the seed experience of self-reflective consciousness contain within it the farthest reaches of conscious evolution.

When we tune in to our moment-to-moment experiencing with persistence and patience, our experience of "self" is gradually though profoundly transformed. The boundaries between the "self-in-here" and the "world-out-there" begin to dissolve as we refine the precision with which we watch ourselves moving through life. The inner and outer person gradually merge into one continuous flow of experience. In other words, in the next stage beyond self-reflective consciousness the duality of "watcher and watched" merges into the unity of an integrated flow of conscious experiencing.

The capacity to ultimately experience the totality of existence as an unbounded and unbroken whole is not confined to any particular culture, race, or religion. This experience of ineffable unity is sometimes referred to as the Perennial Wisdom because it appears throughout recorded history in the writings of every major spiritual tradition in the world: Christianity, Buddhism, Hinduism, Taoism, Judaism, Islam, and more. Each tradition records that if we gently though persistently look into our own experience, we will ultimately discover that who "we" are is not different or separate from that which we call God, Cosmic Consciousness, Unbounded Wholeness, the Tao, Nirvana, and countless other names for this ultimately unnameable experience. The common experience found at the core of every major spiritual tradition is suggested in the following statements:

> The Kingdom of Heaven is within you.
> —words of Jesus

> Look within, thou are the Buddha.
> —words of Gautama Buddha

> Atman (the essence of the individual) and Brahman (the ultimate reality) are one.
> —words from the Hindu tradition

> He who knows himself knows his Lord.
> —words of Muhammad

The experience of unity or wholeness or love lies at the core of every major spiritual tradition. This does not mean there exists a universal theology; rather it means that we are all human beings and there are common experiences we share. For example, the capacity to experience love is not confined to any particular culture, race, or religion. It is a universal human experience. The theologian Paul Tillich described the ultimate nature of love as the experience of life in its actual unity. If the experience of love is the experience of life in its actual unity, then consciousness is the vehicle whereby that experience is known. When we become fully conscious of life, we find that it is an unbroken whole in and, turn we may describe this experience of wholeness as "love."

Enabling Qualities of Living More Consciously

There are a variety of ways in which the capacity for reflective consciousness is empowering and enabling. Being more consciously attentive to our moment-to-moment experience enhances our ability to see the world accurately. Given the distracting power of our thoughts (as lightning-fast movements of inner fantasy-dialogue), it is no small task to see things clearly. If we are not paying attention to our flow through life, then we will find that we have more accidents along the way, we will misunderstand others more often, and we will tend to overlook important things. Conversely, if we are being attentive to ourselves moving through the countless small happenings that comprise our daily lives, then we will tend to be more productive; we will tend to listen more carefully and understand more fully; we will have fewer accidents along the way; and we will be more present and available in our relationships with others.

Living more consciously has a straightforward and practical relevance, both for our lives as individuals and as a civilization in a period of stressful transition. As we develop the skills of living more consciously, we are able not only to examine the underpinnings of our personally constructed reality (as habitual patterns of thought and behavior), but additionally to examine our socially constructed reality (as equally habitual patterns of thought and behavior that characterize an entire culture). Socially, we are more able to penetrate through the political posturings, glib advertisements, and cultural myths that sustain the status quo. In an era dominated by hideously complex problems of global dimension, the ability to see the world more clearly is essential to the survival and well-being of the human family.

Developing the capacity for self-reflective consciousness also enables us to respond more quickly to subtle feedback that something is amiss. In being more attentive to our situation as a society, we do not have to be shocked or bludgeoned into remedial action by, for example, massive famines or catastrophic environmental accidents. Instead, more subtle signals suffice to indicate that corrective actions are warranted. In the context of an increasingly interdependent world—where the strength of the whole web of social, environmental, and economic relations is increasingly at the mercy of the weakest links—the capacity to respond quickly to subtle warnings that we are getting off a healthy track in our social evolution is indispensable to our long-run survival.

Further, living more consciously expands our range of choice and allows us to respond to situations with greater flexibility and creativity. In seeing our habitual patterns of thought and behavior more clearly, we have greater choice in how we respond. This does not mean that we will always make the "right" choices; rather, with conscious attention our actions and their consequences become much more visible to us and they become a potent source of learning. And with learning comes increasing skillfulness of action.

Reflective consciousness also promotes an ecological orientation toward the rest of life. With conscious attention to our moment-to-moment experience, we begin to directly sense the subtle though profound connectedness of all life. We begin to experience that the entirety of existence is an unbroken whole. Awareness of our intimate relationship with the rest of life naturally fosters feelings of compassion. Our range of caring is expanded enormously, and this brings with it a strong feeling of worldly engagement and responsibility.

A witnessing or reflective consciousness has profound relevance for humanity's evolution toward a sustainable society. The ecological crisis we now face has emerged, in no small part, from the gross disparity that exists between our relatively underdeveloped inner faculties and the extremely powerful external technologies now at our disposal. With humanity's powers magnified enormously through our technologies, we can do irreparable damage to the planet. The reach of our technological power exceeds the grasp of our inner learning. Unless we expand our interior learning to match our technological advances, we will be destined to act to the detriment of ourselves and the rest of life on the planet. We must correct the imbalance by developing a level of interior maturation that is at least commensurate with the enormous technological development that has occurred over the last several centuries.

Just as the faculty of the human intellect had to be developed by entire cultures in order to support the emergence of the industrial revolution, so, too, must we now begin to develop the faculty of consciousness if we are to build a sustainable future. There are many paths for this journey of awakening. Whichever path is selected, we must begin to live more consciously as a species if we are to survive the coming decades and make a successful transition to some form of sustainable, global civilization.

. . .

from Voluntary Simplicity

The Nature of Human Nature

Some people believe that "you can't change human nature," so the idea of an evolving human consciousness is no more than unwarranted idealism. Yet, what is human "nature"? The dictionary defines *nature* as the "inherent character or basic constitution of a person or thing—its essence." Does the inherent character and essence of a person ever change? We can gain insight into this key issue by asking an analogous question: Does the inherent character of a seed change when it grows into a tree? Not at all. The potential for becoming a tree was always resident within the seed. When a seed grows into a tree, it only represents a change in the degree to which its potential, always inherent in its original nature, is realized. Similarly, human nature does not change; yet, like the seed with the potential of becoming a tree, human nature is not a static "thing" but a spectrum of potentials. Human beings can grow from a primitive to an enlightened condition without that unfolding representing a change in our basic human nature.

There is, however, a crucial difference between the manner in which the tree and the person realize their innate potentials. For the seed to realize its full expression, it only has to find fertile soil, and the organic cycle of growth unfolds automatically. However, human beings do not develop in an equally automatic manner. For we humans to actualize our potentials, at some point there must be a shift from embedded to self-reflective consciousness (and beyond) if maturation is to continue.

Our culture provides the soil—either moist and fertile or dry and barren—within which we grow. However, the ultimate responsibility for growth, irrespective of cultural setting, remains with the individual. Overall, human nature is not a static condition but an unfolding spectrum of potentials. We can move along that spectrum without changing our basic human nature. That we do progress is vividly illustrated by the fact that humanity has moved from primitive nomad to the edge of global civilization in an instant of geological time. Despite the enormity and speed of our evolution of culture and consciousness, we are far from being fully developed. We are, I think, still in the adolescence of our species and have not yet begun collectively to imagine where our journey could lead in the future.

Conclusion

Throughout history few people have had the opportunity to develop their interior potentials consciously because much of the evolutionary journey of humanity has been preoccupied with the struggle for survival. The present era of relative abundance— particularly in industrial nations—contrasts sharply with the material adversity and poverty of the past. With simplicity, equity, and compassion we can have both freedom from want and the freedom to evolve our potentials in cooperation with other members of the human family. The Industrial Revolution may be viewed as a major breakthrough that could provide the material basis to support the pervasive evolution of individual and sociocultural awareness.

The cumulative effects of even a modest degree of development of the capacity for self-reflective consciousness would result, in my estimation, in a quantum increase in the effectiveness of self-regulating behavior that is conscious of, and responsive to, the needs of the larger world. The actions of countless individuals would arise from a deeper ground of shared awareness and this, in turn, would tend to produce a larger pattern of coherent and harmonious behavior. Self-reflective consciousness now moves from the status of a spiritual luxury for the few in a more rudimentary and fragmented social setting to that of a social necessity for the many in a highly complex and enormously enlarged social setting. Just as the faculty of the intellect had to be developed by entire cultures to support the emergence of the Industrial Revolution, so, too, I think, must we now begin to cultivate the development of the "knowing faculty," or consciousness, if we are to support the emergence of revitalized civilizations. No small part of our contemporary civilizational challenge is to acknowledge, and then begin consciously to develop, these vitally important potentials.

forgiveness

—◇—

from

LOVINGKINDNESS

by Sharon Salzberg

Sharon Salzberg (born 1952) has studied a variety of Buddhist traditions, working with teachers from India, Burma, Nepal, Bhutan and Tibet. Her work as a writer and teacher reflects her experience of loving-kindness meditation, which cultivates elements of love, compassion, joy and equanimity.

—◇—

Hatred can never cease by hatred.
Hatred can only cease by love.
This is an eternal law.

—The Buddha

When I first practiced medition with Sayadaw U Pandita, in 1984, I went through a period of disturbing memories about all the terrible things I had ever done. Memories of spurning childhood friends, of telling lies from seemingly good motives, of holding on to things when I was perfectly capable of giving them up, all came up to haunt me. I did not even want to tell the Sayadaw that I was experiencing this, but I did. I said, "You know, I just keep thinking of event after event after event—all of these bad things I've done. I feel terrible. I feel horrible. I feel awful."

U Pandita looked at me and asked, "Well, are you finally seeing the truth about yourself?" I was shocked at his response. Even though I was enveloped in self-judgment and criticism, something in his comment made me want to challenge it. I thought to myself, "No, I'm not seeing the truth about myself." And then he simply said, "Stop thinking about it." Only later would I understand the wisdom of his advice. Who among us has not done things to hurt people or to harm other creatures, or the earth itself? Through actions born of the mind state of aversion, we harm others and we harm ourselves. We experience aversion through a host of afflictions—anger, fear, guilt, impatience, grief, disappointment, dejection, anxiety, despair. Because hatred and aversion are the opposite of the state of love, they are considered the "far enemy" of metta.

The near enemy of metta, desire, is a subtler hindrance because it brings us temporary satisfaction. These states of aversion, by contrast, tear us apart; we burn when we are caught in them. The Buddha described the states of aversion as being of great consequence but easily overcome. They are of great consequence because they easily provoke strong action, leading us to perform unskillful deeds that hurt both ourselves and others. But even though such states are dangerous, nonetheless the pain of them is obvious, tangible, and easily felt. From beginning to end they bring great pain, so we are naturally moved to let them go.

The force of aversion manifests through us in two primary ways. One is outflowing, such as anger or rage. Such states have a lot of energy; they are powerful and expressive. We also experience aversion in a held-in way, as in grief, fear, disappointment, and despair. Here aversion's energy is frozen and paralyzing. Whether we are directing aversion toward ourselves or others, whether we are containing the aversion within our minds or expressing it toward others, these are the same mind states appearing in different forms.

One of the ways in which we direct aversion toward ourselves is in the form of guilt. As I experienced with Sayadaw U Pandita, as we go deeper in practice, we often begin spontaneously to review everything harmful we have ever done. These things just start coming up. People recall having disappointed a friend twenty-six years previously by not going to her sweet sixteen party, or the bitter retorts made to a partner no longer a part of their life. People suffer from having committed insurance fraud that remained undetected, or from the subtle, ongoing fear in a current friendship because of a lie told. It is very important to be able to acknowledge such things, to experience the pain, and then, as Sayadaw advised me, to just let them go—"stop thinking about it." Otherwise, we actually enhance a mistaken sense of self.

Buddhist psychology makes an interesting distinction between guilt and remorse. The feeling of guilt, or hatred directed toward oneself, lacerates. When we experience a strong feeling of guilt in the mind, we have little or no energy available for transformation or transcendence. We are defeated by the guilt itself, because it depletes us. We also feel very alone. Our thoughts focus on our worthlessness: "I'm the worst person in the world. Only I do these terrible things." However, such an attitude is actually very "self"-promoting. We become obsessed with "self" in the egotistical sense.

Remorse, by contrast, is a state of recognition. We realize that we have at some point done something or said something unskillful that caused pain, and we feel the pain of that recognition. But, crucially, remorse frees us to let go of the past. It leaves us with some energy to move on, resolved not to repeat our mistakes.

And guilt can be deceptive. We may feel that guilt can be a noble force to motivate us to so serve others or perform wholesome actions. But guilt does not actually work in that way. When one is motivated by guilt or grief, one's own pain is center stage, just as when one is motivated by anger, one's outrage is center stage. When such feelings take the central role, we may lose consideration of what somebody else may actually need. There is not enough freedom from self-centeredness in our consciousness to see clearly, to be connected fully. Our own feelings overwhelm consciousness. We end up serving ourselves. How far this is from the invocation of Rabindranath Tagore: "Oh Lord, make me a better instrument through which you can blow."

Cultivating this mistaken concept of a permanent self also leads to aversion in the form of self-hatred or judgment. When we see the self as a fixed entity, we develop a strong habit of mind that drives our lives. If through our practice we can see the impersonal nature of the forces that arise and pass away, we experience a very different reality. For example, we can see anger, guilt, or grief arising in the mind as forces that come and go. Aversion is like a rainstorm, arising and passing away. It is not I, not me, not mine. It is not you or yours, either. In this recognition of emptiness, we look at other beings and see ourselves. Here is the birth of metta.

Self-hatred impedes this flowering of our practice. When the Dalai Lama visited Insight Meditation Society in 1979, somebody asked him, "I am a beginning meditation student and I feel quite worthless as a person. What can you say about that?" The Dalai Lama replied, "You should never think like that; that is completely wrong thinking. You have the power of thought, and therefore the power of mind, and that is all you need." He was recognizing that we all have the potential for enlightenment, and therefore we should not denigrate that capacity by saying we are worthless.

We need to recollect this potential for awakening in order to see ourselves clearly. When we fall into aversion, we lose this perspective. I once approached my very first meditation teacher, S. N. Goenka, in an accusatory fashion and demanded to know, "Isn't there an easier way?" I was fed up and hated all my aches and pains. I think I actually thought he *did* know an easier way and was purposely withholding it from me so that I could suffer. It is quite amusing to look back on it, because he was a very compassionate person. After I asked that question, he just looked at me for a while. I fell into his eyes, which were radiant with a vastness of perspective, which never overlooked my capacity for freedom. From the point of view of a lifetime of spiritual endeavor, my sleepiness and knee pain did not seem so momentous and terrible. Whenever we forget the larger perspective, we become lost in the moment's little drama. Lost in aversion, we forget our capacity to love.

Once I received quite an angry letter from someone. It was one of those letters you would really rather not get, listing a lot of situations and circumstances that had happened. It basically said, "That was your fault, and that was your fault, and that was your fault, and *that* was your fault, too." It was not very pleasant. Throughout the rest of the day, I found myself composing responses in my mind to this letter. Mostly they ran along the lines of, "Well, actually, that's not my fault. It's your fault. And that was your fault, and that was your fault, and that was your fault, and *that* was your fault, too." I spent much of that day spinning it all out.

This kind of self-righteous anger solidifies into an almost choking sense of "I" and "other." Anger is such a grievous state because it means the death of the possibility of love or connection in that moment, in that situation. But what do we do when we feel anger or aversion?

There is a confusion in contemporary society about how to relate to feelings of aversion. For example, it is difficult to understand the difference between *feeling* anger and *venting* anger. When we undertake a spiritual practice, it is important that we open to all that arises, that we recognize, acknowledge, and accept everything we feel. We have a long conditioning of self-deception, of keeping certain things outside the sphere of our awareness, of repressing them. Overcoming our denial and repression and opening to states of aversion can be very healing. But in the process, we may pay the price of becoming lost in anger if, through misunderstanding, we indulge it.

Most contemporary psychological research shows that when one expresses anger quite often in one's life, it leads to the easy expression of anger. Expressing anger becomes a habit. Many people assume that we have a certain amount of anger inside, and that if we do not want to keep it inside, we have to put it outside; somehow if it is outside, it is not going to be inside anymore. Anger seems like a solid thing. But, in fact, we discover, if we observe carefully, that anger has no solidity. In reality it is merely a conditioned response that arises and passes away. It is crucial for us to see that when we *identify* with these passing states as being solid and who we truly are, we let them rule us, and we are compelled to act in ways that cause harm to ourselves and others. Our opening needs to rest on a basis of *nonidentification*. Recognizing aversion or anger in the mind as transitory is very different from identifying with them as being who we really are, and then acting on them.

Anger is a very complex emotion, with a lot of different components. There are strands of disappointment, fear, sadness, all woven together. If the emotions and thoughts are taken as a whole, anger appears as one solid thing. But if we break it down and see its various aspects, we can see the ultimate nature of this experience. We can see that anger is impermanent, and it arises and passes away like a wave that comes and goes. We can see that anger is unsatisfactory; it does not bring us lasting joy. We can see that anger is empty of a "self" determining it; it does not arise according to our will, or whim, or wish. It arises when conditions are right for it to arise. We can see that it is not ours; we do not own it, we do not possess it. We cannot control anger's arising. We can only learn to relate to it in a skillful way.

If we look at the force of anger, we can, in fact, discover many positive aspects in it. Anger is not a passive, complacent state. It has incredible energy. Anger can impel us to let go of ways we may be inappropriately defined by the needs of others; it can teach us to say no. In this way it also serves our integrity, because anger can motivate us to turn from the demands of the outer world to the nascent voice of our inner world. It is a way to set boundaries and to challenge injustice at every level. Anger will not take things for granted or simply accept them mindlessly.

Anger also has the ability to cut through surface appearances; it does not just stay on a superficial level. It is very critical; it is very demanding. Anger has the power to pierce through the obvious to things that are more hidden. This is why anger may be transmuted to wisdom. By nature, anger has characteristics in common with wisdom.

Nevertheless, the unskillful aspects of anger are immense, and they far outweigh the positive aspects. The Buddha described it in this way: "Anger, with its poisoned source and fevered climax, murderously sweet, that you must slay to weep no more." It is sweet indeed! But the satisfaction we get from expressing anger is very short-lived, while the pain endures for a long time and debilitates us.

According to Buddhist psychology, the characteristic of anger is savageness. The function of anger is to burn up its own support, like a forest fire. It leaves us with nothing; it leaves us devastated. Just like a forest fire that ranges free and wild, anger can leave us in a place very far from where we intended to go. The deluding quality of anger is responsible for our losing ourselves in this way. When we are lost in anger, we do not see many options before us, and so we strike out recklessly.

Anger and aversion express themselves in acts of hostility and persecution. The mind becomes very narrow. It isolates someone or something, fixates on it, develops tunnel vision, sees no way out, fixes that experience, that person, or that object as being forever unchanging. Such aversion supports an endless cycle of harm and revenge. We see this reality politically: with racial struggle, with class struggle, with national struggle, with religious hatreds. Anger can bind people to each other as strongly as desire, so that they drag each other along, connected through various kinds of revenge and counterrevenge, never being able to let go, never being able to be still. The playwright and statesman Vaclav Havel has noted insightfully that hatred has much in common with desire, that it is "the fixation on others, the dependence on them, and in fact the delegation of a piece of one's own identity to them. . . . The hater longs for the object of his hatred."

So it never ends, as long as people continue to relate in the same way. We see an oppressed people being hurt and then often taking power and behaving in exactly the same way toward some other people. Someone sends a letter accusing me, and I accuse them back.

How can we let go in such a situation? How can we change it? We can focus our attention more on the *suffering* of the situation, both our own and the suffering of others, rather than on our *anger*. We can ask ourselves whom we are really angry at. Mostly what we are angry at is the anger in the other person. It is almost as if the other person were an instrument for the anger that moves through them and motivates them to act in unskillful ways. We do not become angry at somebody's mouth when they are shouting at us; we are angry at the anger that is motivating them to shout. If we add anger to anger, we only serve to increase it.

In a well-known phrase, the Buddha said, "Hatred can never cease by hatred. Hatred can only cease by love. This is an eternal

Sharon Salzberg

law." We can begin to transcend the cycle of aversion when we can stop seeing ourselves personally as agents of revenge. Ultimately, all beings are the owners of their own karma. If someone has caused harm, they will suffer. If we have caused harm, we will suffer. As the Buddha said in the *Dhammapada:*

> We are what we think.
> All that we are arises with our thoughts.
> With our thoughts we make the world.
> Speak or act with an impure mind
> And trouble will follow you
> As the wheel follows the ox that draws the cart. . . .
> Speak or act with a pure mind
> And happiness will follow you
> As your shadow, unshakable.

Happiness and unhappiness depend upon our actions.

That does not mean that we sit back with glee, thinking, "You'll get yours in this life or the next." Rather, we understand that we do not have to be agents of revenge, that if people have caused suffering, they will suffer. This is an impersonal law, affecting us as well.

On the eve of his enlightenment, the Buddha, then known as the Bodhisattva, sat under the Bodhi Tree, determined not to move until he attained enlightenment. Mara, a mythic figure in the Buddhist cosmology, the "killer of virtue" and the "killer of life," recognizing that his kingdom of delusion was greatly jeopardized by the Bodhisattva's aspiration to awaken, came with many different challenges. Attempting to get the Bodhisattva to give up his resolve, he challenged him through lust, anger, and fear. He showered him with hailstorms, mud storms, and other travails. No matter what happened, the Bodhisattva sat serenely, unmoved and unswayed in his determination.

168

from Lovingkindness

The final challenge of Mara was self-doubt. He said to the Bodhisattva, "By what right are you even sitting there with that goal? What makes you think you have the right even to aspire to full enlightenment, to complete awakening?" In response to that challenge, the Bodhisattva reached over and touched the earth. He called upon the earth itself to bear witness to all of the lifetimes in which he had practiced generosity, patience, and morality. Lifetime after lifetime he had built a wave of moral force that had given him the right to that aspiration.

When I think of the law of karma, I sometimes think of this story. The earth *is* bearing witness, and if we have caused suffering, we will suffer; if others have caused suffering they will suffer. Understanding this truth, we can let go. We can be free.

It so happened that on the very evening of the day I received that letter I reacted to so strongly, a friend brought a Tibetan lama to visit us at Insight Meditation Society. This lama had lived in a cave in the Himalayas for about fifteen years without ever leaving it. He was a master of the Tibetan practice of *tumo,* raising the body heat through the power of mind.

This lama had been approached in his cave and asked if he would consider going to America to be studied. He was told about how scientists, as they try to understand meditation, like to have effects that are measurable. Clearly, raising one's body heat through concentrating the mind is a very measurable thing. Because the Dalai Lama himself had made this request, the monk agreed to go. He came out of his cave and went straight to Boston. He was taken from the airport directly to the hospital, where he spent many days meditating while researchers kept taking his temperature.

At some point, our friend who had brought the lama there suggested that he take a break to come out to Insight Meditation Society, which is not too far from Boston. He came. When he walked through the door, the first thing he said was, "This place seems so different from the rest of America. What do you do here?" So we told him, and we ended up talking and spending the evening together.

This master of *tumo* had with him a young, articulate interpreter. The interpreter told us that this monk was considered quite extraordinary within the Tibetan tradition. He had become a monk quite late in life for that tradition, and he had gone very far in his meditation practice very fast, despite the fact that he had "skipped over" many aspects of spiritual training that the Tibetans consider necessary for such progress. He had not done the preliminary study or any of the preliminary meditation practices, which are considered to be absolutely essential in building a foundation before mastering more difficult and subtle practices. So the Tibetans considered him quite an anomalous puzzle.

We asked the lama, "Do you have any idea why you should have made such extraordinary progress in your practice, even though you did not fulfill these usual preliminaries?"

"Yes," he answered, "I do have an idea. When I was a layperson in Tibet, for many years I was a guerrilla fighter. Often I captured people and tortured and killed them. Then at some point in my life, I was captured myself by the Chinese and put in prison. I was tortured, and I underwent tremendous suffering. I made a commitment at that time not to hate the Chinese people."

The lama explained that he saw his situation in quite classical Buddhist terms. What he was experiencing at the hands of the Chinese, he understood to be the karmic fruit of his own previous actions. He pointed out that even if he had not seen it in those terms, he understood that nobody other than himself could *make* him suffer mentally. So he made a decision not to add the fires of hatred and bitterness to the terrible torment he was undergoing physically. He told us that he thought it was this decision that allowed him to make such extraordinary progress in his practice.

As this remarkable being was speaking, I was sitting there having images in my mind of the letter that I had been composing all day, saying, "That was your fault, and that was your fault, and *that* was your fault, too." I realized that I did not have to write it that way. Thanks to the propitious, timely example of the lama, I understood what is genuinely possible for human beings with a human heart. I understood, as the Buddha said, that "hatred will never cease by hatred." Never. "Hatred can only cease by love."

When our minds are full of anger and hatred toward others, in fact *we* are the ones who are actually suffering, caught in this mind state. But it is not so easy to access that place inside of us which can forgive, which can love. In some ways to be able to forgive, to let go, is a type of dying. It is the ability to say, "I am not that person anymore, and you are not that person anymore." Forgiveness allows us to recapture some part of ourselves that we left behind in bondage to a past event. Some part of our identity may also need to die in that letting go, so that we can reclaim the energy bound up in the past.

All of these teachings are available to us if we can be aware of what we are feeling in the deepest possible way, so that nothing is blocked from our consciousness. Then we can examine: What is our struggle? Why are we struggling? It is important to understand that no one thing makes us feel a certain way. Nothing stands alone in this conditioned world. We live in an interdependent reality, where we have the situation of the present moment and everything we are bringing to it as well.

Somebody could get up and do something in the middle of a room. Some people would become excited. Other people would be afraid. Some people would become angry. Other people would be amused. It is not that a given action, whatever it is, dictates a certain response. There is the situation, and there is everything we bring to it.

So we must take responsibility for our own mind. We live, hopefully, not just to drift along in the wake of different reactions, going up and down all of the time. Having a sense of purpose, such as the development of a loving heart, is the key to living a liberating practice.

If we can learn to see and understand all of these painful mind states of anger, fear, grief, disappointment, and guilt as states of aversion, we can learn to be free of them. Being free does not mean that aversion will never come up in our experience. Being free means that we can purify it. We can see it clearly, understand it, and learn not to be ruled by it. And having seen it clearly, which is the function of wisdom, we can also hold it in the vast, transforming field of acceptance.

Exercise: Forgiveness

In order to be released from deeply held aversion for ourselves and for others, we must be able to practice forgiveness. Forgiveness has the power to ripen forces of purity such as love, and affirms the qualities of patience and compassion. It creates the space for renewal, and a life free from bondage to the past.

When we are held prisoner by our own past actions, or the actions of others, our present life cannot be fully lived. The resentment, the partially experienced pain, the unwelcome inheritance we carry from the past, all function to close our hearts and thereby narrow our worlds.

The intention of forgiveness meditation is not to force anything, or to pretend to anything, or to forget about ourselves in utter deference to the needs of others. In fact, it is out of the greatest compassion for ourselves that we create the conditions for an unobstructed love, which can dissolve separation and relieve us of the twin burdens of lacerating guilt and perpetually unresolved outrage.

It is much more difficult to forgive than not to forgive. Political leaders seem to rely on this fact: it may be much easier to unite people with a bond of common hatred than with shared love. It is not so easy to access that place inside of us which can forgive, which can love. Remember, to be able to forgive is so deep a letting go that it is a type of dying. We must be able to say, "I am not that person anymore, and you are not that person anymore."

Forgiveness does not mean condoning a harmful action, or denying injustice or suffering. It should never be confused with being passive toward violation or abuse. Forgiveness is an inner relinquishment of guilt or resentment, both of which are devastating to us in the end. As forgiveness grows within us, it may take any outward form: we may seek to make amends, demand justice, resolve to be treated better, or simply leave a situation behind us.

The sense of psychological and spiritual well-being that comes from practicing forgiveness comes directly because this practice takes us to the edge of what we can accept. Being on the edge is challenging, wrenching, and transforming. The process of forgiveness demands courage and a continual remembering of where our deepest happiness lies. As Goethe said, "Our friends show us what we can do; our enemies show us what we must do."

It is indeed a process, which means that as you do the reflections, many conflicted emotions may arise: shame, anger, a sense of betrayal, confusion, or doubt. Try to allow such states to arise without judging them. Recognize them as natural occurrences, and then gently return your attention to the forgiveness reflection.

The reflection is done in three parts: asking forgiveness from those you have harmed; offering forgiveness to those who have harmed you; and offering forgiveness to yourself.

Sit comfortably, close your eyes, and let your breath be natural and uncontrolled. Begin with the recitation (silent or not, as you prefer): "If I have hurt or harmed anyone, knowingly or unknowingly, I ask their forgiveness." If different people, images, or scenarios come up, release the burden of guilt and ask for forgiveness: "I ask your forgiveness."

After some time, you can offer forgiveness to those who have harmed you. Don't worry if there is not a great rush of loving feeling; this is not meant to be an artificial exercise, but rather a way of honoring the powerful force of intention in our minds. We are paying respects to our ultimate ability to let go and begin again. We are asserting the human heart's capacity to change and grow and love. "If anyone has hurt or harmed me, knowingly or unknowingly, I forgive them." And, as different thoughts or images come to mind, continue the recitation, "I forgive you."

In the end, we turn our attention to forgiveness of ourselves. If there are ways you have harmed yourself, or not loved yourself, or not lived up to your own expectations, this is the time to let go of unkindness toward yourself because of what you have done. You can include any inability to forgive others that you may have discovered on your part in the reflection immediately preceding—that is not a reason to be unkind to yourself. "For all of the ways I have hurt or harmed myself, knowingly or unknowingly, I offer forgiveness."

Continue this practice as a part of your daily meditation, and allow the force of intention to work in its own way, in its own time.

Exercise: Seeing Goodness
Since the proximate cause, or most powerful conditioning force, for metta to arise is seeing the good in someone, we make an effort

to turn our attention to any good we can find in a difficult person. We may be able to find one good quality even in someone with great character flaws, though we might feel reluctant to try.

The first time I was given the instruction to look for one good quality in a person I found difficult, I rebelled. I thought, "That's what superficial, gullible people do—they just look for the good in someone. I don't want to do that!" As I actually did the practice, however, I discovered that it had an important and powerful effect. In fact, it was doing just what it was supposed to do: looking for the good in someone did not cover up any of the genuine difficulties I found with that person, but allowed me to relate to them without my habituated defensiveness and withdrawal.

There was a person working at our center who was a source of conflict for almost everyone around. He was bombastic and cutting. One of the other people working there was diagnosed at that time with a progressive, painful, and potentially fatal disease. She had huge adjustments to make in terms of her self-image, aspirations, and level of functioning. One day I happened to witness an exchange between the two of them, where the difficult person was relating to my ill friend with compassion, humor, and grace. Whenever I thought about him afterward, I tried to remember that moment. In doing so, I noticed that the positive recollection did not function to deny my problems with his general behavior. Instead, it created a sense of warmth and spaciousness, a greater ease from which I could genuinely open to him.

There may be people who absolutely defy our ability (or willingness) to think of even one good thing about them. In that case, focus on the universal wish to be happy, which this difficult person also shares. All beings want to be happy, yet so very few know how. It is out of ignorance that any of us cause suffering, for ourselves or for others.

. . .

Exercise: The Difficult Person

As we come to sending metta to a person with whom we experience conflict, fear, or anger—known in the traditional texts as the enemy—we can reflect on this line from Rainer Maria Rilke: "Perhaps everything terrible is in its deepest being something that needs our love."

It is useful to begin with someone with whom the difficulty is relatively mild—not starting right away with an attempt to send metta to the one person who has hurt us the most in this lifetime. It is important to approach increasingly difficult people gradually. When I was first practicing metta in Burma, I received the instruction to send metta to a benefactor repeatedly, for about three weeks. The whole time I was secretly frustrated, thinking, "Why am I spending all this time sending metta to someone I already love? That's easy—I should be sending metta to my worst enemy. That's the only kind of love that really counts." Finally I expressed some of this to U Pandita, who laughed and said, "Why do you want to do things in the hardest way possible?" This practice is not meant to induce suffering, though it may reveal it. If a particular person has harmed us so grievously that it is very difficult to include them in the field of our loving care, then we approach sending them metta slowly, with a lot of care and compassion for ourselves.

Sending lovingkindness to a person with whom we have difficulty can be quite a challenge. We initiate the cultivation of metta by visualizing a benefactor, one toward whom it is most easy for us to feel love. In the same way that cultivating lovingkindness toward a benefactor is easy, feeling kindness toward an adversary can be just as difficult. In order to begin to develop metta toward a person with whom we have problems, we must first separate our vision of the person from the actions they commit that may upset or harm us. All beings are deserving of care, of well-being, of the gift of lovingkindness. In developing metta, we put aside the unpleasant traits of such a being and try instead to get in touch with the part of them that deserves to be loved.

Perhaps you can most easily feel metta for a difficult person if you imagine them as a vulnerable infant, or on their deathbed (but not with eager anticipation—be careful). You should allow yourself to be creative, daring, even humorous, in imagining situations where you can more readily feel kindness toward a difficult person. One student of mine chose as a difficult person someone who was loud, intrusive, and extremely talkative. She found she could only start sending this person metta if she imagined her sitting in a chair, bound and gagged. Another student was so afraid of his difficult person that he could only send him metta while imagining him well restrained in prison. As the strength of our metta grows, we can eventually reach a place where we sincerely extend wishes of well-being to the difficult people in our lives, even while we work to counter their actions and activities of which we disapprove.

Sit comfortably, and start with directing the metta phrases toward yourself, enveloping yourself with your own loving care. After some time, direct the phrases toward a benefactor, then a friend. If you have found a neutral person, you can then include them. You should turn your attention to the difficult person only after spending some time sending metta toward yourself and to those you find it relatively easy to feel metta for. Imagine the difficult person in any situation you wish. Get a sense of them by visualizing them or saying their name. If you can, contemplate one good thing about them. If you can't, remember that this person, just like ourselves, wishes to be happy, and makes mistakes out of ignorance. Direct the metta phrases toward them, whichever phrases you have been using. If saying, "May *you* be free from danger, may *you* be happy," brings up too much fear or sense of isolation for you, you can include yourself in the recitation: "May *we* be free from danger. May *we* be happy."

Gently continue to direct metta toward the difficult person, and accept the different feelings that may come and go. There may be sorrow, grief, anger—allow them to pass through you. If they become overwhelming, go back to sending metta to yourself or a good friend. You can also do some reflections to help hold those feelings in a different perspective. A classical one is to ask yourself, "Who is the one suffering from this anger? The person who has harmed me has gone on to live their life (or perhaps has died), while I am the one sitting here feeling the persecution, burning, and constriction of anger. Out of compassion for myself, to ease my own heart, may I let go."

Another reflection is done by turning your mind to the suffering of the difficult person, rather than viewing their actions only as bad or wrong. Compassion is the refinement of love that opens to suffering. When we feel anger, fear, or jealousy, if we feel open to the pain of these states rather than disgraced by their arising, then we will have compassion for ourselves. When we see others lost in states of anger, fear, and so on, and we remember how painful those states are, we can have compassion for those people as well.

When you can, return to directing the metta phrases toward the difficult person. You can go back and forth between yourself, a friend, the reflections, and the difficult person.

You may find yourself expressing greater lovingkindness in actual life situations before you experience a greater depth of loving feeling in your formal meditation practice. Sometimes in difficult encounters there is more patience than before, more willingness to listen than before, and more clarity than before. I had a student who did an intensive metta retreat and chose a former partner in his firm as his difficult person. Negotiations for the partner's departure from the firm were still going on and were highly acrimonious. My student dutifully spent his time sending metta to his former partner, but felt mostly either boredom or irritation. He was astonished upon returning to work, and the next negotiation session, to find himself greeting his former partner with some warmth. The partner was astonished as well. He looked at my friend for some time and then said, "Is that *you*?"

Be patient with yourself in this practice, and try not to hold rigid expectations of what you should be experiencing. Strong expectations detract from our capacity for joy and will often lead to more anger. When we have rigid expectations, we can feel a great sense of helplessness if those expectations are not quickly met. We see our actions as being fruitless, not going anywhere, and we get lost in contempt or self-condemnation. Remember that whatever anger, fear, or sorrow arises will pass away, and we can always return to the intention to care for ourselves and for all beings. Beginning again and again is the actual practice, not a problem to be overcome so that one day we can come to the "real" meditation.

Exercise: Difficult Aspects of Oneself
As an alternative to choosing a difficult person, you can experiment with directing metta toward a difficult aspect of yourself. There may be physical or emotional aspects of yourself you have struggled with, denied, avoided, been at war with. Sit quietly, sending yourself metta. After some time, turn your attention to the loneliness, anger, disability, addiction, or whatever aspect of your mind or body you feel most estranged from. Healing begins with the open, compassionate acknowledgment of these unpleasant

aspects of our lives. Surround the painful element of your experience with the warmth and acceptance of metta. You can use phrases such as, "May I accept this," "May I be filled with lovingkindness toward this," "May I use the pain of this experience for the welfare of all." Feel free to use whatever phrases come to your mind, and return periodically to directing metta to yourself with your customary phrases.

children

———◇———

from

EVERYDAY BLESSINGS

by Myla and Jon Kabat-Zinn

Jon Kabat-Zinn works to integrate mindfulness meditation into mainstream medicine and society. His book with Myla Kabat-Zinn draws on lessons the couple learned raising their three children in a spirit of awareness. These passages offer a sense of the rewards that await parents who are physically, intellectually and emotionally present for their children.

—◇—

Boys

The elemental exuberance of boys, this endless fascination and wonder at the world, and the thousands of ways this energy express-es itself in play and in times of quiet and stillness offer countless challenges and opportunities for fathers to reconnect with this same elemental energy in ourselves as we nurture them and provide them with guidance and models as they grow to manhood.

As a father, I revel in a special joy that comes in and from the times I have spent with my son at different ages, encountering the world together and watching him grow day by day as he explored it on his own. His exuberance made everything an adventure.

When he was fascinated with dinosaurs, we would go to the science museum and stare at the huge *Tyrannosaurus*, so ferocious-looking, first at eye level from the second floor, then from the bottom, looking up. Then we would explore the rest of the museum. When

I went out for a run, I would sometimes take him along when he was little, holding the handle of a toy motorcycle as he rode alongside around the big pond where so many people went to run or to walk their dogs. Later, on occasion, we ran together. I loved to read to him in the evenings, or on camping trips we took, and to tell him special stories involving him, which I made up as I went along.

We wrestled a lot, rolling around on the living-room floor grappling like lions until we were exhausted. We did that for years, until he became a wrestler in high school and the risk of an accidental injury to me got significantly higher.

When he was very young, I trained regularly in Zen sword fighting (*Shim Gum Do*—the "Mind Sword" Path) and he would come to the *dojo* with me and watch us work out. Later, I stopped training, but for years he and I would sometimes practice stylized fighting forms with wooden swords, bowing to each other before and after each bout. He had a short sword that he could wield easily. It was exhilarating to block each other's strikes with our swords, to see that we could protect ourselves from scary blows coming from different directions while remaining calm and stable, grounded in the movement, the rhythm, and the sounds of the sticks clashing.

On rare occasions, we clashed in anger, not with swords but when our strong wills pushed or pulled in different directions. Gradually, I learned to control my own fiery temper and make more room for him—lessons I learned with difficulty as I struggled to grow beyond the vestiges of my own childhood. I worked hard at being as present as possible when I was with him. It was made easier because we loved so many of the same things. As he got older, more and more he did things with his friends.

Different boys, according to their temperaments and interests, need different things as they are growing up. One thing they need a lot of is space to grow on their own, and to find things out away from their parents. As a boy growing up on the streets of New York City, I learned incomparable lessons I could never have learned from my parents by spending countless hours in the streets playing ball, or just hanging out, which we developed into a fine art, watching the underbelly of city life. But I also came home for dinner every night, and learned other things from my parents.

In addition to all their various activities and pursuits, solitary and with their friends, boys have an abiding and overriding need for their fathers, and also their grandfathers and other men, to be present, to care about them, to show interest and share time with them, and to tell them stories and listen to theirs. I sometimes encounter the poignant longing for adult male attention and energy from small boys who do not see their fathers much, if at all, for whatever reasons, when I go into schools or playgroups. I have noticed that for boys who do not live with a man in the house, my presence and proximity is of interest, and they tend to gravitate around me like inner planets hugging a sun. They limb on me or just touch my arm or hold on to my leg. They want to play, or just be close to a man.

Boys need male guidance in exploring their own power and its limits, and in how to use it for their own good and the good of others. Boys need to learn how to know and respect their own strength, and yet not exaggerate it or flaunt it. They need to learn how to listen to the world and know its power and their own limits; how to listen to their own feelings and respect them, and how to express them, to find their voices, and to know the importance of honesty and of keeping one's word. They need to learn how to listen to and respect the feelings of others; and to know the sacredness of life, and its interconnectedness.

These lessons are all picked up by exploration and by example over time, by doing things with them, or spending time together in non-doing, which sometimes looks like fishing, or playing catch, or hanging out in a field, looking at the clouds; not by lectures or sermons. Such lessons take time, and can only come from fully embodied adults, fathers or other men who care and who make it a point to be around.

Is it possible for us as fathers to commit ourselves, inadequate as we may sometimes feel about the task, and hamstrung, even imprisoned by our jobs and by material and professional obligations and attractions, to support our boys in knowing their strength, in finding meaningful expressions for their desire for power and mastery, and also to create an environment where feeling things deeply is not only acceptable but seen as important, and respected. Such an orientation is not fundamentally different from what we believe girls need as well.

The prevalent culture seems quite polarized around the question of how men should be, and this polarization is damaging to fathers and sons alike. One ubiquitous stereotype, premiered in beer commercials, is the tough, macho, beer-drinking, fun-seeking, happy-go-lucky, womanizing, perhaps alienated and misogynistic male. Another stereotype is the sensitive, in-touch-with-his-feelings, considerate, and somewhat wimpy-with-women male. Fathers need to help their sons become aware of and interpret the various subtle and not-so-subtle messages and images the culture puts out, many of them demeaning of women and girls, so that they are less likely to get caught up in such stereotypic images and thinking—and the behaviors that follow from them—and can find their own ways of being.

Many of these images of men and women are products of what

Robert Bly calls the "sibling society," a world in which the father is absent physically or spiritually, and where the prevalent role models are synthesized by the media. In this world, there is precious little mentoring by elders and initiation into adulthood and into the collective knowledge and wisdom of those who came before. It is a world in which the past is rejected and condemned without even being known. Deep mutual alienation leads to the young attempting to raise and socialize themselves. Much of the dominant culture has an exploitative and predatory feel to it, even as progress is being made to protect the rights of children and women.

We have to ask ourselves what a boy (or a girl) will need in order to survive (for it *is* a matter of survival, survival of the soul, as well as of the body) and to live wisely in this world that is emerging at the turn of the millennium. In the absence of a culture that honors and values children and takes some collective responsibility for their spiritual growth and their entry into the world of adults, parents are going to have to do yeoman's and yeowoman's work to guide their children.

As fathers, we need to be strong ourselves—and wise, and present. We may have to look deeply into our very cells and genes in order to find our human strength and our own sovereign nature, and what is best of our lineage, whether Native American, African, Asian, European, Christian, Jewish, Muslim, Buddhist, Hindu, "none of the above," or "other." The alternative is a living death for ourselves and for our children, the death of not knowing who we are, and perhaps not caring, the death of having no "people," no community in which we are known and have a place.

Boys need the presence of competent, embodied men in their lives, men who *do* know who they are and are not afraid of or numb to how they feel, men who are empathic and accepting, playful, wild and soulful, who are not enslaved by their work, and don't fear or hate women. The presence of a strong, empathic man in the role of father, grandfather, or mentor is always important for young boys, but it is needed more and more as boys move into adolescence. The transition from boy to man requires a vision, a new way of seeing, and a new way of being in the body.

Boys need elders, and rituals led by elders, to help them make this transition. They hunger for the close proximity of their fathers and of other trustworthy men they can respect as guides and role models. Boys have a deep need to feel loved and valued by men and to understand how these men see the world, so that they will be able touch their creative energies and learn to channel and use their own power wisely. They need to come to appreciate mystery and the unknown, including other people and customs, and not be swept up in a tribal mentality that makes absolute distinctions between "us" and "them," and then, out of fear and prejudice, plunges into war and violence to vanquish "the other," not realizing that "them is us."

Boys receive essential sustenance from a loving, nurturing relationship with their mothers. Being held in the aura of a mother's love, without being controlled or having to take care of her emotional needs, creates a foundation of inner security and emotional grounding needed for the separations and adventures into the world that have to come as the boy gets older. But they need fathers from their earliest moments as well, as do girls. And the fathers need their sons. If we are not present at key moments in our sons' lives, we will not know them. If we see them born, hold them constantly when they are little, dream dreams with them as they sleep on our shoulders, walk with them in the world and speak with them of what they see, offer them tools to work with and projects to bend their arms and their minds to, get down on the floor with them and play and invent games, watch the sun go down and the rain fall, dig in the mud and build castles at the beach, throw rocks in the water and carve sticks, climb mountains and sit by waterfalls, mess around in rowboats and canoes, sing songs, get together in groups, watch them sleeping and wake them gently—then our souls will know their souls; our spirits will know their spirits.

Fathers and sons can help each other grow and find beauty and meaning. And as the sons grow, they will find other sons who share their passions, and form friendships that endure and that are based on getting high on life. Music and drumming, wilderness and woods and fields, city life, sports, literature and the arts, all beckon, through periods of light and darkness, offering worlds of meaning and value, serving as mirrors in which boys and men can see themselves and continue growing, living their moments fully, trusting their own power, grounded in their bodies, and becoming full, planetary adults as they participate in the mysteries of generativity and the generations, and of finding their own paths and their own places in the world.

> "When they were four or five we would go over to Bald Mountain on foot and we could look back and see our place. When they were seven and eight, we went up to Grouse Ridge on foot and we could look down from Grouse Ridge and see Bald Mountain from which you can see our place. A few years later we went on up to the High Sierra and got up to 8,000 foot English Mountain from which you can see Grouse Ridge. And then we went on over to

Castle Peak which is the highest peak in that range which is 10,000 feet high and climbed that and you can see English Mountain from there. Then we went on north and we climbed Sierra Buttes and Mount Lassen—Mount Lassen is the farthest we've been out now. So from Mount Lassen, you can see Castle Peak, you can see English Peak, you can see Grouse Ridge, you can see Bald Mountain and you can see our place. That is the way the world should be learned. It's an intense geography that is never far removed from your body."

—Gary Snyder

Pond Hockey

When the temperature rises for a day or two and then freezes again without a snowstorm, the winter ponds in New England beckon for a good game of ice hockey. At times like these, if it was on the weekend or over vacation, my son and I (jkz) would put on layers of warm clothing, grab our sticks and pucks and skates, and head down to the pond below the hill. There we would don our skates, struggling with the long laces with freezing fingers until they were pulled tight enough; waddle over the remaining feet of snow; and touch new freedom at the ice edge.

We would skate around for a while, inspecting the ice all over the pond, adjusting to the feeling of being on skates once again. Then we would carefully select a spot and set up a goal with a pair of boots a few feet apart.

We played one on one . . . one of us defending the goal while the other tried to come at it with the puck. The defender had broad latitude to come out of the goal and try to take the puck away from his opponent, so there was lots of fast skating all over the pond, clashing of sticks, racing to get to the puck first. There were fakes and lots of shooting, chases, and bumps, as we maneuvered around each other with exhilarating swiftness and laughter. And of course, there was lots of scoring, and the sheer joy of sensing the puck sail past the defender and through the boots, sometimes on highly improbable trajectories that made us laugh.

As we played, we generated heat. No matter how cold the day, how biting the wind, after a time the hats would come off, and the gloves, then the coats and sweaters. Sometimes we would be down to just shirts on top. As long as we kept skating, we stayed warm. We played for hours. There was never a time that wasn't the best time. Every time was just now, beyond thought, caught up in the joy of sharing what always felt like a particularly male energy in going up against each other time and time again, coming in with the puck, chasing one other, blocking shots, protecting the goal.

Sometimes we played at night, in the orange gloom of one tall floodlight put up by the town, hardly able to see the puck in the shadows. But most of the time, we played in the afternoon, on and on, as the winter sun moved toward its early exit. At times, we had to stop and catch our breath. Lying on our coats spread-open on the snow at the edge of the pond watching the clouds against the deep blue of the sky, or the strands of pinks and golds beginning to show themselves in the west, our breath visible in the air above us, we would revel in silence and perfection.

I would like to say we did this every weekend for years and years, but we didn't, and those days now seem long past. And I would like to say that my girls and I had similar feelings when we played pond hockey, and we did on rare occasions. The girls were drawn to other things. They loved to skate, and skated better than we did, but they lacked interest in the game of stick, puck, goal, and pursuit.

Most of the time, the pond was covered with snow or rough ice and was unskatable. Some winters, it wasn't frozen enough when we wanted it to be. And we had other things calling us as well, and other chances to be together. But none was ever better than playing hockey on the winter pond. . . .

Girls

When our girls were little, I (mkz) took great pleasure in the wide variety of qualities that surfaced in them at different times. They showed enthusiasm and delight in the simplest of activities: picking strawberries and carefully tasting each ripe berry before putting it into their basket; dressing up in old clothes of mine and remnants of cloth, and transforming themselves into queens and princesses; pretending to be baby dolphins, as they swam around me in the ocean. When they saw deeply into things and shared a sudden insight with me, or showed kindness or compassion in some way, I would delight in those wondrous and warmhearted aspects of their being. There were also times when they were fierce, angry, and completely unmovable. Even as I felt thwarted by their indomitable wills, I would find myself cherishing their strength, their power, their one-pointedness.

In those years, both home and school were, for the most part, havens from the broader culture. Their world was simple, with few pressures, expectations, or external distractions. As they got older, of course, things changed. Slowly I became more and more aware of the numerous messages they were getting from the prevailing culture—messages that were ubiquitous and limiting, and that put all sorts of expectations and pressures on them just because they were girls.

Everywhere girls turn, at every checkout counter, in newspapers, magazines, TV, and movies, they are met with sexualized images of women that can deeply affect how they view themselves. These images subtly or not-so-subtly suggest that the greatest power they have is as sexual objects. This message is tremendously limiting and damaging to girls, particularly as they approach adolescence.

Such images are used to sell all manner of products. Not only is the focus constantly on buying and consuming, whole industries are devoted to convincing women and girls that they need to make their bodies more beautiful and more "perfect." Yet most of the images are of bodies that few women naturally have, or only have for a brief time. This "ideal" look, synthesized by the advertising world, can foster in girls a strong dissatisfaction with their own bodies, their hair, their clothes, their skin—virtually every aspect of their physical being.

Appearance is accorded supreme importance. The focus is on cultivating a look, on sculpting a surface. As a result, many girls spend an inordinate amount of time and energy preoccupied with how they look, or don't look. This often happens at the expense of honoring and developing their physical prowess and strength, their creativity, and their inner selves. Parents face a constant struggle to provide an authentic, supportive, balanced view of being a girl or young woman in the face of this very alluring, ever present, enticing media barrage. As difficult as this may be, there are some things we can do.

We might start by becoming aware of the pervasive influence of this industry, so that it is not missed entirely, or taken for granted as an inevitable part of the cultural landscape. Awareness is a first step. Once we start to pay attention to potentially negative influences on our girls, we can begin to see the effects they may be having on their self-image, their self-esteem, their interests and goals. Rather than just continually trying to repair damage that is already done, we can try to prevent damage by limiting their exposure and consumption. We can also discuss with them what we are seeing, in a hopefully non-heavy-handed way so that they can see what lies behind these images of women. They can begin to be aware of the implicit messages and how the desire for buying is fueled in the minds of viewers, readers, and consumers.

A girl who grows up watching all there is to see on television is going to be saturated with many more narrow and demeaning images of women than a girl whose exposure to the media is more limited. Limiting exposure has the added benefit of freeing up time and space for real-life experiences, which hopefully will broaden her view of herself as a whole person with valuable strengths and skills, and many unique qualities. Girls often have such experiences playing sports or engaged in activities or projects, whether artistic, intellectual, or community-oriented, that challenge and develop their creative powers.

At the same time that we try to create some sanctuary from the culture and encourage an awareness of the power of the media, we of necessity have to balance our restrictions and even the expression of our views, or we may end up creating a gulf between ourselves and our children. After all, they are drawn not only by the surface allure of this world of advertising, TV, movies, and music videos, but also by its artistic and entrepreneurial creativity.

This is one reason why mindful parenting is so difficult. As parents, we have to continually work with our fears, our own limitations, our own feelings of powerlessness at times, as we strive to provide some degree of balance in the lives of our children. The fine line we try to walk in our family is to protect and limit at the same time that we stay open and flexible. As the girls get older, this involves more and more negotiation and compromise, and, ultimately, encouraging them to make their own choices thoughtfully.

Children want so much to feel "normal" in what they can do and see, and they compare themselves, naturally enough, to what their friends are allowed to do and watch, and how they behave. What is considered "normal" in our society is often violent, cruel, and much of the time, demeaning to women. It is so ever present that we can become inured to it and hardly see it at all. In the face of this deluge of imagery—which continually connects sex to violence, objectifies girls, and virtually ignores or makes invisible older women, large women, strong women, dark-skinned women, women who don't fit in with the classic, light-skinned, vulnerable, thin-bodied ideal that "sells"—anger would be an appropriate response. But of course women are not supposed to get angry. When we do, we are labeled all sorts of unpleasant and degrading things. We are met with: "What's the matter with *you*?" or, "Why do you take things so seriously?" or, "Where's your sense of humor?" or, "Is it *that* time of the month?"

In parenting girls, we have to continually counter this narrow view of women. When we silently accept the dominant view, we are basically colluding in our society's denigration of women. We have to find and use our own voices as women and as mothers if we are to support our girls so that they don't lose theirs. As their mothers, we need to embody an alternative for them, a different way of being, a different way of viewing the culture they live in. Our girls truly need us as their allies in a culture where their way of seeing things—and what may be most important to them—is often not valued or even acknowledged.

As our daughters experience all the different and sometimes difficult physical and emotional transformations of pre-adolescence through the teen years, fathers need to be particularly mindful of unconscious or habitual ways they may have of relating to women that might influence how they relate to their daughters. This may take the form of being disrespectful or flirtatious, or continually putting their own needs first. A father's need to be loved and adored by his daughter can keep him from seeing what it is that she really needs from him.

Concerned for the well-being of our girls in a culture such as ours, we both feel we have to be fiercely protective of their strengths, their aliveness, and sense of who they are. At the same time, we also have to examine how our own expectations might unwittingly limit their range of expression and their autonomy. We have to ask ourselves, over and over again, are we attached to their being a certain way? Do our girls have to be nice, thoughtful, sensitive, kind, quiet? Do we expect them to smile a lot? Are we taking into account their temperaments, at the same time that we are open to changes in them? Has a sanguine, shy daughter become a fiery, energetic, outgoing, vocal teenager? Do we allow our girls to be angry, to be loud, to be obnoxious in the ways we sometimes *expect* boys to be? Do we allow them their own interests, whether it's quantum mechanics, engineering, clothes, or movie stars? Are we supporting them in finding ways to express their unique abilities, creativity, and strengths?

Our responses to these questions and others like them might change from day to day, or even from moment to moment. But asking them is an essential part of our own work as parents.

A large part of this process is working with other people's expectations of our girls. When we or our daughters become aware of messages that feel inappropriate or limiting or denigrating on the part of an authority figure or their peers, including sexual harassment or sexual stereotyping, we can help them identify and name the troubling attitude or behavior, and support them in their feelings. By doing so, rather than minimizing the problem or denying the validity of their feelings, we are letting them know we are their allies and that when they are unjustly treated or subtly demeaned, feeling angry or hurt is not only okay but a healthy response.

Too often, they are made to feel that it is *their* problem and that there is something the matter with *them* for having the feelings they do. We can support them in learning how to stand up for themselves and speak assertively, giving clear and confident messages that define their boundaries and name unacceptable behaviors on the part of others.

> To keep my mouth shut. To turn away my face. To walk back down the aisle. To slap the bishop back when he slapped me during Confirmation. To hold the word *no* in my mouth like a gold coin, something valued, something possible. To teach the *no* to our daughters. To value their no more than their compliant yes. To celebrate *no*. To grasp the word *no* in your fist and refuse to give it up. To support the boy who says *no* to violence, the girl who will not be violated, the woman who says *no, no, I will not*. To love the

no, to cherish the *no* which is so often our first word.
No—the means to transformation.

       —Louise Erdrich, *The Blue Jay's Dance*

When one of my daughters was eleven, for months she related incidents to me in which she felt her teacher was being disrespectful to her or her classmates. One day she told me the following story. She was talking and laughing exuberantly with her friends at an evening school event when her teacher came up to her, called her by name, and said in a chiding voice, "Be a *lady*!" She told me that she looked her teacher straight in the eye and said, "I *am* being a lady, just a *strong* one!"

Through the experience of having their feelings validated, slowly, over time, girls are better able to see and name attitudes and behaviors that are troubling to them. They can learn to be more readily in touch with what they are feeling, to trust those feelings, and to express them effectively. In this way, they learn to empower themselves and build a repertoire of emotional competencies that will be critical to their further development. Such strengths will be particularly important when they are living on their own in a society that can be deeply disempowering, predatory, and exploitative.

I was in a small store that sells Oriental rugs with my then eleven-year-old daughter. The storekeeper was from another country, and related to us with an exaggerated smile on his face. It made me uneasy, but I quickly proceeded with the business at hand, which was to look at a few rugs. When we got outside, my daughter told me that she felt really uncomfortable because whenever I looked away from him, she noticed he was looking at her in a "weird" way. I made some comment to her about cultural differences. Later, I realized how inadequate my response was and how my focus had been to explain away and excuse his behavior rather than validate her feelings of discomfort.

That evening, as I was saying good-night, I told her that I had been thinking about what happened in the store and that I didn't want something like that to happen again without our having a signal we could use so that she could let me know when something was making her uncomfortable. I suggested that if it happened again, she take my hand and give it a squeeze, and I would know that something wasn't right and we should leave right away. Her eyes lit up and she smiled as she thought about this. . . .

Advocacy, Assertiveness, Accountability

At one point, a friend and I (mkz) had similar experiences being called in to discuss incidents that happened in school with our daughters. The themes were the same: strong-willed girls say how they feel about something, and are seen as "disrespectful."

One afternoon, I was called into the elementary school principal's office. The principal, a woman in her early sixties, said that my daughter and a group of fifth-grade girls were told by an aide that they shouldn't be playing soccer with the boys and that they had to stop. My daughter told the aide she was being sexist, that the girls had just as much of a right to play as the boys. The principal imitated for me my daughter's angry, defiant body language by crossing her arms and putting her head to the side, in a manner that suggested she assumed I would agree that her behavior was not acceptable. She went on to tell me that she had had my daughter brought in to a meeting with the recess aides, and told her that she was not allowed to behave in a manner that was disrespectful, that the aides had to ensure the safety of the children, and that the children had to listen and obey them. The principal assured me that she had asked my daughter for her side of the story and told her she needed to write a note of apology to each of the aides.

I agreed with her that my daughter did need to learn to say how she felt in a more respectful manner. But I said that it sounded to me as if my daughter had felt angry about what she perceived to be an unjust situation and was trying to communicate her feelings to the aides. It also sounded to me as if her concerns and point of view were ignored and she was being labeled as "bad" for expressing them. I asked the principal if she thought that, had a boy crossed his arms and spoken up for himself in a similar way, it would have been seen in such a strongly negative light.

Later on, I told my daughter she needed to learn how to stand up for herself without being disrespectful, that saying someone was being sexist could feel like name-calling if other people didn't understand what she was trying to say. Also that she had to be aware of how she spoke, of her body language and tone of voice, and that not just what she said but *the way* she said it was important. I wanted her to see that her actions affected other people and had consequences, one of which was to influence their ability to hear what she was saying.

Learning how to say how we feel and how we see things in a respectful manner is not easy. It takes lots of practice. We have to give children room to do this, to learn from trying, from making mistakes, and from trying again.

The courage it took for her to speak out was never acknowledged. The message she was given was that she should be quiet and compliant. If my daughter keeps getting this message when she tries to stand up for herself or for others, and if she didn't have parents who accepted her anger and tried to see her point of view, she might start to turn inward, stop speaking up, and perhaps begin to feel badly about herself and lose her self-confidence, as happens to so many girls. At nine they are vital and confident; by the age of fourteen, somehow that strength can become hidden, tentative, unseen, even lost.

fear

—◇—

from

WHEN THINGS FALL APART

by Pema Chödrön

Pema Chödrön (born 1936) is an ordained Buddhist nun and resident teacher at Gampo Abbey in Cape Breton, Nova Scotia. Her three books all explore the need to become intimate with fear and learn its lessons.

—◇—

F ear is a natural reaction to moving closer to the truth. Embarking on the spiritual journey is like getting into a very small boat and setting out on the ocean to search for unknown lands. With wholehearted practice comes inspiration, but sooner or later we will also encounter fear. For all we know, when we get to the horizon, we are going to drop off the edge of the world. Like all explorers, we are drawn to discover what's waiting out there without knowing yet if we have the courage to face it.

If we become interested in Buddhism and decide to find out what it has to offer, we'll soon discover that there are different slants on how we can proceed. With insight meditation we begin practicing mindfulness, being fully present with all our activities and thoughts. With Zen practice we hear teachings on emptiness and are challenged to connect with the open, unbounded clarity of mind. The vajrayana teachings introduce us to the notion of working with the energy of all situations, seeing whatever arises as inseparable from the awakened state. Any of these approaches might hook us and fuel our enthusiasm to explore further, but if we want to go beneath the surface and practice without hesitation, it is inevitable that at some point we will experience fear.

Fear is a universal experience. Even the smallest insect feels it. We wade in the tidal pools and put our finger near the soft, open bodies of sea anemones and they close up. Everything spontaneously does that. It's not a terrible thing that we feel fear when faced with the unknown. It is part of being alive, something we all share. We react against the possibility of loneliness, of death, of not having anything to hold on to. Fear is a natural reaction to moving closer to the truth.

If we commit ourselves to staying right where we are, then our experience becomes very vivid. Things come very clear when there is nowhere to escape.

During a long retreat, I had what seems to me the earthshaking revelation that we cannot be in the present and run our story lines at the same time! It sounds pretty obvious, I know, but when you discover something like this for yourself, it changes you. Impermanence becomes vivid in the present moment; so do compassion and wonder and courage. And so does fear. In fact, anyone who stands on the edge of the unknown, fully in the present without reference point, experiences groundlessness. That's when our understanding goes deeper, when we find that the present moment is a pretty vulnerable place and that this can be completely unnerving and completely tender at the same time.

When we begin our exploration, we have all kinds of ideals and expectations. We are looking for answers that will satisfy a hunger we've felt for a very long time. But the last thing we want is a further introduction to the boogeyman. Of course, people do try to warn us. I remember when I first received meditation instruction, the woman told me the technique and guidelines on how to practice and then said, "But please don't go away from here thinking that meditation is a vacation from irritation." Somehow all the warnings in the world don't quite convince us. In fact they draw us closer.

What we're talking about is getting to know fear, becoming familiar with fear, looking it right in the eye—not as a way to solve problems, but as a complete undoing of old ways of seeing, hearing, smelling, tasting, and thinking. The truth is that when we really begin to do this, we're going to be continually humbled. There's not going to be much room for the arrogance that holding on to ideals can bring. The arrogance that inevitably does arise is going to be continually shot down by our own courage to step forward a little further. The kinds of discoveries that are made through practice have nothing to do with believing in anything. They have much more to do with having the courage to die, the courage to die continually.

Instructions on mindfulness or emptiness or working with energy all point to the same thing: being right on the spot nails us. It nails us right to the point of time and space that we are in. When we stop there and don't act out, don't repress, don't blame it on anyone else, and also don't blame it on ourselves, then we meet with an open-ended question that has no conceptual answer. We also encounter our heart. As one student so eloquently put it, "Buddha nature, cleverly disguised as fear, kicks our ass into being receptive."

I once attended a lecture about a man's spiritual experiences in India in the 1960s. He said he was determined to get rid of his negative emotions. He struggled against anger and lust; he struggled against laziness and pride. But mostly he wanted to get rid of his fear. His meditation teacher kept telling him to stop struggling, but he took that as just another way of explaining how to overcome his obstacles.

Finally the teacher sent him off to meditate in a tiny hut in the foothills. He shut the door and settled down to practice, and when it got dark he lit three small candles. Around midnight he heard a noise in the corner of the room, and in the darkness he saw a very large snake. It looked to him like a king cobra. It was right in front of him, swaying. All night he stayed totally alert, keeping his eyes on the snake. He was so afraid that he couldn't move. There was just the snake and himself and fear.

Just before dawn the last candle went out, and he began to cry. He cried not in despair but from tenderness. He felt the longing of all the animals and people in the world; he knew their alienation and their struggle. All his meditation had been nothing but further separation and struggle. He accepted—really accepted wholeheartedly—that he was angry and jealous, that he resisted and struggled, and that he was afraid. He accepted that he was also precious beyond measure—wise and foolish, rich and poor, and totally unfathomable. He felt so much gratitude that in the total darkness he stood up, walked toward the snake, and bowed. Then he fell sound asleep on the floor. When he awoke, the snake was gone. He never knew if it was his imagination or if it had really been there, and it didn't seem to matter. As he put it at the end of the lecture, that much intimacy with fear caused his dramas to collapse, and the world around him finally got through.

No one ever tells us to stop running away from fear. We are very rarely told to move closer, to just be there, to become familiar with fear. I once asked the Zen master Kobun Chino Roshi how he related with fear, and he said, "I agree. I agree." But the advice we usually get is to sweeten it up, smooth it over, take a pill, or distract ourselves, but by all means make it go away.

We don't need that kind of encouragement, because dissociating from fear is what we do naturally. We habitually spin off and freak out when there's even the merest hint of fear. We feel it coming and we check out. It's good to know we do that—not as a way to beat ourselves up, but as a way to develop unconditional compassion. The most heartbreaking thing of all is how we cheat ourselves of the present moment.

Sometimes, however, we are cornered; everything falls apart, and we run out of options for escape. At times like that, the most profound spiritual truths seem pretty straightforward and ordinary. There's nowhere to hide. We see it as well as anyone else—*better* than anyone else. Sooner or later we understand that although we can't make fear look pretty, it will nevertheless introduce us to all the teaching we've ever heard or read.

So the next time you encounter fear, consider yourself lucky. This is where the courage comes in. Usually we think that brave people have no fear. The truth is that they are intimate with fear. When I was first married, my husband said I was one of the bravest people he knew. When I asked him why, he said because I was a complete coward but went ahead and did things anyhow.

The trick is to keep exploring and not bail out, even when we find out that something is not what we thought. That's what we're going to discover again and again and again. Nothing is what we thought. I can say that with great confidence. Emptiness is not what we thought. Neither is mindfulness or fear. Compassion—not what we thought. Love. Buddha nature. Courage. These are code words for things we don't know in our minds, but any of us could experience them. These are words that point to what life really is when we let things fall apart and let ourselves be nailed to the present moment.

. . .

from When Things Fall Apart

> When things fall apart and we're on the verge of we
> know not what, the test of each of us is to stay on
> that brink and not concretize. The spiritual journey
> is not about heaven and finally getting to a place
> that's really swell.

Gampo Abbey is a vast place where the sea and the sky melt into each other. The horizon extends infinitely, and in this vast space float seagulls and ravens. The setting is like a huge mirror that exaggerates the sense of there being nowhere to hide. Also, since it is a monastery, there are very few means of escape—no lying, no stealing, no alcohol, no sex, no exit.

Gampo Abbey was a place to which I had been longing to go. Trungpa Rinpoche asked me to be the director of the abbey, so finally I found myself there. Being there was an invitation to test my love of a good challenge, because in the first years it was like being boiled alive.

What happened to me when I got to the abbey was that everything fell apart. All the ways I shield myself, all the ways I delude myself, all the ways I maintain my well-polished self-image—all of it fell apart. No matter how hard I tried, I couldn't manipulate the situation. My style was driving everyone else crazy, and I couldn't find anywhere to hide.

I had always thought of myself as a flexible, obliging person who was well liked by almost everyone. I'd been able to carry this illusion throughout most of my life. During my early years at the abbey, I discovered that I had been living in some kind of misunderstanding. It wasn't that I didn't have good qualities, it was just that I was not the ultimate golden girl. I had so much invested in that image of myself, and it just wasn't holding together anymore. All my unfinished business was exposed vividly and accurately in living Technicolor, not only to myself, but to everyone else as well.

Everything that I had not been able to see about myself before was suddenly dramatized. As if that weren't enough, others were free with their feedback about me and what I was doing. It was so painful that I wondered if I would ever be happy again. I felt that bombs were being dropped on me almost continuously, with self-deceptions exploding all around. In a place where there was so much practice and study going on, I could not get lost in trying to justify myself and blame others. That kind of exit was not available.

A teacher visited during this time, and I remember her saying to me, "When you have made good friends with yourself, your situation will be more friendly too."

I had learned this lesson before, and I knew that it was the only way to go. I used to have a sign pinned up on my wall that read: "Only to the extent that we expose ourselves over and over to annihilation can that which is indestructible be found in us." Somehow, even before I heard the Buddhist teachings, I knew that this was the spirit of true awakening. It was all about letting go of everything.

Nevertheless, when the bottom falls out and we can't find anything to grasp, it hurts a lot. It's like the Naropa Institute motto: "Love of the truth puts you on the spot." We might have some romantic view of what that means, but when we are nailed with the truth, we suffer. We look in the bathroom mirror, and there we are with our pimples, our aging face, our lack of kindness, our aggression and timidity—all that stuff.

This is where tenderness comes in. When things are shaky and nothing is working, we might realize that we are on the verge of something. We might realize that this is a very vulnerable and tender place, and that tenderness can go either way. We can shut down and feel resentful or we can touch in on that throbbing quality.

There is definitely something tender and throbbing about groundlessness.

It's a kind of testing, the kind of testing that spiritual warriors need in order to awaken their hearts. Sometimes it's because of illness or death that we find ourselves in this place. We experience a sense of loss —loss of our loved ones, loss of our youth, loss of our life.

I have a friend dying of AIDS. Before I was leaving for a trip, we were talking. He said, "I didn't want this, and I hated this, and I was terrified of this. But it turns out that this illness has been my greatest gift." He said, "Now every moment is so precious to me. All the people in my life are so precious to me. My whole life means so much to me." Something had really changed, and he felt ready for his death. Something that was horrifying and scary had turned into a gift.

Things falling apart is a kind of testing and also a kind of healing. We think that the point is to pass the test or to overcome the problem, but the truth is that things don't really get solved. They come together and they fall apart. Then they come together again and fall apart again. It's just like that. The healing comes from letting there be room for all of this to happen: room for grief, for relief, for misery, for joy.

When we think that something is going to bring us pleasure, we don't know what's really going to happen. When we think something is going to give us misery, we don't know. Letting there be room for not knowing is the most important thing of all. We try to do what we think is going to help. But we don't know. We never know if we're going to fall flat or sit up tall. When there's a big disappointment, we don't know if that's the end of the story. It may be just the beginning of a great adventure.

I read somewhere about a family who had only one son. They were very poor. This son was extremely precious to them, and the only thing that mattered to his family was that he bring them some financial support and prestige. Then he was thrown from a horse and crippled. It seemed like the end of their lives. Two weeks after that, the army came into the village and took away all the healthy, strong men to fight in the war, and this young man was allowed to stay behind and take care of his family.

Life is like that. We don't know anything. We call something bad; we call it good. But really we just don't know.

When things fall apart and we're on the verge of we know not what, the test for each of us is to stay on that brink and not concretize. The spiritual journey is not about heaven and finally getting to a place that's really swell. In fact, that way of looking at things is what keeps us miserable. Thinking that we can find some lasting pleasure and avoid pain is what in Buddhism is called samsara, a hopeless cycle that goes round and round endlessly and causes us to suffer greatly. The very first noble truth of the Buddha points out that suffering is inevitable for human beings as long as we believe that things last—that they don't disintegrate, that they can be counted on to satisfy our hunger for security. From this point of view, the only time we ever know what's really going on is when the rug's been pulled out and we can't find anywhere to land. We use these situations either to wake ourselves up or to put ourselves to sleep. Right now—in the very instant of groundlessness—is the seed of taking care of those who need our care and of discovering our goodness.

I remember so vividly a day in early spring when my whole reality gave out on me. Although it was before I had heard any Buddhist teachings, it was what some would call a genuine spiritual experience. It happened when my husband told me he was having an affair. We lived in northern New Mexico. I was standing in front of our adobe house drinking a cup of tea. I heard the car drive up and the door bang shut. Then he walked around the corner, and without warning he told me that he was having an affair and he wanted a divorce.

I remember the sky and how huge it was. I remember the sound of the river and the steam rising up from my tea. There was no time, no thought, there was nothing—just the light and a profound, limitless stillness. Then I regrouped and picked up a stone and threw it at him.

When anyone asks me how I got involved in Buddhism, I always say it was because I was so angry with my husband. The truth is that he saved my life. When that marriage fell apart, I tried hard—very, very hard—to go back to some kind of comfort, some kind of security, some kind of familiar resting place. Fortunately for me, I could never pull it off. Instinctively I knew that annihilation of my old dependent, clinging self was the only way to go. That's when I pinned that sign up on my wall.

Life is a good teacher and a good friend. Things are always in transition, if we could only realize it. Nothing ever sums itself up in the way that we like to dream about. The off-center, in-between state is an ideal situation, a situation in which we don't get caught and we can open our hearts and minds beyond limit. It's a very tender, nonaggressive, open-ended state of affairs.

To stay with that shakiness—to stay with a broken heart, with a rumbling stomach, with the feeling of hopelessness and wanting to get revenge—that is the path of true awakening. Sticking with that uncertainty, getting the knack of relaxing in the midst of chaos, learning not to panic—this is the spiritual path. Getting the knack of catching ourselves, of gently and compassionately catching ourselves, is the path of the warrior. We catch ourselves one zillion times as once again, whether we like it or not, we harden into resentment, bitterness, righteous indignation—harden in any way, even into a sense of relief, a sense of inspiration.

Every day we could think about the aggression in the world, in New York, Los Angeles, Halifax, Taiwan, Beirut, Kuwait, Somalia, Iraq, everywhere. All over the world, everybody always strikes out at the enemy, and the pain escalates forever. Every day we could reflect on this and ask ourselves, "Am I going to add to the aggression in the world?" Every day, at the moment when things get edgy, we can just ask ourselves, "Am I going to practice peace, or am I going to war?"

> We can meet our match with a poodle or with a raging guard dog, but the interesting question is—what happens next?

Generally speaking, we regard discomfort in any form as bad news. But for practitioners or spiritual warriors—people who have a certain hunger to know what is true—feelings like disappointment, embarrassment, irritation, resentment, anger, jealousy, and fear, instead of being bad news, are actually very clear moments that teach us where it is that we're holding back. They teach us to perk up and lean in when we feel we'd rather collapse and back away. They're like messengers that show us, with terrifying clarity, exactly where we're stuck. This very moment is the perfect teacher, and, lucky for us, it's with us wherever we are.

Those events and people in our lives who trigger our unresolved issues could be regarded as good news. We don't have to go hunting for anything. We don't need to try to create situations in which we reach our limit. They occur all by themselves, with clockwork regularity.

Each day, we're given many opportunities to open up or shut

down. The most precious opportunity presents itself when we come to the place where we think we can't handle whatever is happening. It's too much. It's gone too far. We feel bad about ourselves. There's no way we can manipulate the situation to make ourselves come out looking good. No matter how hard we try, it just won't work. Basically, life has just nailed us.

It's as if you just looked at yourself in the mirror, and you saw a gorilla. The mirror's there; it's showing you, and what you see looks bad. You try to angle the mirror so you will look a little better, but no matter what you do, you still look like a gorilla. That's being nailed by life, the place where you have no choice except to embrace what's happening or push it away.

Most of us do not take these situations as teachings. We automatically hate them. We run like crazy. We use all kinds of ways to escape—all addictions stem from this moment when we meet our edge and we just can't stand it. We feel we have to soften it, pad it with something, and we become addicted to whatever it is that seems to ease the pain. In fact, the rampant materialism that we see in the world stems from this moment. There are so many ways that have been dreamt up to entertain us away from the moment, soften its hard edge, deaden it so we don't have to feel the full impact of the pain that arises when we cannot manipulate the situation to make us come out looking fine.

Meditation is an invitation to notice when we reach our limit and to not get carried away by hope and fear. Through meditation, we're able to see clearly what's going on with our thoughts and emotions, and we can also let them go. What's encouraging about meditation is that even if we shut down, we can no longer shut down in ignorance. We see very clearly that we're closing off. That in itself begins to illuminate the darkness of ignorance. We're able to see how we run and hide and keep ourselves busy so that we never have to let our hearts be penetrated. And we're also able to see how we could open and relax.

Basically, disappointment, embarrassment, and all these places where we just cannot feel good are a sort of death. We've just lost our ground completely; we are unable to hold it together and feel that we're on top of things. Rather than realizing that it takes death for there to be birth, we just fight against the fear of death.

Reaching our limit is not some kind of punishment. It's actually a sign of health that, when we meet the place where we are about to die, we feel fear and trembling. A further sign of health is that we don't become undone by fear and trembling, but we take it as a message that it's time to stop struggling and look directly at what's threatening us. Things like disappointment and anxiety are messengers telling us that we're about to go into unknown territory.

Our bedroom closet can be unknown territory for some of us. For others, it's going into outer space. What evokes hope and fear for me is different from what brings it up for you. My aunt reaches her limit when I move a lamp in her living room. My friend completely loses it when she has to move to a new apartment. My neighbor is afraid of heights. It doesn't really matter what causes us to reach our limit. The point is that sooner or later it happens to all of us.

The first time I met Trungpa Rinpoche was with a class of fourth graders who asked him a lot of questions about growing up in Tibet and about escaping from the Chinese Communists into India. One boy asked him if he was ever afraid. Rinpoche answered that his teacher had encouraged him to go to places like graveyards that scared him and to experiment with approaching things he didn't like. Then he told a story about traveling with his attendants to a monastery he'd never seen before. As they neared the gates, he saw

a large guard dog with huge teeth and red eyes. It was growling fero-
ciously and struggling to get free from the chain that held it. The
dog seemed desperate to attack them. As Rinpoche got closer, he
could see its bluish tongue and spittle spraying from its mouth.
They walked past the dog, keeping their distance, and entered the
gate. Suddenly the chain broke and the dog rushed at them. The
attendants screamed and froze in terror. Rinpoche turned and ran
as fast as he could—straight at the dog. The dog was so surprised that
he put his tail between his legs and ran away.

We can meet our match with a poodle or with a raging guard
dog, but the interesting question is—what happens next?

The spiritual journey involves going beyond hope and fear,
stepping into unknown territory, continually moving forward.
The most important aspect of being on the spiritual path may be to
just keep moving. Usually, when we reach our limit, we feel exactly
like Rinpoche's attendants and freeze in terror. Our bodies freeze
and so do our minds.

How do we work with our minds when we meet our match?
Rather than indulge or reject our experience, we can somehow let
the energy of the emotion, the quality of what we're feeling, pierce
us to the heart. This is easier said than done, but it's a noble way
to live. It's definitely the path of compassion—the path of cultivating human bravery and kindheartedness.

In the teachings of Buddhism, we hear about egolessness. It
sounds difficult to grasp: what are they talking about, anyway?
When the teachings are about neurosis, however, we feel right at
home. That's something we really understand. But egolessness?
When we reach our limit, if we aspire to know that place fully—
which is to say that we aspire to neither indulge nor repress—a
hardness in us will dissolve. We will be softened by the sheer force
of whatever energy arises—the energy of anger, the energy of disap-

pointment, the energy of fear. When it's not solidified in one direction or another, that very energy pierces us to the heart, and it opens us. This is the discovery of egolessness. It's when all our usual schemes fall apart. Reaching our limit is like finding a doorway to sanity and the unconditional goodness of humanity, rather than meeting an obstacle or a punishment.

The safest and most nurturing place to begin working this way is during formal meditation. On the cushion, we begin to get the hang of not indulging or repressing and of what it feels like to let the energy just be there. That is why it's so good to meditate every single day and continue to make friends with our hopes and fears again and again. This sows the seeds that enable us to be more awake in the midst of everyday chaos. It's a gradual awakening, and it's cumulative, but that's actually what happens. We don't sit in meditation to become good meditators. We sit in meditation so that we'll be more awake in our lives.

The first thing that happens in meditation is that we start to see what's happening. Even though we still run away and we still indulge, we see what we're doing clearly. One would think that our seeing it clearly would immediately make it just disappear, but it doesn't. So for quite a long time, we just see it clearly. To the degree that we're willing to see our indulging and our repressing clearly, they begin to wear themselves out. Wearing out is not exactly the same as going away. Instead, a wider, more generous, more enlightened perspective arises.

How we stay in the middle between indulging and repressing is by acknowledging whatever arises without judgment, letting the thoughts simply dissolve, and then going back to the openness of this very moment. That's what we're actually doing in meditation. Up come all these thoughts, but rather than squelch them or obsess with them, we acknowledge them and let them go. Then we come back to just being here. As Sogyal Rinpoche puts it, we simply "bring our mind back home."

After a while, that's how we relate with hope and fear in our daily lives. Out of nowhere, we stop struggling and relax. We stop talking to ourselves and come back to the freshness of the present moment.

This is something that evolves gradually, patiently, over time. How long does this process take? I would say it takes the rest of our lives. Basically, we're continually opening further, learning more, connecting further with the depths of human suffering and human wisdom, coming to know both those elements thoroughly and completely, and becoming more loving and compassionate people. And the teachings continue. There's always more to learn. We're not just complacent old fogies who've given up and aren't challenged by anything anymore. At the most surprising times, we still meet those ferocious dogs.

We might think, as we become more open, that it's going to take bigger catastrophes for us to reach our limit. The interesting thing is that, as we open more and more, it's the big ones that immediately wake us up and the little things that catch us off guard. However, no matter what the size, color, or shape is, the point is still to lean toward the discomfort of life and see it clearly rather than to protect ourselves from it.

In practicing meditation, we're not trying to live up to some kind of ideal—quite the opposite. We're just being with our experience, whatever it is. If our experience is that sometimes we have some kind of perspective, and sometimes we have none, then that's our experience. If sometimes we can approach what scares us, and sometimes we absolutely can't, then that's our experience. "This very moment is the perfect teacher, and it's always with us" is really a most profound instruction. Just seeing what's going on—that's the teaching right there. We can be with what's happening and not

217

dissociate. Awakeness is found in our pleasure and our pain, our confusion and our wisdom, available in each moment of our weird, unfathomable, ordinary everyday lives.

> Once we know this instruction, we can put it into practice. Then it's up to us what happens next. Ultimately, it comes down to the question of just how willing we are to lighten up and loosen our grip. How honest do we want to be with ourselves?

The meditation instruction that Chögyam Trungpa Rinpoche gave to his students is called *shamatha-vipashyana* meditation. When Trungpa Rinpoche first taught in the West, he told his students to simply open their minds and relax. If thoughts distracted them, they could simply let the thoughts dissolve and just come back to that open, relaxed state of mind.

After a few years, Rinpoche realized that some of the people who came to him found this simple instruction somewhat impossible to do and that they needed a bit more technique in order to proceed. At that point, without really changing the basic intent of the meditation, he nevertheless began to give the instructions a bit differently. He put more emphasis on posture and taught people to put very light attention on their out-breath. Later he said that the out-breath was as close as you could come to simply resting the mind in its natural open state and still have an object to which to return.

He emphasized that it should be just the ordinary out-breath, not manipulated in any way, and that the attention should be soft, a sort of touch-and-go approach. He said that about 25 percent of the attention should be on the breath, so that one was still aware of one's surroundings and didn't consider them an intrusion or an obstacle to meditation. Years later he used a humorous analogy comparing a meditator to someone all dressed up in a costume and holding a spoonful of water. One could be happily sitting there in one's fancy costume and still be quite undistracted from the spoonful of water in one's hand. The point was not to try to achieve some special state or to transcend the sounds and movement of ordinary life. Rather we were encouraged to relax more completely with our environment and to appreciate the world around us and the ordinary truth that takes place in every moment.

Most meditation techniques use an object of meditation—something you return to again and again no matter what's going on in your mind. Through rain, hail, snow, and sleet, fair weather and foul, you simply return to the object of meditation. In this case, the out-breath is the object of meditation—the elusive, fluid, everchanging out-breath, ungraspable and yet continuously arising. When you breathe in, it's like a pause or a gap. There is nothing particular to do except wait for the next out-breath.

I once explained this technique to a friend who had spent years doing a very focused concentration on both the in- and out-breaths as well as another object. When she heard this instruction, she said, "But that's impossible! No one could do this! There's a whole part where there's nothing to be aware of!" That was the first time I realized that built right into the instruction was the opportunity to completely let go. I'd heard Zen teachers talk of meditation as the willingness to die over and over again. And there it was—as each breath went out and dissolved, there was the chance to die to all that had gone before and to relax instead of panic.

Rinpoche asked us as meditation instructors not to speak of "concentrating" on the out-breath but to use more fluid language. So we would tell students to "touch the out-breath and let it go" or to "have a light and gentle attention on the out-breath" or to "be one with the breath as it relaxes outward." The basic guideline was still to open and relax without adding anything extra, without conceptualizing, but to keep returning to the mind just as it is, clear, lucid, and fresh.

After some time, Rinpoche added another refinement to the instruction. He began to ask us to label our thoughts "thinking." We'd be sitting there with the out-breath, and before we knew what had happened, we were gone—planning, worrying, fantasizing—completely in another world, a world totally made of thoughts. At the point when we realized we'd gone off, we were instructed to say to ourselves "thinking" and, without making it a big deal, to simply return again to the out-breath.

I once saw someone do a dance about this. The dancer came on stage and sat in the meditation posture. In a few seconds, thoughts of passion began to arise. The dancer moved through the process, becoming more and more frenzied as just a tiny glimpse of passion began to escalate until it was a full-blown sexual fantasy. Then a small bell rang, and a calm voice said "thinking," and the dancer relaxed back into the meditation posture. About five seconds later, the dance of rage began, again starting as a small irritation and then exploding more and more wildly. Then came the dance of loneliness, then the dance of drowsiness, and each time the bell would ring, and the voice would say "thinking," and the dancer would simply relax for a little longer and a little longer into what began to feel like the immense peace and spaciousness of simply sitting there.

Saying "thinking" is a very interesting point in the meditation. It's the point at which we can consciously train in gentleness and in developing a nonjudgmental attitude. The word for loving-kindness in Sanskrit is *maitri*. Maitri is also translated as unconditional friendliness. So each time you say to yourself "thinking," you are cultivating that unconditional friendliness toward whatever arises in your mind. Since this kind of unconditional compassion is difficult to come by, this simple and direct method for awakening it is exceedingly precious.

Sometimes we feel guilty, sometimes arrogant. Sometimes our thoughts and memories terrify us and make us feel totally miserable. Thoughts go through our minds all the time, and when we sit, we are providing a lot of space for all of them to arise. Like clouds in a big sky or waves in a vast sea, all our thoughts are given the space to appear. If one hangs on and sweeps us away, whether we call it pleasant or unpleasant, the instruction is to label it all "thinking" with as much openness and kindness as we can muster and let it dissolve back into the big sky. When the clouds and waves immediately return, it's no problem. We just acknowledge them again and again with unconditional friendliness, labeling them as just "thinking" and letting them go again and again and again.

Sometimes people use meditation to try to avoid bad feelings and disturbing thoughts. We might try to use the labeling as a way to get rid of what bothers us, and if we connect with something blissful or inspiring, we might think we've finally *got* it and try to stay where there's peace and harmony and nothing to fear.

So right from the beginning it's helpful to always remind yourself that meditation is about opening and relaxing with whatever arises, without picking and choosing. It's definitely not meant to repress anything, and it's not intended to encourage grasping, either. Allen Ginsberg uses the expression "surprise mind." You sit down and—wham!—a rather nasty surprise arises. Okay. So be it. This part is not to be rejected but compassionately acknowledged as "thinking" and let go. Then—wow!—a very delicious surprise appears. Okay. So be it. This part is not to be clung to but compassionately acknowledged as "thinking" and let go. These surprises are, we find, endless. Milarepa, the twelfth-century Tibetan yogi, sang wonderful songs about the proper way to meditate. In one song he says that mind has more projections than there are dust motes in a sunbeam and that even hundreds of spears couldn't put an end to that. So as meditators we might as well stop struggling against our thoughts and realize that honesty and humor are far more inspiring and helpful than any kind of solemn religious striving for or against anything.

In any case, the point is not to try to get rid of thoughts, but rather to see their true nature. Thoughts will run us around in circles if we buy into them, but really they are like dream images. They are like an illusion—not really all that solid. They are, as we say, just thinking.

Over the years, Rinpoche continued to refine the instructions on posture. He said it was never a good idea to struggle in meditation. So if our legs or back were hurting, we were told it was fine to move. However, it became clear that by working with proper posture, it was possible to become far more relaxed and settled in one's body by making very subtle adjustments. Large movements brought comfort for about five or ten minutes, and then we just wanted to shift again. Eventually we began following the six points of good posture as a way to really settle down. The six points are: (1) seat, (2) legs, (3) torso, (4) hands, (5) eyes, and (6) mouth, and the instruction is as follows.

> 1. Whether sitting on a cushion on the floor or in a chair, the seat should be flat, not tilting to the right or left or to the back or front.
>
> 2. The legs are crossed comfortably in front of

you—or, if you're sitting in a chair, the feet are flat
on the floor, and the knees are a few inches apart.
3. The torso (from the head to the seat) is upright,
with a strong back and an open front. If sitting in a
chair, it's best not to lean back. If you start to
slouch, simply sit upright again.
4. The hands are open, with palms down, resting on
the thighs.
5. The eyes are open, indicating the attitude of
remaining awake and relaxed with all that occurs.
The eye gaze is slightly downward and directed about
four to six feet in front.
6. The mouth is very slightly open so that the jaw is
relaxed and air can move easily through both mouth
and nose. The tip of the tongue can be placed on
the roof of the mouth.

Each time you sit down to meditate, you can run through these six
points, and anytime you feel distracted during your meditation,
you can bring your attention back to your body and run through
the six points. Then, with a sense of starting afresh, return once
again to the out-breath. If you find that thoughts have carried you
away, don't worry about it. Simply say to yourself, "thinking," and
come back to the openness and relaxation of the out-breath. Again
and again just come back to being right where you are.

In the beginning people sometimes find this meditation excit-
ing. It's like a new project, and you think that if you do it, perhaps
all the unwanted stuff will go away and you'll become open, non-
judgmental, and unconditionally friendly. But after a while the
sense of project wears out. You just find time each day, and you sit

down with yourself. You come back to that breath over and over, through boredom, edginess, fear, and well-being. This persever-ance and repetition—when done with honesty, a light touch, humor, and kindness—is its own reward.

Once we know this instruction, we can put it into practice. Then it's up to us what happens next. Ultimately, it comes down to the question of just how willing we are to lighten up and loosen our grip. How honest do we want to be with ourselves?

What makes maitri such a different approach is that we are not trying to solve a problem. We are not striving to make pain go away or to become a better person. In fact, we are giving up control altogether and letting concepts and ideals fall apart.

I get many letters from "the worst person in the world." Sometimes this worst person is getting older and feels he has wasted his life. Sometimes she is a suicidal teenager reaching out for help. The people who give themselves such a hard time come in all ages, shapes, and colors. The thing they have in common is that they have no loving-kindness for themselves.

Recently I was talking with a man I've known for a long time. I've always considered him to be a shy, good-hearted person who spends more time than most helping other people. On this day he was completely despondent and feeling like a hopeless case. Intending to be facetious, I asked him, "Well, don't you think that somewhere on this planet there might be someone worse than you?" He answered with heartbreaking honesty, "No. If you want to know what I really feel, it's that there's no one as bad as me."

It made me think of a Gary Larson cartoon I once saw. Two women are standing behind their locked door peeking out the window at a monster standing on their doorstep. One of the ladies is saying, "Calm down, Edna. Yes, it is a giant hideous insect, but it may be a giant hideous insect in need of help."

The most difficult times for many of us are the ones we give ourselves. Yet it's never too late or too early to practice loving-kindness. It's as if we had a terminal disease but might live for quite a while. Not knowing how much time we have left, we might begin to think it was important to make friends with ourselves and others in the remaining hours, months, or years.

It is said that we can't attain enlightenment, let alone feel contentment and joy, without seeing who we are and what we do, without seeing our patterns and our habits. This is called maitri—developing loving-kindness and an unconditional friendship with ourselves.

People sometimes confuse this process with self-improvement or building themselves up. We can get so caught up in being good to ourselves that we don't pay any attention at all to the impact that we're having on others. We might erroneously believe that maitri is a way to find a happiness that lasts; as advertisements so seductively promise, we could feel great for the rest of our lives. It's not that we pat ourselves on the back and say, "You're the greatest," or "Don't worry, sweetheart, everything is going to be fine." Rather it's a process by which self-deception becomes so skillfully and compassionately exposed that there's no mask that can hide us anymore.

What makes maitri such a different approach is that we are not trying to solve a problem. We are not striving to make pain go away or to become a better person. In fact, we are giving up control altogether and letting concepts and ideals fall apart.

This starts with realizing that whatever occurs is neither the beginning nor the end. It is just the same kind of normal human experience that's been happening to everyday people from the beginning of time. Thoughts, emotions, moods, and memories come and they go, and basic nowness is always here.

It is never too late for any of us to look at our minds. We can always sit down and allow the space for anything to arise. Sometimes we have a shocking experience of ourselves. Sometimes we try to hide. Sometimes we have a surprising experience of ourselves. Often we get carried away. Without judging, without buying into likes and dislikes, we can always encourage ourselves to just be here again and again and again.

The painful thing is that when we buy into disapproval, we are practicing disapproval. When we buy into harshness, we are practicing harshness. The more we do it, the stronger these qualities become. How sad it is that we become so expert at causing harm to ourselves and others. The trick then is to practice gentleness and letting go. We can learn to meet whatever arises with curiosity and not make it such a big deal. Instead of struggling against the force of confusion, we could meet it and relax. When we do that, we gradually discover that clarity is always there. In the middle of the worst scenario of the worst person in the world, in the midst of all the heavy dialogue with ourselves, open space is always there.

We carry around an image of ourselves, an image we hold in our minds. One way to describe this is "small mind." It can also be described as *sem*. In Tibetan there are several words for mind, but two that are particularly helpful to know are *sem* and *rikpa*. Sem is what we experience as discursive thoughts, a stream of chatter that's always reinforcing an image of ourselves. Rikpa literally means "intelligence" or "brightness." Behind all the planning and worrying, behind all the wishing and wanting, picking and choosing, the unfabricated, wisdom mind of rikpa is always here. Whenever we stop talking to ourselves, rikpa is continually here.

In Nepal the dogs bark all night long. Every twenty minutes or so, they all stop at once, and there is an experience of immense relief and stillness. Then they all start barking again. The small mind of sem can feel just like that. When we first start meditating, it's as if the dogs never stop barking at all. After a while, there are those gaps. Discursive thoughts are rather like wild dogs that need taming. Rather than beating them or throwing stones, we tame them with compassion. Over and over we regard them with the precision and kindness that allow them to gradually calm down. Sometimes it feels like there's much more space, with just a few yips and yaps here and there.

Of course the noise will continue. We aren't trying to get rid of those dogs. But once we've touched in with the spaciousness of rikpa, it begins to permeate everything. Once we've even had a glimpse of spaciousness, if we practice with maitri, it will continue to expand. It expands into our resentment. It expands into our fear. It expands into our concepts and opinions about things and into who we think we are. We might sometimes even get the feeling that life is like a dream.

When I was about ten, my best friend started having nightmares: she'd be running through a huge dark building pursued by hideous monsters. She'd get to a door, struggle to open it, and no sooner had she closed it behind her than she'd hear it opened by the rapidly approaching monsters. Finally she'd wake up screaming and crying for help.

One day we were sitting in her kitchen talking about her nightmares. When I asked her what the demons looked like, she said she didn't know because she was always running away. After I asked her that question, she began to wonder about the monsters. She wondered if any of them looked like witches and if any of them had knives. So on the next occurrence of the nightmare, just as the demons began to pursue her, she stopped running and turned around. It took tremendous courage, and her heart was pounding, but she put her back up against the wall and looked at them. They all stopped right in front of her and began jumping up and down, but none of them came closer. There were five in all, each looking something like an animal. One of them was a gray bear, but instead of claws, it had long red fingernails. One had four eyes. Another had a wound on its cheek. Once she looked closely, they appeared less like monsters and more like the two-dimensional drawings in comic books. Then slowly they began to fade. After that she woke up, and that was the end of her nightmares.

There is a teaching on the three kinds of awakening: awakening from the dream of ordinary sleep, awakening at death from the dream of life, and awakening into full enlightenment from the dream of delusion. These teachings say that when we die, we experience it as waking up from a very long dream. When I heard this teaching, I remembered my friend's nightmares. It struck me right then that if all this is really a dream, I might as well spend it trying to look at what scares me instead of running away. I haven't always found this all that easy to do, but in the process I've learned a lot about maitri.

Our personal demons come in many guises. We experience them as shame, as jealousy, as abandonment, as rage. They are anything that makes us so uncomfortable that we continually run away.

We do the big escape: we act out, say something, slam a door, hit someone, or throw a pot as a way of not facing what's happening in our hearts. Or we shove the feelings under and somehow deaden the pain. We can spend our whole lives escaping from the monsters of our minds.

All over the world, people are so caught in running that they forget to take advantage of the beauty around them. We become so accustomed to speeding ahead that we rob ourselves of joy.

from When Things Fall Apart

Once I dreamt that I was getting a house ready for Khandro Rinpoche. I was rushing around cleaning and cooking. Suddenly her car drove up, and there she was with her attendant. As I ran up and greeted them, Rinpoche smiled at me and asked, "Did you see the sun come up this morning?" I answered, "No, Rinpoche, I didn't. I was much too busy to see the sun." She laughed and said, "Too busy to live life!"

Sometimes it seems we have a preference for darkness and speed. We can protest and complain and hold a grudge for a thousand years. But in the midst of the bitterness and resentment, we have a glimpse of the possibility of maitri. We hear a child crying or smell that someone is baking bread. We feel the coolness of the air or see the first crocus of spring. Despite ourselves we are drawn out by the beauty in our own backyard.

The way to dissolve our resistance to life is to meet it face to face. When we feel resentment because the room is too hot, we could meet the heat and feel its fieriness and its heaviness. When we feel resentment because the room is too cold, we could meet the cold and feel its iciness and its bite. When we want to complain about the rain, we could feel its wetness instead. When we worry because the wind is shaking our windows, we could meet the wind and hear its sound. Cutting our expectations for a cure is a gift we can give ourselves. There is no cure for hot and cold. They will go on forever. After we have died, the ebb and flow will still continue. Like the tides of the sea, like day and night—this is the nature of things. Being able to appreciate, being able to look closely, being able to open our minds—this is the core of maitri.

When the rivers and air are polluted, when families and nations are at war, when homeless wanderers fill the highways, these are traditional signs of a dark age. Another is that people become poisoned by self-doubt and become cowards.

Practicing loving-kindness toward ourselves seems as good a way as any to start illuminating the darkness of difficult times.

Being preoccupied with our self-image is like being deaf and blind. It's like standing in the middle of a vast field of wildflowers with a black hood over our heads. It's like coming upon a tree of singing birds while wearing earplugs.

There's so much resentment and so much resistance to life. In all nations, it's like a plague that's gotten out of control and is poisoning the atmosphere of the world. At this point it might be wise to wonder about these things and begin to get the knack of loving-kindness.

therapy

—◇—

from

AWAKENING THE HEART

by John Welwood

Some psychotherapists are intrigued by meditation's potential to address issues that arise in therapy. John Welwood (born 1943), a therapist and clinical psychologist, argues that therapy and meditation can play complementary but very distinct roles in personal growth.

—◇—

As Eastern psychologies and meditative practices have an increasing influence in our culture, questions about the relationship between psychotherapy and meditation frequently arise in people's minds. If a person is dissatisfied with the course of his life, where should he turn for guidance? Is psychotherapy or a meditative practice more likely to help him find his way? Do therapy and meditation cover the same territory, or are they oriented in quite different directions? How far can psychotherapy take a person, and at what point might meditation be a more appropriate vehicle for growth?

No clear consensus about the proper domain of meditation and psychotherapy exists today. My own perspective on these questions, which are not readily amenable to definitive answers, has kept changing over the years. Part of the difficulty in addressing these issues is that the terms "psychotherapy" and "meditation" are both used loosely to refer to a very diverse range of practices, so that discussions about them are often not very precise or meaningful. To go beyond loose generalizations, it is necessary to look more clearly at the specifics of change and development in these two different modalities. For this purpose, I will base my reflections here on my practice with experiential Focusing, within a context of existential therapy, and mindfulness meditation, within the context of Buddhist psychology.

Therapeutic Change and Unfolding
According to one body of research, what seems essential for change to occur in psychotherapy is that clients speak *from* their immediate experience, rather than from familiar thoughts, feelings, beliefs, or judgments *about* their experience. And yet it is not all that easy to speak from our immediate experience. For instance, if you ask yourself how you are feeling right now, the first sense you may have is "I don't know. I'm not quite sure." Since it is easy to give up looking further at this point, we have to learn how to follow and stay with what is still unclear in our felt experience, if we are to let it unfold and reveal itself to us. The research mentioned above suggests that therapy is successful when a person can attend to this fresh yet unclear edge in his experience, gently question it, and allow himself to sense and gradually unfold its meanings. Focusing developed as a way of teaching clients how to do this.

With any given problem or situation, there are aspects of it that we know and understand, and other aspects that we are not aware of (these are the ones that usually give us the most trouble). But though we do not know all the ramifications of a situation and how it affects us, we usually have some kind of global *felt sense* of the situation. For instance, if you pick a problem in your life right now, and ask yourself how it feels to you as a whole (aside from all your familiar thoughts and feelings about it), the overall, perhaps fuzzy, feeling-texture it has for you is a "felt sense." A felt sense is a wider way our body holds or "knows" many aspects of a situation all at once—subverbally, holistically, intuitively. It is concretely *felt*—in the body—as a *sense*—something not yet cognitively clear or distinct. It is not yet clear because it contains many aspects of the situation— it needs to be "unpacked" or "unfolded." Contacting and unfolding the wider felt sense of a situation we are in often leads to important therapeutic changes.

Let me illustrate this by taking a somewhat simplified case example. A certain client comes in feeling angry, along with a familiar round of thoughts and emotional stories surrounding the anger. Instead of having him talk *about* the anger and try to figure it out, I ask him to sense how he is holding it in his body right now. "Something is sitting in my gut, weighing me down, eating at me from the inside," he says, describing a felt sense. The next step is to feel out this sense more fully. Resting with the unknown, waiting, and letting it take shape is one of the most important, though subtle and difficult, moments in therapy, which often takes patience and practice.

As he sits with his felt sense in this way, he is going underneath the familiar feelings and thoughts associated with anger to contact its *fresh* quality in *this* situation. He spends more time sighing and shifting around in his chair, but he is beginning to get in touch with where it gets to him right now: "It's frustrating living with her." Pause. "And disappointing . . . she let me down really badly this time." Another pregnant pause. "I've invested too much in her . . . for so many years I've wanted so badly to really communicate with her." There is a vitality to his words and tone of voice now that tells me he is moving further into new territory here. "But you know, it's not really her I'm angry at . . . I'm angry and disappointed in myself. That's what's got me right now." Another sigh, and a deep breath. I give him plenty of space to let that sink in, to let him feel out the ramifications of this new edge of the felt sense. "Things used to be so good between us, and now we don't even listen to each other." His voice is shaky, alerting me that he is still exploring new ground. His next words really crack it open: "I'm just now realizing I haven't let her know how much I care about her in a long time. That's what feels so heavy in my gut—I've sat on my love for the past six months. No wonder she is giving me such a hard time." A really deep breath this time, his head is nodding, and he sits up straight. By unfolding the meanings in the felt sense, he is released from its grip. In getting to the crux of his anger, the client has experienced a *felt shift*. He smiles at this point and talks about how much he really does care for her.

In going beneath his anger to feel out the unknown dimensions of it, he becomes a larger awareness that can question the anger and have it speak to him. When it has its say, its contraction in his stomach can release, and he can leave not only with a new resolve to relate to his wife in a new way, but also with a fresh sense of his aliveness. In this way, psychotherapy can often provide a glimpse of how we live in a larger way that is not entangled in problems. Insofar as it can tap into this larger sense of life when releasing a person from the grip of personal problems, psychotherapy can also serve as a bridge to meditation.

Psychotherapy and Meditation: Differences
When I first discovered it in the mid-sixties, Focusing seemed to resemble what writers such as D. T. Suzuki and Alan Watts were describing in their books on Zen. I wondered whether the diffuse feeling of a felt sense was the same as what Zen referred to as *emptiness*, and how a felt shift might be akin to the famous *satori*. In those

days, before I actually started meditating, I used to speculate that psychotherapy could be a Western equivalent of meditation and other Eastern paths of liberation. But after practicing meditation for many years, their similarities do not seem as great to me as the following major differences between the orientation of therapy and meditation.

Expanding Identity or Letting Go of Identity

The basic task of psychotherapy is to expand a person's sense of who he is by integrating the parts of himself that he treats as alien— what Freud described by saying, "Where there was id (it), there shall ego (I) be." This kind of work can help people develop personal stability, self-respect, and an expanded sense of what they can feel and do. Meditation practice, however, goes one step further. Instead of expanding or shoring up the "I," meditation is a way of inquiring into what this "I" consists of.

Before proceeding further, I should describe the practice of mindfulness meditation more fully. It involves sitting straight, following the breath, and letting thoughts come and go, without trying to control them or direct them in more pleasant directions. As soon as we give up control and let ourselves be in this way, the confusion of churning thoughts and feelings may become more noticeable. In observing our thoughts, which graphically portray what is driving us, we get a very intimate sense of the areas of our life where we are afraid, fixated, or grasping too tightly. Meditation provides an opportunity to let this confusion arise and be there, rather than, as therapy does, trying to sort out the confusion.

Gently bringing our attention back to the breath helps keep us from getting lost in the chaos of thoughts and feelings, so that we can let the confusion arise without identifying with it, and eventually go to its root. We begin to learn how to "keep our seat," how not to get thrown or carried away by the wild horse of the mind, but rather to stay alert and keep riding no matter where the mind may go. In so doing, the mind begins to slow down (the horse gets tired!), and we get glimpses of another way of being. Instead of being driven and carried away by our thoughts, we can begin to tap into a deeper, wider awareness, which is quite refreshing.

Meditation takes us directly to the root of confusion. It allows us to see how we are driven by fear, which arises from our uncertainty about who we are amidst the constantly changing flux of life. Meditation provides an opportunity to directly experience how we keep trying to manufacture and hold onto a fixed identity as a defense against the uncertainties surrounding our lives. The Tibetan word for ego-identity (*dagdzin*) literally means "holding on to oneself." We create this seemingly solid identity out of various stories we tell ourselves about who we are and what we like or don't like, as well as from unconscious scripts that we act out over and over again, which seem to imply that we are a predictable "somebody." In the Buddhist view, this attempt to maintain a solid identity is the root of certain universal tendencies that produce suffering, called the five *kleshas*: hatred, greed, envy, pride, and ignorance. Although psychotherapy works with the specific manifestations of these *kleshas* in a person's life, it does not provide a means of going to their source, which is our ingrained habit of trying to hold onto and shore up "I." And while therapy can help us let go of specific objects of hatred, envy, greed, and so on, meditation can teach us to let go of this "I-fixation" altogether. This is essential for coming to terms with the essential questions of human life, such as change and impermanence, aging, adversity, love and death.

The process of meditation reveals a deeper core of well-being beyond ego strength in the therapeutic sense of a well-adjusted, functioning personality structure. If psychotherapy can heal the

self-defeating splits between different parts *within ourselves*, meditation allows us to go one step further, by starting to dissolve the
fortress of "I," and heal *our split from life as a whole.* Then a wider way
of perceiving life can arise, which is known in Buddhism as *vipassana. Vipassana* is a panoramic awareness that includes the surrounding environment and helps us see situations in a larger way, beyond
how they just affirm or negate "I." This larger awareness is the basis
for compassionate action and service to others, which is perhaps
the ultimate orientation of meditation and spiritual practice in
general.

Building Meaning-Structure or Dissolving Meaning-Structure
Psychotherapy focuses on and observes the personal world. It takes
the question, "Who am I?" seriously, in order to untangle and
straighten out the unconscious scripts that may be driving us to act
in self-defeating ways. Then we can develop more positive mean-
ing-structures that support an active, wholesome lifestyle. The
therapeutic search is to find meaning in our experience where it was
previously unclear or misunderstood. For example, the client mentioned above suffered digestive problems, which had no particular
meaning for him until he focused on his anger and saw how he was
blocking his caring about himself and his communication with his
wife. Unfolding these meanings changed how he related to this situation, which not only cleared up his digestion, but also gave him
new energy for working on his marriage. Yet although therapy can
help free a person from emotional and personal entanglements, it
does not generally provide a path for accessing or deepening the
larger sense of freedom and aliveness that arises in a moment of
shift and opening, when old scripts and story-lines fall away.

Meditation can provide such a path, taking us further into the
larger sense of aliveness that opens up in moments of release and

shift, because it focuses not on personal issues, but on the nature and process of mind as a whole. The question "Who am I?" from a meditative point of view has no answer. Since we are never able to pin down this "I," meditation helps dissolve fixation on "I" altogether. Then we may begin to experience pure, open moments of just being here, which feel very spacious because they are free of personal needs, meanings, and interpretations. Meditation can teach us how to contact this larger space or emptiness that lies beyond the constant search for personal meaning. This can effect a radical transformation in the way we live. As we begin to give up holding onto ourselves so tightly, this larger sense of aliveness starts permeating everything we do.

Goal Orientation or Letting Be

Psychotherapy is more goal-oriented than medication. If there were no specific goals for therapy, termination of therapy would not be possible.

Mindfulness practice, on the other hand, does not have specific goals, but is open ended. It could easily be practiced for a whole lifetime, for broadening and deepening awareness has no limit. Meditation does not have the aim of solving problems or making us feel better; rather it provides a space in which we can let ourselves be, just as we are, and thus discover our basic nature (beyond all our stories and problems). As Suzuki Roshi once said, "As long as you think you are practicing meditation for the sake of something, that is not true practice. You may feel as if you are doing something special, but it is only the expression of your true nature."

In letting oneself remain open toward whatever comes along in this way, considerable anxiety may arise. Yet in meditation this anxiety is not considered to be a particular problem. By not trying to find release from the anxiety that goes along with openness, but letting it be, facing it mindfully, the meditator strengthens the "muscles" that allow him to ride his mind and accept whatever arises in his life.

Maitri: The Common Ground of Psychotherapy and Meditation

If the differences between psychotherapy and meditation could always be so clearly demarcated, there would not be so much confusion about their relative effectiveness. But the fact is that the effects of these two practices overlap in certain important ways as well. Not only can therapy often help people tap into a larger transpersonal sense of aliveness, but meditation can also help ground people, so that their personal lives take a more satisfying direction.

Though therapy and meditation both may take a person through many stages of development, I see their major point of overlap as helping to develop what is known in Buddhism as *maitri*, or "unconditional friendliness to oneself." Usually we are friendly with people (or parts of ourselves) because they are pleasant or praiseworthy in some way. *Maitri* is a kind of friendliness with ourselves that is not conditional in any way. It means being friendly toward our experience, not because we are necessarily enjoying it (in fact, it may be painful or unpleasant), but just because is is what we are experiencing. Instead of trying to get ourselves to live up to how we think we *should* be, *maitri* involves accepting ourselves unconditionally and allowing ourselves to be human. How do therapy and meditation at their best help develop this friendliness with ourselves, which is an important first step in awakening the heart?

First, both psychotherapy and meditation involve a certain disciplined attention. Although such a formal practice of inquiry into our experience may at first seem contrived or difficult, is is often necessary to help us break through the habitual thought patterns that prevent us from contacting our experience more fully. Unfortunately, many of us associate discipline with harsh or coercive measures, either using it to "whip ourselves into shape," or else rebelling against it. Yet there is a more natural kind of discipline that is an expression of caring for ourselves and the quality of our lives.

Secondly, therapy and meditation can teach us how to "make space" for whatever obstacles arise, instead of getting caught in struggling with them, judging them, or pushing them away. Fighting with our feelings only gives them a greater charge of energy, and thus more power over us. Making space for whatever feelings we have to be there, by contrast, allows us to become larger than them, not by "rising above them," but by stretching to include them. When we can include pain in our lives, then it no longer has such a hold over us.

One client of mine who was experiencing fear said, "I don't like this fear. I want to be strong." She was trying to get rid of her fear, keep it down, suppress it because it did not suit her image of herself. This was the opposite of *maitri*. So I said to her, "Can you make a space for your fear to be there? And then make another space for your dislike of the fear? They can both be there, and one does not have to negate the other." When she could let her fear be in this way, she found that it immediately lessened, as it no longer had to keep struggling to be recognized.

Mindfulness meditation works in a similar way, as the meditator neither suppresses nor indulges the thoughts and feelings that arise while sitting. It is important in both therapy and meditation to develop a "light touch"—the ability to contact our experience directly but not, bogged down in any particular content.

Thirdly, both therapy and meditation can help us respect the unknown in our lives, out of which new ways of being can arise. To face and admit our uncertainties is a way of being kind to ourselves. Trying to fit an image of being "on top of things" can be aggressive and self-destructive, for it forces us to deny and manipulate what we are actually experiencing. Admitting uncertainty, rather than trying to fit our experience into preconceived ideas and images, allows natural, spontaneous directions and insights to emerge, which are likely to serve us better than our old concept and beliefs.

Being friendly with ourselves means living in our bodies in a more wholesome way as well. For example, in both Focusing and mindfulness meditation positive life directions emerge out of coming down to earth—grounding ourselves more fully in the body. A process such as Focusing undermines the tendency to explain or figure out experience "from the top (head) down" by letting experience speak to us "from the ground (body) up." In meditation, the posture itself is a *mudra* (symbolic gesture) expressing our connection with the earth and a willingness to slow down and face our experience directly. Rinzai Zen has a word—*kufu*—for the process of placing a *koan* or question in the abdomen and waiting for an answer to come from there. D. T. Suzuki describes *kufu* as "not just thinking with the head but the state when the whole body is involved in and applied to the solving of a problem." This does not sound so very different from those crucial moments in therapy when we ask questions and wait for answers to emerge from a bodily felt sense.

In helping us overcome fear of our own experience in these ways, psychotherapy and meditation can point us toward a core of strength and well-being underneath all our problems and neurotic patterns. If a client can stay with and unfold his negative feelings, they will eventually yield or point to some more positive, wholesome direction underneath them. In meditation, the practice of being with parts of ourselves that we would rather not look at builds confidence as we realize that nothing inside is as bad as our avoidance or rejection of it. By not running away from our experience, but staying with ourselves through thick and thin, we begin to accept ourselves in a new way and appreciate the basic openness and sensitivity at the root of our being.

Recognizing the Whole Range of Human Development
One of the most important contributions of the East to Western psychology has been in helping us extend our vision of the whole range of human development beyond the normal aims of psychological adjustment. The Eastern psychologies have helped many Western psychologists realize that there is another dimension of growth beyond merely finding fulfillment in achieving personal goals. Beyond the desire for self-actualization—the tendency to realize ourselves as individuals and live full and rich personal lives— we seem to have a need to go beyond ourselves, to step outside our familiar safe boundaries and taste life on a larger scale. Important as personal fulfillment is it does not prepare us for dealing with impermanence, death, aloneness, or the basic pain that is inherent in having an open heart, apart from any specific personal problems.

On the other side, the contribution of Western psychology to the East/West dialogue is in pointing out that we cannot begin to transcend self-centeredness if we do not first "have" a strong sense of self. The Eastern teachings about emptiness and selflessness can be confusing to people who may not yet know what it is to feel the fullness of life or have a self they can respect. And it is certainly true that many people take refuge in meditation or spiritual groups as a way of escaping from the normal developmental tasks of growing up. A certain kind of self-deception is common among such persons: exposure to the great ideas of the spiritual traditions may cause them to imagine themselves to be more detached and enlightened than they actually are. They may become inflated and carried away with themselves, or else emotionally flat, lacking color and personal warmth.

One person who came to me for counseling vividly illustrated this confusion of wrongly applying the Eastern teachings, which speak about the higher stages of human development, to her situation. She had difficulties with men, giving herself to them too soon, so that she always wound up being hurt and abandoned. This exacerbated her feelings of worthlessness and distrust of the opposite sex. She had read widely in Eastern literature, which led her to believe that she should give up self-importance, but the task facing her was clearly the opposite: to develop a sense of self-worth, to respect herself, and to start setting limits, drawing boundaries, learning to say no and to protect her own space. Like many others who use spiritual teachings to avoid normal developmental tasks, she tended to dismiss and belittle her own needs and feelings. In Buddhist terms, she was confusing absolute and relative truth. From an *absolute* point of view, no solid, permanent self exists; therefore distinctions between self and other are highly arbitrary and ultimately false. However, from a *relative* point of view, distinctions between self and other are quite real and functional. If self doesn't get out of the way of other's car, then there will be no one around to appreciate absolute truth. If distinctions between self and other are muddled or confused, as in psychosis, then they can never really be transcended in the larger panoramic awareness of big mind.

The kind of confusion exemplified by this client is familiar to many psychotherapists and meditation teachers. The Eastern teachings assume that a person already has a healthy self-structure. However, in modern society it may be dangerous to make such an assumption. The breakdown of family, tradition, and community has undermined the whole fabric of meaning and supports that help people develop a realistic sense of themselves, their possibilities and limitations. Especially if a person has not developed the ability to relate to others in a wholesome way or is unable to acknowledge and express feelings, psychotherapy may be the first treatment of choice before he can even begin to consider meditation. Psychotherapy helps people understand themselves in a very pragmatic way. To attempt to skip over this area of our development in favor of some spiritual bliss beyond is asking for trouble.

In short, therapy and meditation have their own proper domains, which should not be confused. People often ask me whether I teach my therapy clients to meditate. I generally do not try to mix these two paths, partly because my clients do not come to me for meditation, and in most cases do not seem ready for it. Since mindfulness is the most powerful method I know for dissolving the rigidity of ego-clinging, introducing it as a purely therapeutic technique for feeling better would be to risk treating it as a "mental health gimmick," as Harvey Cox warns against doing. And as Robin Skynner points out in chapter two of this book, "the more powerful a technique is, the more dangerous it can be in preventing real change if it is misused." Moreover, for certain clients like the one mentioned above, mindfulness practice might even reinforce distance from feelings.

Some psychotherapists have introduced meditation into therapy as a way of helping clients to see through their egos, but this could be problematic. It is not so hard to help people see through ego-clinging—this can happen in many moments of crisis, intoxication, or altered perception. But helping a person live beyond ego in a genuine or lasting way takes an enormous commitment on the part of both a teacher and a student of meditation. This kind of commitment is inappropriate for the therapy relationship, which is limited by professional and monetary constraints.

A teacher in one of the meditative traditions, moreover, has typically undergone lengthy, intensive training and discipline, and has been allowed to teach by one of his own teachers, who has carefully tested his realization. A psychotherapist who has not had such training or testing could run the danger of confusing the two roles and becoming inflated by pretensions to a level of spiritual understanding and authority he may not genuinely possess.

For these reasons, I prefer to maintain a clear distinction between psychotherapy and meditation in my work with clients, seeing them as complementary, sometimes overlapping paths that apply to different aspects of human development. Psychotherapy has different levels and functions to it, depending on the goals and the understanding of the client and the therapist. Act the very least, it is an effective way of solving life problems and developing a functional sense of self. Beyond that, it can also help people deepen feelings and their sense of their inner life. Finally, it may help people begin to break through the protective shell that surrounds the heart, so that they can let the world in and go out to meet others more fully. In this way especially, psychotherapy can serve as a stepping stone to meditative practices, which can take the process of awakening the heart still further.

It is important not to blur the distinction between therapy and meditation, for this may lead to confusing self-integration and self-transcendence. This confusion could weaken the effectiveness of therapy to help us find ourselves—by crying to make it achieve something more than it is designed for. And it could dilute the power of meditation, distorting the larger reality it can reveal, thereby diminishing its unique potential to open our eyes to a radically fresh vision of who we are and what we are capable of.

time

◇

from
FULL CATASTROPHE LIVING
by Jon Kabat-Zinn

Most people who consider adopting a meditation practice wonder how to find the time for it. Jon Kabat-Zinn, founder and former director of the Stress Reduction Center at the University of Massachusetts, suggests that meditation offers its own answer to the question.

—◇—

"Practice not-doing and everything will fall into place."
—Lao-tzu, *Tao Te Ching*

In our society, time has become one of our biggest stressors. At some stages of life it may feel as if there is never enough time to do what we need to do. Often we don't know where time has gone, the years pass by so fast. At other stages, time may weigh heavily upon us. The days and the hours can seem interminable. We don't know what to do with all our time. Crazy as it may sound, we are going to suggest that the antidote to time stress is intentional non-doing, and that non-doing is applicable whether you are suffering from not having "enough time" or suffering from having "too much time." The challenge here is for you to put this proposition to the test in your own life, to see for yourself whether your relationship to time can be transformed through the practice of non-doing.

248

If you feel completely overwhelmed by the pressures of time, you might wonder how it could possibly help to take time away from what you "have to do" in order to practice non-doing. And on the other hand, if you are feeling isolated and bored and have nothing but time on your hands, you might wonder how it could possibly help to fill this burden of time unfilled with "nothing."

The answer is simple and not at all farfetched. *Inner peace exists outside of time.* If you commit yourself to spending some time each day in inner stillness, even if it is for two minutes, or five, or ten, for those moments you are stepping out of the flow of time altogether. The calmness, relaxation, and centering that come from letting go of time transform your experience of time when you go back into it. Then it becomes possible to flow along with time during your day rather than constantly fighting against it or feeling driven by it, simply by bringing awareness to present-moment experience.

The more you practice making some time in your day for non-doing, the more your whole day becomes non-doing; in other words, is suffused with an awareness grounded in the present moment and therefore outside of time. Perhaps you have already experienced this if you have been practicing the sitting meditation or the body scan or the yoga. Perhaps you have observed that being aware takes no extra time, that awareness simply rounds out each moment, makes it more full, breathes life into it. So if you are pressed for time, being in the present gives you more time by giving you back the fullness of each moment that you have. No matter what is happening, you can be centered in perceiving and accepting things as they are. Then you can be aware of what still needs to be done in the future without it causing you undue anxiety or loss of perspective. Then you can move to do it, with your doing coming out of your being, out of peace.

On the other hand, let's suppose you are in a life situation in which you don't know what to do with all the time you have. Time weighs on your hands. Perhaps you feel empty, disconnected from the world and from all the meaningful things being done in it. Perhaps you can't go out, or hold down a job, or get out of bed for long, or even read much to "pass the time." Perhaps you are alone, without friends and relatives or far from them. How could non-doing possibly help you? You are already not doing anything and it is driving you nuts!

Actually you are probably doing a lot even though you are unaware of it. For one thing, you may be "doing" unhappiness, boredom, and anxiety. You are probably spending at least some time, and perhaps a great deal of time, dwelling in your thoughts and memories, reliving pleasant moments from the past or unhappy events. You may be "doing" anger at other people for things that happened long ago. You may be "doing" loneliness or resentment or self-pity or hopelessness. These inner activities of mind can drain your energy. They can be exhausting and make the passage of time seem interminable.

Our subjective experience of time passing seems linked to the activity of thought in some way. We *think* about the past, we *think* about the future. Time is measured as the space between our thoughts and in the never-ending stream of them. As we practice watching our thoughts come and go, we are cultivating an ability to dwell in the silence and stillness behind the stream of thought itself, in a timeless present. Since the present is always here, now, it is already outside of time passing.

Non-doing means letting go of *everything*. Above all, it means see-ing and letting go of your thoughts as they come and go. It means letting yourself be. If you feel trapped in time, non-doing is a way that you can step out of all the time on your hands by stepping into timelessness. In doing so you also step out, at least momentarily, from your isolation and your unhappiness and from your desire to be engaged, busy, a part of things, doing something meaningful. By connecting with yourself outside of the flow of time, you are already doing the most meaningful thing you could possibly do, namely coming to peace within your own mind, coming into contact with your own wholeness, reconnecting with yourself.

> Time past and time future
> Allow but a little consciousness.
> To be conscious is not to be in time.
> —T. S. Eliot, "Burnt Norton," *Four Quartets*

You could look at all the time you have as an opportunity to engage in the inner work of being and growing. Then, even if your body doesn't work "right" and you are confined to the house or to a bed, the possibility is still there to turn your life into an adventure and to find meaning in each moment. If you commit yourself to the work of mindfulness, your physical isolation might take on a different meaning for you. Your inability to be active in outer ways and the pain and regret that you may feel from it may become balanced by the joy of other possibilities, by a new perspective on yourself, one in which you are seeing optimistically, reframing the time that weighed on your hands as time to do the work of being, the work of non-doing, the work of self-awareness and understanding.

There is no end to this work, of course, and no telling where it might lead. But wherever that is, it will be away from suffering, away from boredom and anxiety and self-pity and toward healing. Negative mental states cannot survive for long when timelessness is being cultivated. How could they when you are embodying peace? Your concentrated awareness serves as a crucible in which negative mental states can be contained and then transmuted.

And if you are able-bodied enough to do at least some things in the outside world, dwelling in non-doing will likely lead to insights as to how you might connect up with people and activities and events that might be meaningful to you as well as helpful and useful to others. Everybody has something to offer to the world—in fact, something that no other person can offer, something unique and priceless, *one's own being.* If you practice non-doing, you may find that, rather than having all this time on your hands, the days may not be long enough to do what needs doing. In this work, you will never be unemployed.

If you take a more cosmic perspective on time, none of us is here for very long anyway. The total duration of human life on the planet has itself been the briefest of eye blinks, our own individual lives infinitesimal in the vastness of geological time. Stephen Jay Gould, the paleontologist, points out that "the human species has inhabited this planet for only 250,000 years or so—roughly 0.0015 percent of the history of life, the last inch of the cosmic mile." Yet the way minds represent time, it feels as if we have a long time to live. In fact we often delude ourselves, especially early in life, with feelings of immortality and of our own permanence. At other times we are only too keenly aware of the inevitability of death and the rapidity of the passage of our lives.

Perhaps it is the knowledge of death, conscious or unconscious, that ultimately drives us to feel pressed for time. The word *deadline* certainly carries the message. We have many deadlines, those imposed by our work and by other people and those we impose on ourselves. We rush here and there, doing this and that, trying to get it all done "in time." Often we are so stressed by the squeeze of time that we do what we are doing just to get through with it, to be able to say to ourselves, "At least *that* is out of the way." And then it's on to the next thing that needs doing, pressing on, pressing through our moments.

Some doctors believe that time stress is a fundamental cause of disease in the present era. Time urgency was originally featured as one of the salient characteristics of coronary-disease-prone, or Type A, behavior. The Type-A syndrome is sometimes described as "hurry sickness." People who fit into this category are driven by a sense of time pressure to speed up the doing of all their daily activities and to do and think more than one thing at a time. They tend to be very poor listeners. They are constantly interrupting and finishing other people's sentences for them. They tend to be very impatient. They have great difficulty sitting and doing nothing or standing in lines, and they tend to speak rapidly and to dominate in social and professional situations. Type A's also tend to be highly competitive, easily irritated, cynical and hostile. As we have seen, the evidence to date seems to be pointing toward hostility and cynicism as the most toxic elements of coronary-prone behavior. But, even if further research shows that time urgency by itself is not a major factor in heart disease, it nevertheless has a toxicity of its own. Time stress can easily erode the *quality* of a person's life and threaten health and well-being.

Dr. Robert Eliot, a cardiologist and well-known stress researcher, described his own mental state and his relationship to time prior to his heart attack as follows:

> My body cried out for rest, but my brain wasn't lis-
> tening. I was behind schedule. My timetable read
> that by the age of forty I should be the chief of car-
> diology at a major university. I was forty-three when

I left the University of Florida at Gainesville and
accepted the position of chief of cardiology at the
University of Nebraska in 1972. All I had to do was
run a little faster and I'd be back on track.

Yet he found himself running into roadblocks of various kinds in
his efforts to establish an innovative cardiovascular research center.

I came to feel that the walls were closing in on me
and that I would never break free to make my dream
a reality.

Desperately I did what I had been doing all my life. I picked up
the pace. I tried to force things through. I crisscrossed the state to
provide on-the-spot cardiology education to rural Nebraska
physicians and build support among them for the university's cardiovascular program. I scheduled academic lectures across the
country, continually flying in and out at a moment's notice. I
remember that on one trip on which my wife, Phyllis, helped with
the business arrangements, a seminar went superbly, and on the
plane ride home Phyllis wanted to savor the memory. Not me. I was
rushing through the evaluation forms, worrying about how to make
the next seminar better.

I had no time for family and friends, relaxation and diversion. When
Phyllis bought me an exercise bike for Christmas, I was offended.
How could I possibly find time to sit down and pedal a bicycle?

I was often overtired, but I put that out of my mind. I wasn't
concerned about my health. What did I have to worry about? I was
an expert in diseases of the heart, and I knew I didn't have any of
the risk factors. My father had lived to be seventy-eight and my
mother, at eighty-five, showed no sign of heart disease. I didn't
smoke. I wasn't overweight. I didn't have high blood pressure. I

didn't have high cholesterol. I didn't have diabetes. I thought I was immune to heart disease.

But I was running a big risk for other reasons. I had been pushing too hard for too long. Now all my efforts seemed futile. . . . A feeling of disillusionment descended on me, a sense of *invisible entrapment*.

I didn't know it then, but my body was continuously reacting to this inner turmoil. For nine months I was softened for the blow. It came two weeks after my forty-fourth birthday.

As he described it, after a disappointing confrontation one day, he got very angry and was unable to calm down. After a sleepless night and a long drive to a speaking engagement, he gave a medical lecture. Following a heavy lunch, he tried to diagnose cases, but his mind was foggy, his eyes were blurry. He felt dizzy. These were the conditions immediately preceding his heart attack.

Dr. Eliot's heart attack led him to write a book called *Is It Worth Dying For?* in which he describes how he came to answer that question with a resounding *no* and went on to change his relationship to time and to stress. He described his life leading up to his heart attack as "a joyless treadmill."

Norman Cousins described the conditions leading up to his heart attack in much the same way in his book *The Healing Heart:*

> The main source of stress in my life for some years
> had been airports and airplanes, necessitated by a
> heavy speaking and conference schedule. Battling
> traffic congestion en route to airports, having to
> run through air terminals . . . , having to queue up
> for boarding passes at the gate and then being
> turned away because the plane had been over-

booked, waiting at baggage carousels for bags that never turned up, time-zone changes, irregular meals, insufficient sleep—these features of airline transportation had been my melancholy burdens for many years and were especially profuse in the latter part of 1980. . . . I returned from a hectic trip to the East Coast just before Christmas only to discover that I was due to leave again in a few days for the Southeast. I asked my secretary about the possibility of a postponement or a cancellation. She carefully reviewed with me the special facts in each case that made it essential to go through with the engagements. It was obvious . . . that only the most drastic event would get me out of it. My body was listening. The next day I had my heart attack.

Notice the sense of time pressure and urgency in the words themselves in both these passages: "behind schedule," career "timetable," "I picked up the pace," "I tried to force things through," "no time for family or friends," "joyless treadmill," "battling traffic," "having to run" to make the plane, "having to queue up," "waiting" for baggage, dealing with "time-zone changes."

Time pressures are not the limited province of successful executives, physicians, and academicians who travel a lot. In our postindustrial society, all of us are exposed to the stress of time. We strap on our watches in the morning and we get *going*. We conduct our lives by the clock. The clock dictates when we have to be where, and woe to us if we forget too often. Time and the clock drive us from one thing to the next. It has become a "way of life" for many of us to feel driven every day by all our obligations and responsibilities and then to fall into bed exhausted at the end of it all. If we keep up this pattern for long stretches without adequate rest and without replenishing our own energy reserves, breakdown will inevitably occur in one way or another. No matter how stable your homeostatic mechanisms are, they can eventually be pushed over the edge if they are not reset from time to time.

Nowadays we even transmit time urgency to our children. How many times have you found yourself saying to little children, "Hurry up, there's no time" or "I don't have time"? We hurry them to get dressed, to eat, to get ready for school. By what we say, by our body language, by the way we rush around ourselves, we are giving them the clear message that there is simply never enough time.

This message has been getting through to them all too clearly. It is not uncommon now for children to feel stressed and hurried at an early age. Instead of being able to follow their own inner rhythms, they are scooped up onto the conveyor belt of their parents' lives and taught to hurry and to be time-conscious. This may ultimately have deleterious effects on their biological rhythms and cause various kinds of physiological disregulation as well as psychological distress, just as it does in adults. For instance, high blood pressure begins in childhood in our society, with small but significant elevations detectable even in five-year-olds. This is not true in nonindustrial societies, where high blood pressure is virtually unknown. Something in the stress of our way of life beyond just dietary factors is probably responsible for this. Perhaps it is the stress of time.

In earlier times our activities were much more in step with the cycles of the natural world. People stayed put more. They didn't travel very far. Most died in the same place they were born and knew everybody in their town or village. Daylight and night dictated very different life rhythms. Many tasks just could not be done at night for lack of light. Sitting around fires at night, their only sources of heat and light, had a way of slowing people down— it was calming as well as warming. Staring into the flames and the embers, the mind could focus on the fire, always different, yet always the same. People could watch it moment by moment and night after night, month after month, year after year, through the seasons—and see time stand still in the fire. Perhaps the ritual of sitting around fires was mankind's first experience of meditation.

In earlier times, the rhythms of people were the rhythms of nature. A farmer could only plow so much by hand or with an ox in one day. You could only travel so far on foot or even with a horse. People were in touch with their animals and their needs. The animals' rhythm dictated the limits of time. If you valued your horse, you knew not to push him too fast or too far.

Now we can live largely independent of those natural rhythms. Electricity has given us light in the darkness, so that there is much less of a distinction between day and night—we can work after the sun goes down if we have to, or want to. We never have to slow down because the light has failed. We also have cars and tractors, telephones and jet travel, radios and televisions, photocopying machines, and now personal computers and fax machines. These have shrunk the world and reduced by a staggering amount the time that it takes to do things or find things out or communicate or go someplace or finish a piece of work. Computers have amplified to such an extent the ability to get paperwork and computations done that, although they are tremendously liberating in some ways, people can find themselves under more pressure than ever to get more done in less time. The expectations of oneself and of others just increase as the technology provides us with the power to do more faster. Instead of sitting around fires at night for light and warmth and something to look into, we can throw switches and keep going with whatever we have to *do*. Then, too, we can watch television and think we are relaxing and slowing down. Actually it is just more sensory bombardment.

And in the future, what with cellular phones in our cars and even on our bodies, with portable computers, electronic mail, computer shopping, smart television, narrowcasting, and personal robots, we will have more and more ways to stay busier and busier and to do more and more things simultaneously, with expectations rising accordingly. We can drive *and* do business, we can exercise *and* process information, we can read *and* watch television, or have split screens so that we can watch two or three or four things at once on television. We will never be out of touch with the world. But will we ever be in touch with ourselves?

Four Ways to Free Yourself from the Tyranny of Time
Just because the world has been speeded up through technology is no reason for us to be ruled by it to the point where we are stressed beyond all limits and perhaps even driven to an early grave by the treadmill of modern life. There are many ways you might free yourself from the tyranny of time. The first is to remind yourself that time is a product of thought. Minutes and hours are conventions, agreed upon so that we can conveniently meet and communicate and work in harmony. But they have no absolute meaning, as Einstein was fond of pointing out to lay audiences. To paraphrase what he was supposed to have said in explaining the concept of relativity, "If you are sitting on a hot stove, a minute can seem like an hour, but if you are doing something pleasurable, an hour can seem like a minute."

Of course we all know this from our own experience. Nature is in fact very equitable. We all get twenty-four hours per day to live. How we see that time and what we do with it can make all the difference in whether we feel we have "enough time" or "too much time" or "not enough." So we need to look at our expectations of ourselves. We need to be aware of just what we are trying to accomplish and whether we are paying too great a price for it or, in Dr. Eliot's words, whether it is "worth dying for."

A second way of freeing yourself from the tyranny of time is to live in the present more of the time. We waste enormous amounts of time and energy musing about the past and worrying about the future. These moments are hardly ever satisfying. Usually they produce anxiety and time urgency, thoughts such as "time is running out" or "those were the good old days." As we have seen now many times, to practice being mindful from one moment to the next puts you in touch with life in the only time you have to live it, namely right now. Whatever you are engaged in takes on a greater richness when you drop out of the automatic-pilot mode and into awareness and acceptance. If you are eating, then really eat in this time. It might mean *choosing* not to read a magazine or watch TV while half-consciously "shoveling" food into your body. If you are baby-sitting for your grandchildren, then really *be* with them, become engaged. Time will disappear. If you are helping your children with their homework or just talking with them don't do it on the run. Make the effort to be fully present. Make eye contact. Own those moments. Then you will not see other people as "taking time" away from you. All your moments will be your own. And if you want to reminisce about the past or plan for the future, then do *that* with awareness as well. Remember *in the present*. Plan *in the present*.

The essence of mindfulness in daily life is to make every moment you have your own. Even if you are hurrying, which is

sometimes necessary, then at least hurry mindfully. Be aware of
your breathing, of the need to move fast, and do it with awareness
until you don't have to hurry anymore and then let go and relax
intentionally. If you find your mind making lists and compelling
you to get every last thing on them done, then bring awareness to
your body and the mental and physical tension that may be mounting and remind yourself that some of it can probably wait. If you
get really close to the edge, stop completely and ask yourself, "Is it
worth dying for?" or "Who is running where?"

A third way of freeing yourself from the tyranny of time is take
some of it intentionally each day to just be, in other words to meditate. We need to protect our time for formal meditation practice
because it is so easy to write it off as unnecessary or a luxury; after
all, it is empty of doing. When you do write it off and give this time
over to doing, you wind up losing what may be the most valuable
part of your life, namely time for yourself to just be.

As we have seen, in practicing meditation you are basically stepping out of the flow of time and residing in stillness, in an eternal
present. That doesn't mean that every moment you practice will be
a moment of timelessness. That depends on the degree of concentration and calmness that you bring to each moment. But just
making the commitment to practice non-doing, to let go of striving, to be non-judgmental, slows down that time for you and
nourishes the timeless in you. By devoting some time each day to
slowing down time itself, for giving yourself time for just being,
you are strengthening your ability to operate *out of* your being, in
the present, during the rest of your day, when the pace of the outer
and inner worlds may be much more relentless. That is why it is so
important to organize your life around preserving some time each
day for just being.

A fourth way of freeing yourself from time is to simplify your life in certain ways. As already noted, we once held an eight-week stress reduction program just for judges. Judges tend to be sorely stressed by overwhelming caseloads. One judge complained that he never had enough time to review cases and to do extra background reading to prepare for them and that he didn't feel he had enough time to be with his family. When he explored how he used his time when he was not at work, it turned out that he religiously read three newspapers every day and also watched the news on television for an hour each day. The newspapers alone took up an hour and a half. It amounted to a kind of addiction.

Of course he knew how he was spending his time. But for some reason, he hadn't made the connection that he was choosing to use up two and a half hours a day with news, almost all of which was the same in each newspaper and on TV When we discussed it, he saw in an instant that he could gain time for other things he wanted to do by letting go of two newspapers and the TV news. He intentionally broke his addictive news habit and now reads one paper a day, doesn't watch the news on TV, and has about two more hours a day to do other things.

Simplifying our lives in even little ways can make a big difference. If you fill up all your time, you won't have any. And you probably won't even be aware of why you don't. Simplifying may mean prioritizing the things that you have to and want to do and, at the same time, *consciously choosing to give certain things up.* It may mean learning to say no sometimes, even to things you want to do or to people you care about and want to help so that you are protecting and preserving some space for silence, for non-doing.

After an all-day session, a woman who had been in pain for a number of years discovered that the next day she had no pain at all. She also woke up feeling differently about time that morning. It felt precious to her in a new way. When she got a routine call from her son, saying that he was bringing over the children so that she and her husband could baby-sit for them, she found herself telling him not to bring them, that she couldn't do it, that she needed to be alone. She felt she needed to protect this amazing moment of freedom from pain. She felt she had to preserve the preciousness of the stillness she was experiencing that morning rather than to fill it, even with her grandchildren, whom she of course loved enormously. She wanted to help her son out, but this time she needed to say no and to do something for herself. And her husband, sensing something different in her, perhaps her inner peacefulness, uncharacteristically supported her.

Her son couldn't believe it. She had never said no before. She didn't even have anything she was doing that day. To him it seemed nuts. But she knew, perhaps for the first time in quite a while, that some moments are worth protecting, just so that nothing can happen. Because that "nothing" is a very rich nothing.

There is a saying: "Time is money." But some people may have enough money and not enough time. It wouldn't hurt them to think about giving up some of their money for some time. For many years I worked three or four days a week and got paid accordingly. I needed the full-time money, but I felt the time was more important, especially when my children were very little. I wanted to be there for them as much as I could. Now I work full-time. This means I'm away from home more and I feel the pressure of time more in many ways. But I try to practice non-doing within the domain of doing and to remember not to overcommit myself.

I was lucky enough to have some outer control over how much I worked. Most people don't. But there are still many ways in which it is possible to simplify your life. Maybe you don't need to run around so much or have so many obligations or commitments. Maybe you don't have to have the TV on all the time in your house. Maybe you don't need to use your car so much. And maybe you don't really need so much money. Giving some thought and attention to the ways in which you might simplify things will probably start you on the road toward making your time your own. It is yours anyway, you know. You might as well enjoy it.

Mahatma Gandhi was once asked by a journalist, "You have been working at least fifteen hours a day, every day for almost fifty years. Don't you think it's about time you took a vacation?" To which Gandhi replied, "I am always on vacation."

Of course, the word *vacation* means "empty, vacant." When we practice being completely in the present, life in its fullness is totally accessible to us at all times, precisely because we are out of time. Time becomes empty and so do we. Then we, too, can always be on vacation. We might even learn how to have better vacations if we practiced all year long.

> But only in time can the moment in the rose-
> garden
> The moment in the arbour where the rain beat,
> The moment in the draughty church at smokefall
> Be remembered; involved with past and future.
> Only through time is time conquered.
> —T. S. Eliot, "Burnt Norton," *Four Quartets*

pain

⟶◇

from

WHO DIES?

by Stephen Levine

—◇—

A few years ago a friend requested we meet with a young
woman who was dying in a great deal of pain. She had a
tumor wrapped around her spine. Her legs hurt much of
the time because of the pressure on the sciatic nerve. Her back felt
as though it were on fire.

In the first minutes of our meeting, it was clear that this woman
had worked hard in her confrontation with cancer and opening to
the possibility of her death. Indeed, in the three years since her
cancer diagnosis, she had become a very skillful counselor and
caregiver and had been with several people at the time of their
death.

She told me of the various pain meditations and techniques she
had learned from the healers and holistic clinics she had attended.
She knew several methods of dispersing pain from the various
Eastern and American Indian traditions as well as more recent

holistic visualizations and meditations. Techniques for placing the awareness elsewhere so that pain would not be experienced.

She had become so adept at the use of these techniques that her therapists and counselors had asked her to participate in helping teach at their workshops. She had been invited to participate in healing festivals by some of the most respected healers of the Native American tradition. She said, though, that now that her body was in such agony, most of what she had learned was of very little help. The pain was so intense she could hardly concentrate. She said she had worked with the pain for more than two years, but now it had grown to a point where she just prayed for some release.

With considerable difficulty, she lay down on the couch as I sat on the coffee table next to her. And we began working with a guided meditation to investigate pain, which has been used with many people in similar predicaments. It is an attempt to begin to soften around pain, to open to the intensity of the experience, beyond the concepts of pain and the conditioned fearful responses, the confusion that so often amplifies the experience of intense discomfort.

Directing her attention to the sensations arising in her back and legs, she began to soften around the pain, began to allow the pain— perhaps for the first time—to just be there, so she could uncover what its real nature actually might be. To notice the resistance that seemed almost to form a fist around the pain, and slowly to loosen the fingers that closed around the pain. Bringing her awareness to the mass of sensations in her legs and back, she started to soften the flesh, the tissues, the muscles, the ligaments, all about the pain, allowing the resistance to soften and stretch, encouraging the opening at almost the cellular level. Not trying to change the pain, but letting it float free, letting it just be there in space, not even trying to get rid of it. Just opening to the pain as it was.

When pain arises in the body, it is very common to close around it. But our resistance and fear, our dread of the unpleasant, magnify pain. It is like closing your hand around a burning ember. The tighter you squeeze, the deeper you are seared.

We have seen that much of what is called pain is actually resistance, a mental tightening reflected and experienced in the body.

As she began softening around the pain, allowing it to float free in the body, she then began to soften around the ideas and fears in the mind. Thoughts of "pain," "tumor," "cancer," which intensified the resistance and magnified the scope of pain. The concepts and models that turn reality into an emergency.

Without the least force, doing no violence to the mind or body, she began to let such thoughts and fear-producing images dissolve, giving them space, allowing them to be gently let go of. Reminding the body to be allowing and soft, she was no longer at war with her pain. Not reinforcing the compulsive resistance whose goal is the elimination of the unpleasant. She began to enter into the sensations, to investigate what indeed this thing called pain might actually be. It was a process which, she noted later, was quite different from any way she had previously related to her pain. Taking her attention and directing it into the pain, she began to explore the moment-to-moment truth of her experience. As she said later, "I was in pain for years but before going into it and examining it I would have been hard put to describe what pain is." She began to investigate: What is the texture of this sensation? Is it hot? Or cold? Does it stay in one place? Is it moving? Does it vibrate? What color is it? What is its shape? Does it have tendrils? What actually is the experience that mind so quickly calcifies with labels of pain and emergency?

To cultivate the relaxation and sensitivity that allow this soft awareness and spaciousness to develop.

She entered the sensations arising in her back and legs with an acceptance and openness she had not previously encouraged. She began to explore that which her whole life had encouraged her to escape from. She penetrated the moment-to-moment intensity of sensation. Later, she related back to this moment of moving into, instead of pulling back from, her pain and said, "There was a spaciousness, a gentleness involved in this investigation that I never associated with my condition." The direct experience of her pain was quite different from what she had imagined. She said that indeed most of what she had called pain was actually resistance. Yes, there was pressure and intensity. But the word "pain" didn't quite suit the experience. She gained considerable satisfaction from entering into that which she had always attempted to elude.

As she began to soften, moments of resistance would tighten around the pain and cause it to be amplified, creating a knot of tension all about it. Her aversion to the pain had become a hell-realm for her, reinforcing and intensifying each day's discomfort. The more she resisted, the fiercer the pain became. The more frightened the mind, the more she tried to hide, but the only place to hide was in hell. Now though as she opened into it, she found the space to see what was actually happening.

She said she could almost see the waves of resistance that came to meet this new openness ripple along the nerve to magnify the pain. Letting go of resistance allowed a softness, an ease that made room for the pain and allowed it to float free as she had never imagined possible.

She said it was ironic, because it was the first time in these years she had directly experienced that which was so much a part of her life. In opening and entering into the sensation, she noticed that actually the pain didn't stay in one place or even maintain one shape. That it was amoeba-like, vibrating and constantly changing.

It was not the burning hot laser beam she had imagined. Not some solid knot of pain. But rather a mass of multiple changing sensations. Sometimes experienced as heat, sometimes as a tingling or pressure. And that in letting go of resistance, much restlessness seemed to dissolve in the mind. Concentrating on the moment-to-moment change of sensations allowed her to become one with her experience. And it brought a quietness to the mind because pain is such a clear object of investigation. She said it was like looking into a bright sun that she had at first wanted to pull back from, but that as she penetrated into the instant-to-instant experience her eyes became accustomed to the brilliance and could almost see the particles of light that made up the blazing orb. See Pain Meditation III.

She said she felt that all the techniques she had acquired for ridding herself of pain were, by their very nature, subtly cultivating the resistance that so amplified her suffering. That until she looked directly into the experience of her pain, those methods whose goal was the removal of pain subtly reinforced her desire to withdraw, her resistance. She had for a moment become one with that which she had always so desperately sought to stay apart from. The pushing away of pain had, she said, subtly intensified her desire for control and her fear of death.

Using her reaction to pain as a mirror for her resistance to life, she saw how much holding there was in the mind, how much fear of life and death. Once she had some insight into the nature of pain and resistance, pain was no longer the enemy and she was able to employ other methods to alleviate discomfort. No longer trying to pry her awareness away from pain she was able to trust her pain, to open around it and to direct her awareness toward some sense of peace.

Much of our pain is reinforced by those around us who wish us not to be in pain. Indeed, many of those who want to help—

doctors, nurses, loved ones, therapists—because of their own fear of pain project resistance with such comments as, "Oh, you poor baby!" Or a wincing around the eyes that reinforces the pain of those they are treating. Those who have little room for their own pain, who find pain in no way acceptable, seldom encourage another to enter directly into their experience, to soften the resistance and holding that so intensifies suffering. Pain for most is treated like a tragedy. Few recognize the grace of deeper investigation. As one person said after opening to and exploring their pain, "It isn't just the pain in my spine or my head or my bones, it's all the pains in my life that I have pulled back from that have imprisoned me. Watching this pain in my body makes me see how little of the pain in my life, in my mind, I've given any space to."

Many who have worked with these exercises have said that it wasn't just the pain in their body that they hadn't understood, it was also the fear, the boredom, the restlessness, the self-doubt, the anger which they had always pulled back from, which they had never allowed themselves to enter into. That they had never fully met themselves in life or dealt with death because they had always been encouraged to withdraw from anything that was unpleasant. The unpleasant had always acted as their jailer.

Many have told us that their opening to pain has allowed them to begin to open to what has made life difficult. Has allowed them to begin to understand what anger is, what fear is, what life itself might be. Life begins to open when we begin to recognize the enormity of our opposition. As painful as the body can become, the mind's fearfulness is so much more discomforting. Many begin to make friends with their pain, to meet it as softly as possible, to investigate it as it is. Not just the pain in the body but the suffering in the mind. To look beneath the anger and discover the frustration, the blocked and unfilled desires at things not being as we

wished. Investigating this frustration we find beneath it a great sadness and yet letting go deeper the most immense love is discovered.
Starting to examine all these states of mind which have imprisoned
us in the past becomes a fascinating meeting with ourselves. To
penetrate into each state of mind, into each sensation in the body,
and to experience it fully so that they no longer have some strange
mystique but are seen simply as clouds constantly changing in den-
sity and form yet always floating in the spaciousness of being.

Many who have spent their whole life withdrawing from pain
come to see that by withdrawing they have never gone beyond their
pain. That their whole life has been a juggling act, always trying to
keep one ball in the air, never quite grounded in life. They begin
to cut the bonds of fear that the investigation of their reaction to
physical pain has made them aware of. They move fully into life
and, at the moment of their death, leave the body behind without
resistance or struggle, in an openheartedness and love that become
a legacy of wisdom.

Ironically, we have found that those people we have worked with
who have been in the greatest pain are those who tended to go
deepest into an exploration of what has kept them bound to fear
and resistance. In pain, they have seen how shallow their philosophies or imaginings have been. They come right to their edge in
the investigation of life they were never prodded to undertake
before. Their pain acted like a fierce and loving teacher that
reminded them again and again to go beyond their holding, to
investigate deeper, to let this moment be as it is and observe what
arises in the fullness of the next.

Then it is not the death of one who wishes at any cost to be rid
of pain. It is an opening to how life has been blocked. A clear
reception of life that allows one to go beyond death. These are
people who go naked into the truth. . . .

enlightenment

—◇—

from

THE THREE PILLARS OF ZEN

by Roshi Philip Kapleau

Philip Kapleau (born 1912) studied Zen in Japan for thirteen years, and in 1966 founded the Rochester Zen Center in Rochester, New York. *The Three Pillars of Zen* includes these accounts by Zen practitioners of their enlightenment experiences.

—◇—

The Experiences of Mr. K. Y., a Japanese executive, age 47
November 27, 1953

Dear Nakagawa-roshi:

Thank you for the happy day I spent at your monastery. You remember the discussion which arose about Self-realization centering around that American. At that time I hardly imagined that in a few days I would be reporting to you my own experience.

The day after I called on you I was riding home on the train with my wife. I was reading a book on Zen by Son-o, who, you may recall, was a master of Soto Zen living in Sendai during the Genroku period [1688-1703]. As the train was nearing Ofuna station I ran across this line: "I came to realize clearly that Mind is no other than mountains and rivers and the great wide earth, the sun and the moon and the stars."

I had read this before, but this time it impressed itself upon me so vividly that I was startled. I said to myself: "After seven or eight years of zazen I have finally perceived the essence of this statement," and couldn't suppress the tears that began to well up. Somewhat ashamed to find myself crying among the crowd, I averted my face and dabbed at my eyes with my handkerchief.

Meanwhile the train had arrived at Kamakura station and my wife and I got off. On the way home I said to her: "In my present exhilarated frame of mind I could rise to the greatest heights." Laughingly she replied: "Then where would I be?" All the while I kept repeating that quotation to myself.

It so happened that that day my younger brother and his wife were staying at my home, and I told them about my visit to your monastery and about that American who had come to Japan again only to attain enlightenment. In short, I told them all the stories you had told me, and it was after eleven thirty before I went to bed.

At midnight I abruptly awakened. At first my mind was foggy, then suddenly that quotation flashed into my consciousness: "I came to realize clearly that Mind is no other than mountains, rivers, and the great wide earth, the sun and the moon and the stars." And I repeated it. Then all at once I was struck as though by lightning, and the next instant heaven and earth crumbled and disappeared. Instantaneously, like surging waves, a tremendous delight welled up in me, a veritable hurricane of delight, as I laughed loudly and wildly: "Ha, ha, ha, ha, ha, ha! There's no reasoning here, no reasoning at all! Ha, ha, ha!" The empty sky split in two, then opened its enormous mouth and began to laugh uproariously: "Ha, ha, ha!" Later one of the members of my family told me that my laughter had sounded inhuman.

I was now lying on my back. Suddenly I sat up and struck the bed with all my might and beat the floor with my feet, as if trying to smash it, all the while laughing riotously. My wife and youngest son, sleeping near me, were now awake and frightened. Covering my mouth with her hand, my wife exclaimed: "What's the matter with you? What's the matter with you?" But I wasn't aware of this until told about it afterwards. My son told me later he thought I had gone mad.

"I've come to enlightenment! Shakyamuni and the patriarchs haven't deceived me! They haven't deceived me!" I remember crying out. When I calmed down I apologized to the rest of the family, who had come downstairs frightened by the commotion.

Prostrating myself before the photograph of Kannon you had given me, the Diamond sutra, and my volume of the book written by Yasutani-roshi, I lit a stick of incense and did zazen until it was consumed half an hour later, though it seemed only two or three minutes had elapsed.

Even now my skin is quivering as I write.

That morning I went to see Yasutani-roshi and tried to describe to him my experience of the sudden disintegration of heaven and earth. "I am overjoyed, I am overjoyed!" I kept repeating, striking my thigh with vigor. Tears came which I couldn't stop. I tried to relate to him the experience of that night, but my mouth trembled and words wouldn't form themselves. In the end I just put my face in his lap. Patting me on the back he said: "Well, well, it is rare indeed to experience to such a wonderful degree. It is termed 'Attainment of the emptiness of Mind.' You are to be congratulated!"

"Thanks to you," I murmured, and again wept for joy. Repeatedly I told him: "I must continue to apply myself energetically to zazen." He was kind enough to give me detailed advice on how to pursue my practice in the future, after which he again whispered in my ear, "My congratulations!" and escorted me to the foot of the mountain by flashlight.

Although twenty-four hours have elapsed, I still feel the after-math of that earthquake. My entire body is still shaking. I spent all of today laughing and weeping by myself.

I am writing to report my experience in the hope that it will be of value to your monks, and because Yasutani-roshi urged me to.

Please remember me to that American. Tell him that even I, who am unworthy and lacking in spirit, can grasp such a wonderful experience when time matures. I would like to talk with you at length about many things, but will have to wait for another time.

P.S. That American was asking us whether it is possible for him to attain enlightenment in one week of sesshin. Tell him this for me: don't say days, weeks, years, or even lifetimes. Don't say millions or billions of *kalpa*. Tell him to vow to attain enlightenment though it take the infinite, the boundless, the incalculable future.

Midnight of the 28th: [These diary entries were made during the next two days.] Awoke thinking it 3 or 4 a.m., but clock said it was only 12:30.

Am totally at peace at peace at peace.

Feel numb throughout body, yet hands and feet jumped for joy for almost half an hour.

Am supremely free free free free free.

Should I be so happy?

There is no common man.

The big clock chimes—not the clock but Mind chimes. The universe itself chimes. There is neither Mind nor universe. Dong, dong, dong!

I've totally disappeared. Buddha is!

"Transcending the law of cause and effect, controlled by the law of cause and effect"—such thoughts have gone from my mind.

Oh, you *are!* You laughed, didn't you? This laughter is the sound of your plunging into the world.

The substance of Mind—this is now luminously clear to me.

My concentration in zazen has sharpened and deepened.

Midnight of the 29th: I am at peace at peace at peace. Is this tremendous freedom of mine the Great Cessation described by the ancients? Whoever might question it would surely have to admit that this freedom is extraordinary. If it isn't absolute freedom or the Great Cessation, what is it?

4 a.m. of the 29th: Ding, dong! The clock chimed. This alone *is!* This alone *is!* There's no reasoning here.

Surely the world has changed [with awakening]. But in what way?

The ancients said the enlightened mind is comparable to a fish swimming. That's exactly how it is—there's no stagnation. I feel no hindrance. Everything flows smoothly, freely. Everything goes naturally. This limitless freedom is beyond all expression. What a wonderful world!

Dogen, the great teacher of Buddhism, said: "Zen is the wide, all-encompassing gate of compassion."

I am grateful, so grateful.

spontaneity

—◇—

from

THE WAY OF ZEN

by Alan Watts

Alan Watts (1915–1973) wrote more than twenty-five books on science, religion and related topics. *The Way of Zen* helped establish his reputation as a leading Western interpreter of Eastern thought. This passage from the book comes to grips with some of Zen Buddhism's most mysterious elements, which in turn have important implications for any meditation practice.

—◇—

"Sitting Quietly, Doing Nothing"

In both life and art the cultures of the Far East appreciate nothing more highly than spontaneity or naturalness (*tzu–jan*). This is the unmistakable tone of sincerity marking the action which is not studied and contrived. For a man rings like a cracked bell when he thinks and acts with a split mind—one part standing aside to interfere with the other, to control, to condemn, or to admire. But the mind, or the true nature, of man cannot actually be split. According to a *Zenrin* poem, it is

> Like a sword that cuts, but cannot cut itself;
> Like an eye that sees, but cannot see itself.

The illusion of the split comes from the mind's attempt to be both itself and its idea of itself, from a fatal confusion of fact with symbol. To make an end of the illusion, the mind must stop trying to act upon itself, upon its stream of experiences, from the standpoint of the idea of itself which we call the ego. This is expressed in another *Zenrin* poem as

> Sitting quietly, doing nothing,
> Spring comes, and the grass grows by itself

This "by itself" is the mind's and the world's natural way of action, as when the eyes see by themselves, and the ears hear by themselves, and the mouth opens by itself without having to be forced apart by the fingers. As the *Zenrin* says again:

> The blue mountains are of themselves blue
> mountains;
> The white clouds are of themselves white clouds.

In its stress upon naturalness, Zen is obviously the inheritor of Taoism, and its view of spontaneous action as "marvelous activity" (*miao-yung*) is precisely what the Taoists meant by the word *te*— "virtue" with an overtone of magical power. But neither in Taoism nor in Zen does it have anything to do with magic in the merely sensational sense of performing superhuman "miracles." The "magical" or "marvelous" quality of spontaneous action is, on the contrary, that it is perfectly human, and yet shows no sign of being contrived.

Such a quality is peculiarly subtle (another meaning of *miao*), and extremely hard to put into words. The story is told of a Zen monk who wept upon hearing of the death of a close relative. When one of his fellow students objected that it was most unseemly for a monk to show such personal attachment he replied, "Don't be stupid! I'm weeping because I want to weep." The great Hakuin was deeply disturbed in his early study of Zen when he came across the story of the master Yen-t'ou, who was said to have screamed at the top of his voice when murdered by a robber. Yet this doubt was dissolved at the moment of his *satori*, and in Zen circles his own death is felt to have been especially admirable for its display of human emotion. On the other hand, the abbot Kwaisen and his monks allowed themselves to be burned alive by the soldiers of Oda Nobunaga, sitting calmly in the posture of meditation. Such contradictory "naturalness" seems most mysterious, but perhaps the clue lies in the saying of Yün-men: "In walking, just walk. In sitting, just sit. Above all, don't wobble." For the essential quality of naturalness is the sincerity of the undivided mind which does not dither between alternatives. So when Yen-t'ou screamed, it was such a scream that it was heard for miles around.

But it would be quite wrong to suppose that this natural sincerity comes about by observing such a platitude as "Whatsoever thy hand findeth to do, do it with all thy might." When Yen-t'ou screamed, he was not screaming *in order* to be natural, nor did he first make up his mind to scream and then implement the decision with the full energy of his will. There is a total contradiction in planned naturalness and intentional sincerity. This is to overlay, not to discover, the "original mind." Thus to try to be natural is an affectation. To try not to try to be natural is also an affectation. As a *Zenrin* poem says:

> You cannot get it by taking thought;
> You cannot seek it by not taking thought.

But this absurdly complex and frustrating predicament arises from a simple and elementary mistake in the use of the mind. When this is understood, there is no paradox and no difficulty. Obviously, the mistake arises in the attempt to split the mind against itself, but to understand this clearly we have to enter more deeply into the "cybernetics" of the mind, the basic pattern of its self-correcting action.

It is, of course, part of the very genius of the human mind that it can, as it were, stand aside from life and reflect upon it, that it can be aware of its own existence, and that it can criticize its own processes. For the mind has something resembling a "feed-back" system. This is a term used in communications engineering for one of the basic principles of "automation," of enabling machines to control themselves. Feed-back enables a machine to be informed of the effects of its own action in such a way as to be able to correct its action. Perhaps the most familiar example is the electrical thermostat which regulates the heating of a house. By setting an upper and a lower limit of desired temperature, a thermometer is so connected that it will switch the furnace on when the lower limit is reached, and off when the upper limit is reached. The temperature of the house is thus kept within the desired limits. The thermostat provides the furnace with a kind of sensitive organ—an extremely rudimentary analogy of human self-consciousness.

The proper adjustment of a feed-back system is always a complex mechanical problem. For the original machine, say, the furnace, is adjusted by the feed-back system, but this system in turn needs adjustment. Therefore to make a mechanical system more and more automatic will require the use of a series of feed-back systems—a second to correct the first, a third to correct the second, and so on. But there are obvious limits to such a series, for beyond a certain point the mechanism will be "frustrated" by its own complexity. For example, it might take so long for the information to pass through the series of control systems that it would arrive at the original machine too late to be useful. Similarly, when human beings think too carefully and minutely about an action to be taken, they cannot make up their minds in time to act. In other words, one cannot correct one's means of self-correction indefinitely. There must soon be a source of information at the end of the line which is the final authority. Failure to trust its authority will make it impossible to act, and the system will be paralyzed.

The system can be paralyzed in yet another way. Every feed-back system needs a margin of "lag" or error. If we try to make a thermostat absolutely accurate—that is, if we bring the upper and lower limits of temperature very close together in an attempt to hold the temperature at a constant 70 degrees—the whole system will break down. For to the extent that the upper and lower limits coincide, the signals for switching off and switching on will coincide! If 70 degrees is both the lower and upper limit the "go" sign will also be the "stop" sign; "yes" will imply "no" and "no" will imply "yes." Whereupon the mechanism will start "trembling," going on and off, on and off, until it shakes itself to pieces. The system is too sensitive and shows symptoms which are startlingly like human anxiety. For when a human being is so self-conscious, so self-controlled that he cannot let go of himself, he dithers or wobbles between opposites. This is precisely what is meant in Zen by going round and round on "the wheel of birth-and-death," for the Buddhist samsara is the prototype of all vicious circles.

Now human life consists primarily and originally in action—in living in the concrete world of "suchness." But we have the power to control action by reflection, that is, by thinking, by comparing the actual world with memories or "reflections." Memories are organized in terms of more or less abstract images—words, signs, simplified shapes, and other symbols which can be reviewed very rapidly one after another. From such memories, reflections, and symbols the mind constructs its idea of itself. This corresponds to the thermostat—the source of information about its own past action by which the system corrects itself. The mind-body must, of course, trust that information in order to act, for paralysis will soon result from trying to remember whether we have remembered everything accurately.

But to keep up the supply of information in the memory, the mind-body must continue to act "on its own." It must not cling too closely to its own record. There must be a "lag" or distance between the source of information and the source of action. This does *not* mean that the source of action must hesitate before it accepts the information. It means that it must not identify itself with the source of information. We saw that when the furnace responds too closely to the thermostat, it cannot go ahead without also trying to stop, or stop without also trying to go ahead. This is just what happens to the human being, to the mind, when the desire for certainty and security prompts identification between the mind and its own image of itself. It cannot let go of itself. It feels that it should not do what it is doing, and that it should do what it is not doing. It feels that it should not be what it is, and be what it isn't. Furthermore, the effort to remain always "good" or "happy" is like trying to hold the thermostat to a constant 70 degrees by making the lower limit the same as the upper.

The identification of the mind with its own image is, therefore, paralyzing because the image is fixed—it is past and finished. But it is a fixed image of oneself in motion! To cling to it is thus to be in constant contradiction and conflict. Hence Yün-men's saying, "In walking, just walk. In sitting, just sit. Above all; don't wobble." In other words, the mind cannot act without giving up the impossible attempt to control itself beyond a certain point. It must let go of itself both in the sense of trusting its own memory and reflection, and in the sense of acting spontaneously, on its own into the unknown.

This is why Zen often seems to take the side of action as against reflection, and why it describes itself as "no-mind' (*wu-hsin*) or "no-thought" (*wu-nien*), and why the masters demonstrate Zen by giving instantaneous and unpremeditated answers to questions. When Yün-men was asked for the ultimate secret of Buddhism, he replied, "Dumpling!" In the words of the Japanese master Takuan:

> When a monk asks, "What is the Buddha?" the
> master may raise his fist; when he is asked, "What is
> the ultimate idea of Buddhism? he may exclaim
> even before the questioner finishes his sentence "A
> blossoming branch of the plum," or "The cypress-
> tree in the court-yard." The point is that the
> answering mind does not "stop" anywhere, but
> responds straightway without giving any thought to
> the felicity of an answer.

This is allowing the mind to act on its own.

But reflection is also action, and Yün-men might also have said, "In acting, just act. In thinking, just think. Above all, don't wobble." In other words, if one is going to reflect, just reflect—but do not reflect about reflecting. Yet Zen would agree that reflection about reflection is also action—provided that in doing it we do just that, and do not tend to drift off into the infinite regression of trying always to stand above or outside the level upon which we are acting. Thus Zen is also a liberation from the dualism of thought and action, for it thinks as it acts—with the same quality of abandon, commitment, or faith. The attitude of *wu-hsin* is by no means an anti-intellectualist exclusion of thinking. *Wu-hsin* is action on any level whatsoever, physical or psychic, without trying *at the same moment* to observe and check the action from outside. This attempt to act and think about the action simultaneously is precisely the identification of the mind with its idea of itself. It involves the same contradiction as the statement which states something about itself—"This statement is false."

The same is true of the relationship between feeling and action. For feeling blocks action, and blocks itself as a form of action, when it gets caught in this same tendency to observe or feel itself indefinitely—as when, in the midst of enjoying myself, I examine myself to see if I am getting the utmost out of the occasion. Not content with tasting the food, I am also trying to taste my tongue. Not content with feeling happy, I want to feel myself feeling happy—so as to be sure not to miss anything.

Whether trusting our memories or trusting the mind to act on its own, it comes to the same thing: ultimately we must act and think, live and die, from a source beyond all "our" knowledge and control. But this source is ourselves, and when we see that, it no longer stands over against us as a threatening object. No amount of care and hesitancy, no amount of introspection and searching of our motives, can make any ultimate difference to the fact that the mind is

Like an eye that sees, but cannot see itself.

In the end, the only alternative to a shuddering paralysis is to leap into action regardless of the consequences. Action in this spirit may be right or wrong with respect to conventional standards. But our decisions upon the conventional level must be supported by the conviction that whatever we do, and whatever "happens" to us, is ultimately "right." In other words, we must enter into it without "second thought," without the *arrière-pensée* of regret, hesitancy, doubt, or self-recrimination. Thus when Yün-men was asked, "What is the Tao?" he answered simply "Walk on! (*ch'ü*)."

But to act "without second thought," without double-mindedness, is by no means a mere precept for our imitation. For we cannot realize this kind of action until it is clear beyond any shadow of doubt that it is actually impossible to do anything else. In the words of Huang-po:

> Men are afraid to forget their own minds, fearing to
> fall through the void with nothing on to which they
> can cling. They do not know that the void is not
> really the void but the real realm of the Dharma. . . .
> It cannot be looked for or sought, comprehended by
> wisdom or knowledge, explained in words, contacted
> materially (i.e., objectively) or reached by merito-
> rious achievement.

Now this impossibility of "grasping the mind with the mind" is, when realized, the non-action (*wu-wei*), the "sitting quietly, doing nothing" whereby "spring comes, and the grass grows by itself." There is no necessity for the mind to try to let go of itself, or to try not to try. This introduces further artificialities. Yet, as a matter of psychological strategy, there is no need for trying to avoid artifi-cialities. In the doctrine of the Japanese master Bankei (1622–1693) the mind which cannot grasp itself is called the "Unborn" (*fusho*), the mind which does not arise or appear in the realm of symbolic knowledge.

A layman asked, "I appreciate very much your

instruction about the Unborn, but by force of habit
second thoughts [*nien*] keep tending to arise, and
being confused by them it is difficult to be in perfect accord with the Unborn. How am I to trust in it
entirely?"

Bankei said, "If you make an attempt to stop the second thoughts
which arise, then the mind which does the stopping and the mind
which is stopped become divided, and there is no occasion for peace
of mind. So it is best for you simply to believe that originally there
is no (possibility of control by) second thoughts. Yet because of
karmic affinity, through what you see and what you hear these
thoughts arise and vanish temporarily, but are without substance.

"Brushing off thoughts which arise is just like washing off blood
with blood. We remain impure because of being washed with
blood, even when the blood that was first there has gone—and if we
continue in this way the impurity never departs. This is from ignorance of the mind's unborn, unvanishing, and unconfused nature.
If we take second thought for an effective reality, we keep going on
and on around the wheel of birth-and-death. You should realize
that such thought is just a temporary mental construction, and not
try to hold or to reject it. Let it alone just as it occurs and just as it
ceases. It is like an image reflected in a mirror. The mirror is clear
and reflects anything which comes before it, and yet no image sticks
in the mirror. The Buddha mind (i.e., the real, unborn mind) is
ten thousand times more clear than a mirror, and more inexpress-
ibly marvelous. In its light all such thoughts vanish without trace.
If you put your faith in this way of understanding, however strongly
such thoughts may arise, they do no harm."

This is also the doctrine of Huang-po, who says again:

If it is held that there is something to be realized or attained apart from mind, and, thereupon, mind is used to seek it, (that implies) failure to understand that mind and the object of its search are one. Mind cannot be used to seek something from mind for, even after the passage of millions of kalpas, the day of success would never come.

One must not forget the social context of Zen. It is primarily a way of liberation for those who have mastered the disciplines of social convention, of the conditioning of the individual by the group. Zen is a medicine for the ill effects of this conditioning, for the mental paralysis and anxiety which come from excessive self-consciousness. It must be seen against the background of societies regulated by the principles of Confucianism, with their heavy stress on propriety and punctilious ritual. In Japan, too, it must be seen in relation to the rigid schooling required in the training of the *samurai* caste, and the emotional strain to which the *samurai* were exposed in times of constant warfare. As a medicine for these conditions, it does not seek to overthrow the conventions themselves, but, on the contrary, takes them for granted—as is easily seen in such manifestations of Zen as the *cha-no-yu* or "tea ceremony" of Japan. Therefore Zen might be a very dangerous medicine in a social context where convention is weak, or, at the other extreme, where there is a spirit of open revolt against convention ready to exploit Zen for destructive purposes.

With this in mind, we can observe the freedom and naturalness of Zen without loss of perspective. Social conditioning fosters the identification of the mind with a fixed idea of itself as the means of self-control, and as a result man thinks of himself a "I"—the ego.

Thereupon the mental center of gravity shifts from the spontaneous or original mind to the ego image. Once this has happened, the very center of our psychic life is identified with the self-controlling mechanism. It then becomes almost impossible to see how "I" can let go of "myself," for I am precisely my habitual effort to hold on to myself. I find myself totally incapable of any mental action which is not intentional, affected, and insincere. Therefore anything I do to give myself up, to let go, will be a disguised form of the habitual effort to hold on. I cannot be intentionally unintentional or purposely spontaneous. As soon as it becomes important for me to be spontaneous, the intention to be so is strengthened; I cannot get rid of it, and yet it is the one thing that stands in the way of its own fulfillment. It is as if someone had given me some medicine with the warning that it will not work if I think of a monkey while taking it.

While I am remembering to forget the monkey, I am in a "double-bind" situation where "to do" is "not to do," and vice versa. "Yes" implies "no," and "go" implies "stop." At this point Zen comes to me and asks, "If you cannot help remembering the monkey, are you doing it on purpose?" In other words, do I have an intention for being intentional, a purpose for being purposive? Suddenly I realize that my very intending is spontaneous, or that my controlling self—the ego—arises from my uncontrolled or natural self. At this moment all the machinations of the ego come to nought; it is annihilated in its own trap. I see that it is actually impossible not to be spontaneous. For what I cannot help doing I am doing spontaneously, but if I am at the same time trying to control it, I interpret it as a compulsion. As a Zen master said, "Nothing is left to you at this moment but to have a good laugh."

In this moment the whole quality of consciousness is changed, and I feel myself in a new world in which, however, it is obvious that I have always been living. As soon as I recognize that my voluntary and purposeful action happens spontaneously "by itself," just like breathing, hearing, and feeling, I am no longer caught in the contradiction of trying to be spontaneous. There is no real contradiction, since "trying" is "spontaneity." Seeing this, the compulsive, blocked, and "tied-up" feeling vanishes. It is just as if I had been absorbed in a tug-of-war between my two hands, and had forgotten that both were mine. No block to spontaneity remains when the trying is seen to be needless. As we saw, the discovery that both the voluntary and involuntary aspects of the mind are alike spontaneous makes an immediate end of the fixed dualism between the mind and the world, the knower and the known. The new world in which I find myself has an extraordinary transparency or freedom from barriers, making it seem that I have somehow become the empty space in which everything is happening.

Here, then, is the point of the oft-repeated assertion that "all beings are in *nirvana* from the very beginning," that "all dualism is falsely imagined," that "the ordinary mind is the Tao" and that there is therefore no meaning in trying to get into accord with it. In the words of the *Cheng-tao Ke:*

> Like the empty sky it has no boundaries,
> Yet it is right in this place, ever profound and clear.
> When you seek to know it, you cannot see it.
> You cannot take hold of it,
> But you cannot lose it.
> In not being able to get it, you get it.
> When you are silent, it speaks;
> When you speak, it is silent.
> The great gate is wide open to bestow alms,
> And no crowd is blocking the way.

. . .

It was through seeing this that, in the moment of his *satori,* Hakuin
cried out, "How wondrous! How wondrous! There is no birth-
and-death from which one has to escape, nor is there any supreme
knowledge after which one has to strive!" Or in the words of
Hsiang-yen:

> At one stroke I forgot all my knowledge!
> There's no use for artificial discipline,
> For, move as I will, I manifest the ancient Way.

Paradoxically, nothing is more artificial than the notion of artifi-
ciality. Try as one may, it is as impossible to go against the spontaneous Tao as to live in some other time than now, or some other
place than here. When a monk asked Bankei what he thought of
disciplining oneself to attain *satori,* the master said, "*Satori* stands in
contrast to confusion. Since each person is the substance of
Buddha, (in reality) there is not one point of confusion. What,
then, is one going to achieve by *satori*?"

Seeing, then, that there is no possibility of departing from the
Tao, one is like Hsüan-chüeh's "easygoing" man who

> Neither avoids false thoughts nor seeks the true,
> For ignorance is in reality the Buddha nature,
> And this illusory, changeful, empty body is the
> Dharmakaya.

One stops trying to be spontaneous by seeing that it is unnecessary to try, and then and there it can happen. The Zen masters
often bring out this state by the device of evading a question
and then, as the questioner turns to go, calling him suddenly by

name. As he naturally replies, "Yes?" the master exclaims, "There it is!"

To the Western reader it may seem that all this is a kind of pantheism, an attempt to wipe out conflicts by asserting that "everything is God." But from the standpoint of Zen this is a long way short of true naturalness since it involves the use of the artificial concept "everything is God" or "everything is the Tao." Zen annihilates this concept by showing that it is as unnecessary as every other. One does not realize the spontaneous life by depending on the repetition of thoughts or affirmations. One realizes it by seeing that no such devices are necessary. Zen describes all means and methods for realizing the Tao as "legs on a snake"—utterly irrelevant attachments.

To the logician it will of course seem that the point at which we have arrived is pure nonsense—as, in a way, it is. From the Buddhist point of view, reality itself has no meaning since it is not a sign, pointing to something beyond itself. To arrive at reality—at "suchness"—is to go beyond *karma*, beyond consequential action, and to enter a life which is completely aimless. Yet to Zen and Taoism alike this is the very life of the universe, which is complete at every moment and does not need to justify itself by aiming at something beyond. In the words of a *Zenrin* poem:

> If you don't believe, just look at September, look at October!
> The yellow leaves falling, falling, to fill both mountain and river.

To see this is to be like the two friends of whom another *Zenrin* poem says:

from The Way of the Zen

Meeting, they laugh and laugh—
The forest grove, the many fallen leaves!

To the Taoist mentality, the aimless, empty life does not suggest anything depressing. On the contrary, it suggests the freedom of clouds and mountain streams, wandering nowhere, of flowers in impenetrable canyons, beautiful for no one to see, and of the ocean surf forever washing the sand, to no end.

Furthermore, the Zen experience is more of a conclusion than a premise. It is never to be used as the first step in a line of ethical or metaphysical reasoning, since conclusions draw to it rather than from it. Like the Beatific Vision of Christianity, it is a "which than which there is no whicher"—the true end of man—not a thing to be used for some other end. Philosophers do not easily recognize that there is a point where thinking—like boiling an egg—must come to a stop. To try to formulate the Zen experience as a proposition—"everything is the Tao"—and then to analyze it and draw conclusions from it is to miss it completely. Like the Crucifixion, it is "to the Jews [the moralists] a stumblingblock and to the Greeks [the logicians] foolishness." To say that "everything is the Tao" almost gets the point, but just at the moment of getting it, the words crumble into nonsense. For we are here at a limit at which words break down because they always imply a meaning beyond themselves—and here there is no meaning beyond.

Zen does not make the mistake of using the experience "all things are of one Suchness" as the premise for an ethic of universal brotherhood. On the contrary, Yüan-wu says:

If you are a real man, you may by all means drive

295

off with the farmer's ox, or grab the food from a
starving man.

This is only to say that Zen lies beyond the ethical standpoint,
whose sanctions must be found, not in reality itself, but in the
mutual agreement of human beings. When we attempt to univer-
salize or absolutize it, the ethical standpoint makes it impossible to
exist, for we cannot live for a day without destroying the life of
some other creature.

If Zen is regarded as having the same function as a religion in
the West, we shall naturally want to find some logical connection
between its central experience and the improvement of human
relations. But this is actually putting the cart before the horse. The
point is rather that some such experience or way of life as this is the
object of improved human relations. In the culture of the Far East
the problems of human relations are the sphere of Confucianism
rather than Zen, but since the Sung dynasty (959–1278) Zen has
consistently fostered Confucianism and was the main source of the
introduction of its principles into Japan. It saw their importance
for creating the type of cultural matrix in which Zen could flourish
without coming into conflict with social order, because the Con-
fucian ethic is admittedly human and relative, not divine and
absolute.

Although profoundly "inconsequential," the Zen experience
has consequences in the sense that it may be applied in any direction, to any conceivable human activity, and that wherever it is so
applied it lends an unmistakable quality to the work. The characteristic notes of the spontaneous life are *mo chih ch'u* or "going ahead
without hesitation," *wu-wei*, which may here be understood as pur-
poselessness, and *wu-shih*, lack of affectation or simplicity.

While the Zen experience does not imply any specific course of action, since it has no purpose, no motivation, it turns unhesitatingly to anything that presents itself to be done. *Mo chih ch'u* is the mind functioning without blocks, without "wobbling" between alternatives, and much of Zen training consists in confronting the student with dilemmas which he is expected to handle without stopping to deliberate and "choose." The response to the situation must follow with the immediacy of sound issuing from the hands when they are clapped, or sparks from a flint when struck. The student unaccustomed to this type of response will at first be confused, but as he gains faith in his "original" or spontaneous mind he will not only respond with ease, but the responses themselves will acquire a startling appropriateness. This is something like the professional comedian's gift of unprepared wit which is equal to any situation.

The master may begin a conversation with the student by asking a series of very ordinary questions about trivial matters, to which the student responds with perfect spontaneity. But suddenly he will say, "When the bath water flows down the drain, does it turn clockwise or counter-clockwise?" As the student stops at the unexpectedness of the question, and perhaps tries to remember which way it goes, the master shouts, "Don't think! Act! This way—" and whirls his hand in the air. Or, perhaps less helpfully, he may say, "So far you've answered my questions quite naturally and easily, but where's your difficulty now?"

The student, likewise, is free to challenge the master, and one can imagine that in the days when Zen training was less formal the members of Zen communities must have had enormous fun laying traps for each other. To some extent this type of relationship still exists, despite the great solemnity of the *sanzen* interview in which the *koan* is given and answered. The late Kozuki Roshi was entertaining two American monks at tea when he casually asked, "And what do you gentlemen know about Zen?" One of the monks flung his closed fan straight at the master's face. All in the same instant the master inclined his head slightly to one side, the fan shot straight through the paper *shoji* behind him, and he burst into a ripple of laughter.

Suzuki has translated a long letter from the Zen master Takuan on the relationship of Zen to the art of fencing, and this is certainly the best literary source of what Zen means by *mo chih ch'u,* by "going straight ahead without stopping." Both Takuan and Bankei stressed the fact that the "original" or "unborn" mind is constantly working miracles even in the most ordinary person. Even though a tree has innumerable leaves, the mind takes them in all at once without being "stopped" by any one of them. Explaining this to a visiting monk, Bankei said, "To prove that your mind is the Buddha mind, notice how all that I say here goes into you without missing a single thing, even though I don't try to push it into you." When heckled by an aggressive Nichiren monk who kept insisting that he couldn't understand a word, Bankei asked him to come closer. The monk stepped forward. "Closer still," said Bankei. The monk came forward again. "How well," said Bankei, "you understand me!" In other words, our natural organism performs the most marvelously complex activities without the least hesitation or deliberation. Conscious thought is itself founded upon its whole system of spontaneous functioning, for which reason there is really no alternative to trusting oneself completely to its working. Oneself *is* its working.

Zen is not merely a cult of impulsive action. The point of *mo chih ch'u* is not to eliminate reflective thought but to eliminate "blocking" in both action and thought, so that the response of the mind is always like a ball in a mountain stream—"one thought after another without hesitation." There is something similar to this in the psychoanalytic practice of free association, employed as a technique to get rid of obstacles to the free flow of thought from the "unconscious." For there is a tendency to confuse "blocking"—a purely obstructive mechanism—with thinking out an answer, but the difference between the two is easily noticed in such a purely "thinking out" process as adding a column of figures. Many people find that at certain combinations of numbers, such as 8 and 5 or 7 and 6, a feeling of resistance comes up which halts the process. Because it is always annoying and disconcerting, one tends also to block at blocking, so that the state turns into the kind of wobbling dither characteristic of the snarled feed-back system. The simplest cure is to feel free to block, so that one does not block at blocking. When one feels free to block, the blocking automatically eliminates itself. It is like riding a bicycle. When one starts falling to the left, one does not resist the fall (i.e., the block) by turning to the right. One turns the wheel to the left—and the balance is restored. The principle here is, of course, the same as getting out of the contradiction of "trying to be spontaneous" through accepting the "trying" as "spontaneous," through not resisting the block.

"Blocking" is perhaps the best translation of the Zen term *nien* as it occurs in the phrase *wu-nien*, "no-thought" or, better, "no second thought." Takuan points out that this is the real meaning of "attachment" in Buddhism, as when it is said that a Buddha is free from worldly attachments. It does not mean that he is a "stone Buddha" with no feelings, no emotions, and no sensations of hunger or pain. It means that he does not block at anything. Thus it is typical of Zen that its style of action has the strongest feeling of commitment, of "follow-through." It enters into everything wholeheartedly and freely without having to keep an eye on itself. It does not confuse spirituality with thinking about God while one is peeling potatoes. Zen spirituality is just to peel the potatoes. In the words of Lin-chi:

> When it's time to get dressed, put on your clothes.
> When you must walk, then walk. When you must sit,
> then sit. Don't have a single thought in your mind
> about seeking for Buddhahood. . . . You talk about
> being perfectly disciplined in your six senses and in
> all your actions, but in my view all this is making
> *karma*. To seek the Buddha (nature) and to seek the
> Dharma is at once to make *karma* which leads to the
> hells. To seek (to be) Bodhisattvas is also making
> *karma,* and likewise studying the *sutras* and commen-
> taries. Buddhas and Patriarchs are people without
> such artificialities. . . . It is said everywhere that
> there is a Tao which must be cultivated and a
> Dharma which must be realized. What Dharma do
> you say must be realized, and what Tao cultivated?
> What do you lack in the way you are functioning
> right now? What will you add to where you are?

As another *Zenrin* poem says:

> There's nothing equal to wearing clothes and eating
> food.
> Outside this there are neither Buddhas nor Patri-
> archs.

This is the quality of *wu-shih,* of naturalness without any con-
trivances or means for being natural, such as thoughts of Zen, of
the Tao, or of the Buddha. One does not exclude such thoughts;

they simply fall away when seen to be unnecessary. "He does not linger where the Buddha is, and where there is no Buddha he passes right on."
For as the *Zenrin* says again:

> To be conscious of the original mind, the original
> nature—
> Just this is the great disease of Zen!

As "the fish swims in the water but is unmindful of the water, the bird flies in the wind but knows not of the wind," so the true life of Zen has no need to "raise waves when no wind is blowing," to drag in religion or spirituality as something over and above life itself. This is why the sage Fa-yung received no more offerings of flowers from the birds after he had had his interview with the Fourth Patriarch, for his holiness no longer "stood out like a sore thumb." Of such a man the *Zenrin* says:

> Entering the forest he moves not the grass;
> Entering the water he makes not a ripple.

No one notices him because he does not notice himself.

It is often said that to be clinging to oneself is like having a thorn in the skin, and that Buddhism is a second thorn to extract the first. When it is out, both thorns are thrown away. But in the moment when Buddhism, when philosophy or religion, becomes another way of clinging to oneself through seeking a spiritual security, the two thorns become one—and how is it to be taken out? This, as Bankei said, is "wiping off blood with blood." Therefore in Zen there is neither self nor Buddha to which one can cling, no good to gain and no evil to be avoided, no thoughts to be eradicated and no mind to be purified, no body to perish and no soul to be saved. At one blow this entire framework of abstractions is shattered to fragments. As the *Zenrin* says:

> To save life it must be destroyed.
> When utterly destroyed, one dwells for the first time
> in peace.
>
> One word settles heaven and earth;
> One sword levels the whole world.

Of this "one sword" Lin-chi said:

> If a man cultivates the Tao, the Tao will not work—
> on all sides evil conditions will head up competi-
> tively. But when the sword of wisdom [*prajna*] comes
> out there's not one thing left.

The "sword of *prajna*" which cuts away abstraction is that "direct pointing" whereby Zen avoids the entanglements of religiosity and goes straight to the heart. Thus when the Governor of Lang asked Yao-shan, "What is the Tao?" the master pointed upwards to the sky and downwards to a water jug beside him. Asked for an explanation, he replied: "A cloud in the sky and water in the jug."

motivation

—◇—

from
Zen Mind, Beginner's Mind
by Shunryu Suzuki

Shunryu Suzuki (1905–1971) was a respected Zen master in Japan when he visited America in 1959. He was so delighted by the open and serious quality of Americans' interest in Zen that he stayed here to teach them. The innocent and enigmatic quality of his work invites and demands a spirit of fresh inquiry: beginner's mind. The more you think you know, the harder it may be for you to understand his words.

—◇—

Now I would like to talk about our zazen posture. When you sit in the full lotus position, your left foot is on your right thigh, and your right foot is on your left thigh. When we cross our legs like this, even though we have a right leg and a left leg, they have become one. The position expresses the oneness of duality: not two, and not one. This is the most important teaching: not two, and not one. Our body and mind are not two and not one. If you think your body and mind are two, that is wrong; if you think that they are one, that is also wrong. Our body and mind are both two *and* one. We usually think that if something is not one, it is more than one: if it is not singular, it is plural. But in actual experience, our life is not only plural but also singular. Each one of us is both dependent and independent.

After some years we will die. If we just think that it is the end of our life, this will be the wrong understanding. But, on the other hand, if we think that we do not die, this is also wrong. We die, and we do not die. This is the right understanding. Some people may say that our mind or soul exists forever, and it is only our physical body which dies. But this is not exactly right, because both mind and body have their end. But at the same time it is also true that they exist eternally. And even though we say mind and body, they are actually two sides of one coin. This is the right understanding. So when we take this posture it symbolizes this truth. When I have the left foot on the right side of my body, and the right foot on the left side of my body, I do not know which is which. So either may be the left or the right side.

The most important thing in taking the zazen posture is to keep your spine straight. Your ears and your shoulders should be on one line. Relax your shoulders, and push up towards the ceiling with the back of your head. And you should pull your chin in. When your chin is tilted up, you have no strength in your posture; you are probably dreaming. Also to gain strength in your posture, press your diaphragm down towards your *hara*, or lower abdomen. This will help you maintain your physical and mental balance. When you try to keep this posture, at first you may find some difficulty breathing naturally, but when you get accustomed to it you will be able to breathe naturally and deeply.

Your hands should form the "cosmic mudra." If you put your left hand on top of your right, middle joints of your middle fingers together, and touch your thumbs lightly together (as if you held a piece of paper between them), your hands will make a beautiful oval. You should keep this universal mudra with great care, as if you were holding something very precious in your hand. Your hands should be held against your body, with your thumbs at about the height of your navel. Hold your arms freely and easily, and slightly away from your body, as if you held an egg under each arm without breaking it.

You should not be tilted sideways, backwards, or forwards. You should be sitting straight up as if you were supporting the sky with your head. This is not just form or breathing. It expresses the key point of Buddhism. It is a perfect expression of your Buddha nature. If you want true understanding of Buddhism, you should practice this way. These forms are not a means of obtaining the right state of mind. To take this posture itself is the purpose of our practice. When you have this posture, you have the right state of mind, so there is no need to try to attain some special state. When you try to attain something, your mind starts to wander about somewhere else. When you do not try to attain anything, you have your own body and mind right here. A Zen master would say, "Kill the Buddha!" Kill the Buddha if the Buddha exists somewhere else. Kill the Buddha, because you should resume your own Buddha nature.

Doing something is expressing our own nature. We do not exist for the sake of something else. We exist for the sake of ourselves. This is the fundamental teaching expressed in the forms we observe. Just as for sitting, when we stand in the zendo we have some rules. But the purpose of these rules is not to make everyone the same but to allow each to express his own self most freely. For instance, each one of us has his own way of standing, so our standing posture is based on the proportions of our own bodies. When you stand, your heels should be as far apart as the width of your own fist, your big toes in line with the centers of your breasts. As in zazen, put some strength in your abdomen. Here also your hands should express your self. Hold your left hand against your chest with fingers encircling your thumb, and put your right hand over it. Holding your thumb pointing downward, and your forearms parallel to

the floor, you feel as if you have some round pillar in your grasp—
a big round temple pillar—so you cannot be slumped or tilted to
the side.

The most important point is to own your own physical body. If
you slump, you will lose your self. Your mind will be wandering
about somewhere else; you will not be in your body. This is not the
way. We must exist right here, right now! This is the key point. You
must have your own body and mind. Everything should exist in the
right place, in the right way. Then there is no problem. If the
microphone I use when I speak exists somewhere else, it will not
serve its purpose. When we have our body and mind in order,
everything else will exist in the right place, in the right way.

But usually, without being aware of it, we try to change something other than ourselves, we try to order things outside us. But it
is impossible to organize things if you yourself are not in order.
When you do things in the right way, at the right time, everything
else will be organized. You are the "boss." When the boss is sleeping, everyone is sleeping. When the boss does something right,
everyone will do everything right, and at the right time. That is the
secret of Buddhism.

So try always to keep the right posture, not only when you practice zazen, but in all your activities. Take the right posture when
you are driving your car, and when you are reading. If you read in
a slumped position, you cannot stay awake long. Try. You will discover how important it is to keep the right posture. This is the true
teaching. The teaching which is written on paper is not the true
teaching. Written teaching is a kind of food for your brain. Of
course it is necessary to take some food for your brain, but it is
more important to be yourself by practicing the right way of life.

That is why Buddha could not accept the religions existing at his
time. He studied many religions, but he was not satisfied with their

practices. He could not find the answer in asceticism or in philosophies. He was not interested in some metaphysical existence, but in his own body and mind, here and now. And when he found himself, he found that everything that exists has Buddha nature. That was his enlightenment. Enlightenment is not some good feeling or some particular state of mind. The state of mind that exists when you sit in the right posture is, itself, enlightenment. If you cannot be satisfied with the state of mind you have in zazen, it means your mind is still wandering about. Our body and mind should not be wobbling or wandering about. In this posture there is no need to talk about the right state of mind. You already have it. This is the conclusion of Buddhism.

Breathing

When we practice zazen our mind always follows our breathing. When we inhale, the air comes into the inner world. When we exhale, the air goes out to the outer world. The inner world is limitless, and the outer world is also limitless. We say "inner world" or "outer world," but actually there is just one whole world. In this limitless world, our throat is like a swinging door. The air comes in and goes out like someone passing through a swinging door. If you think, "I breathe," the "I" is extra. There is no you to say "I." What we call "I" is just a swinging door which moves when we inhale and when we exhale. It just moves; that is all. When your mind is pure and calm enough to follow this movement, there is nothing: no "I," no world, no mind nor body; just a swinging door.

So when we practice zazen, all that exists is the movement of the breathing, but we are aware of this movement. You should not be absent-minded. But to be aware of the movement does not mean to be aware of your small self, but rather of your universal nature, or Buddha nature. This kind of awareness is very important, because we are usually so one-sided. Our usual understanding of life is dualistic: you and I, this and that, good and bad. But actually these discriminations are themselves the awareness of the universal existence. "You" means to be aware of the universe in the form of you, and "I" means to be aware of it in the form of I. You and I are just swinging doors. This kind of understanding is necessary. This should not even be called understanding; it is actually the true experience of life through Zen practice.

So when you practice zazen, there is no idea of time or space. You may say, "We started sitting at a quarter to six in this room." Thus you have some idea of time (a quarter to six), and some idea of space (in this room). Actually what you are doing, however, is just sitting and being aware of the universal activity. That is all. This moment the swinging door is opening in one direction, and the next moment the swinging door will be opening in the opposite direction. Moment after moment each one of us repeats this activity. Here there is no idea of time or space. Time and space are one. You may say, "I must do something this afternoon," but actually there is no "this afternoon." We do things one after the other. That is all. There is no such time as "this afternoon" or "one o'clock" or "two o'clock." At one o'clock you will eat your lunch. To eat lunch is itself one o'clock. You will be somewhere, but that place cannot be separated from one o'clock. For someone who actually appreciates our life, they are the same. But when we become tired of our life we may say, "I shouldn't have come to this place. It may have been much better to have gone to some other place for lunch. This place is not so good." In your mind you create an idea of place separate from an actual time.

Or you may say, "This is bad, so I should not do this." Actually, when you say, "I should not do this," you are doing not-doing in that moment. So there is no choice for you. When you separate the idea of time and space, you feel as if you have some choice but actually, you have to do something, or you have to do not-doing. Not-to-do something is doing something. Good and bad are only in your mind. So we should not say, "This is good," or "This is bad." Instead of saying bad, you should say, "not-to-do"! If you think, "This is bad," it will create some confusion for you. So in the realm of pure religion there is no confusion of time and space, or good or bad. All that we should do is just do something as it comes. *Do* something! Whatever it is, we should do it, even if it is not-doing something. We should live in this moment. So when we sit we concentrate on our breathing, and we become a swinging door, and we do something we should do, something we must do. This is Zen practice. In this practice there is no confusion. If you establish this kind of life you have no confusion whatsoever.

Tozan, a famous Zen master, said, "The blue mountain is the father of the white cloud. The white cloud is the son of the blue mountain. All day long they depend on each other without being dependent on each other. The white cloud is always the white cloud. The blue mountain is always the blue mountain." This is a pure, clear interpretation of life. There may be many things like the white cloud and blue mountain: man and woman, teacher and disciple. They depend on each other. But the white cloud should not not be bothered by the blue mountain. The blue mountain should not be bothered by the white cloud. They are quite independent, but yet dependent. This is how we live, and how we practice zazen.

When we become truly ourselves, we just become a swinging door, and we are purely independent of, and at the same time, dependent upon everything. Without air, we cannot breathe. Each one of us is in the midst of myriads of worlds. We are in the center of the world always, moment after moment. So we are completely dependent and independent. If you have this kind of experience, this kind of existence, you have absolute independence; you will not be bothered by anything. So when you practice zazen, your mind should be concentrated on your breathing. This kind of activity is the fundamental activity of the universal being. Without this experience, this practice, it is impossible to attain absolute freedom.

Control

To live in the realm of Buddha nature means to die as a small being, moment after moment. When we lose our balance we die, but at the same time we also develop ourselves, we grow. Whatever we see is changing, losing its balance. The reason everything looks beautiful is because it is out of balance, but its background is always in perfect harmony. This is how everything exists in the realm of Buddha nature, losing its balance against a background of perfect balance. So if you see things without realizing the background of Buddha nature, everything appears to be in the form of suffering. But if you understand the background of existence, you realize that suffering itself is how we live, and how we extend our life. So in Zen sometimes we emphasize the imbalance or disorder of life.

Nowadays traditional Japanese painting has become pretty formal and lifeless. That is why modern art has developed. Ancient painters used to practice putting dots on paper in artistic disorder. This is rather difficult. Even though you try to do it, usually what you do is arranged in some order. You think you can control it, but you cannot; it is almost impossible to arrange your dots out of order. It is the same with taking care of your everyday life. Even though you try to put people under some control, it is impossible. You cannot do it. The best way to control people is to encourage them to be mischievous. Then they will be in control in its wider sense. To give your sheep or cow a large, spacious meadow is the way to control him. So it is with people: first let them do what they want, and watch them. This is the best policy. To ignore them is not good; that is the worst policy. The second worst is trying to control them. The best one is to watch them, just to watch them, without trying to control them.

The same way works for you yourself as well. If you want to obtain perfect calmness in your zazen, you should not be bothered by the various images you find in your mind. Let them come, and let them go. Then they will be under control. But this policy is not so easy. It sounds easy, but it requires some special effort. How to make this kind of effort is the secret of practice. Suppose you are sitting under some extraordinary circumstances. If you try to calm your mind you will be unable to sit, and if you try not to be disturbed, your effort will not be the right effort. The only effort that will help you is to count your breathing, or to concentrate on your inhaling and exhaling. We say concentration, but to concentrate your mind on something is not the true purpose of Zen. The true purpose is to see things as they are, to observe things as they are, and to let everything go as it goes. This is to put everything under control in its widest sense. Zen practice is to open up our small mind. So concentrating is just an aid to help you realize "big mind," or the mind that is everything. If you want to discover the true meaning of Zen in your everyday life, you have to understand the meaning of keeping your mind on your breathing and your body in the right posture in zazen. You should follow the rules of practice and your study should become more subtle and careful. Only in this way can you experience the vital freedom of Zen.

Dogen-zenji said, "Time goes from present to past." This is absurd, but in our practice sometimes it is true. Instead of time progressing from past to present, it goes backwards from present to past. Yoshitsune was a famous warrior who lived in medieval Japan. Because of the situation of the country at that time, he was sent to the northern provinces, where he was killed. Before he left he bade farewell to his wife, and soon after she wrote in a poem, "Just as you unreel the thread from a spool, I want the past to become present." When she said this, actually she made past time present. In her mind the past became alive and *was* the present. So as Dogen said, "Time goes from present to past." This is not true in our logical mind, but it is in the actual experience of making past time present. There we have poetry, and there we have human life.

When we experience this kind of truth it means we have found the true meaning of time. Time constantly goes from past to present and from present to future. This is true, but it is also true that time goes from future to present and from present to past. A Zen master once said, "To go eastward one mile is to go westward one mile." This is vital freedom. We should acquire this kind of perfect freedom.

But perfect freedom is not found without some rules. People, especially young people, think that freedom is to do just what they want, that in Zen there is no need for rules. But it is absolutely necessary for us to have some rules. But this does not mean always to be under control. As long as you have rules, you have a chance for freedom. To try to obtain freedom without being aware of the rules means nothing. It is to acquire this perfect freedom that we practice zazen.

Mind waves

When you are practicing zazen, do not try to stop your thinking. Let it stop by itself. If something comes into your mind, let it come in, and let it go out. It will not stay long. When you try to stop your

Shunryu Suzuki

thinking, it means you are bothered by it. Do not be bothered by anything. It appears as if something comes from outside your mind, but actually it is only the waves of your mind, and if you are not bothered by the waves, gradually they will become calmer and calmer. In five or at most ten minutes, your mind will be completely serene and calm. At that time your breathing will become quite slow, while your pulse will become a little faster.

It will take quite a long time before you find your calm, serene mind in your practice. Many sensations come, many thoughts or images arise, but they are just waves of your own mind. Nothing comes from outside your mind. Usually we think of our mind as receiving impressions and experiences from outside, but that is not a true understanding of our mind. The true understanding is that the mind includes everything; when you think something comes from outside it means only that something appears in your mind. Nothing outside yourself can cause any trouble. You yourself make the waves in your mind. If you leave your mind as it is, it will become calm. This mind is called big mind.

If your mind is related to something outside itself, that mind is a small mind, a limited mind. If your mind is not related to anything else, then there is no dualistic understanding in the activity of your mind. You understand activity as just waves of your mind. Big mind experiences everything within itself. Do you understand the difference between the two minds: the mind which includes everything, and the mind which is related to something? Actually they are the same thing, but the understanding is different, and your attitude towards your life will be different according to which understanding you have.

That everything is included within your mind is the essence of mind. To experience this is to have religious feeling. Even though waves arise, the essence of your mind is pure; it is just like clear water with a few waves. Actually water always has waves. Waves are the practice of the water. To speak of waves apart from water or water apart from waves is a delusion. Water and waves are one. Big mind and small mind are one. When you understand your mind in this way, you have some security in your feeling. As your mind does not expect anything from outside, it is always filled. A mind with waves in it is not a disturbed mind, but actually an amplified one. Whatever you experience is an expression of big mind.

The activity of big mind is to amplify itself through various experiences. In one sense our experiences coming one by one are always fresh and new, but in another sense they are nothing but a continuous or repeated unfolding of the one big mind. For instance, if you have something good for breakfast, you will say, "This is good." "Good" is supplied as something experienced some time long ago, even though you may not remember when. With big mind we accept each of our experiences as if recognizing the face we see in a mirror as our own. For us there is no fear of losing this mind. There is nowhere to come or to go; there is no fear of death, no suffering from old age or sickness. Because we enjoy all aspects of life as an unfolding of big mind, we do not care for any excessive joy. So we have imperturbable composure, and it is with this imperturbable composure of big mind that we practice zazen.

Mind weeds

When the alarm rings early in the morning, and you get up, I think you do not feel so good. It is not easy to go and sit, and even after you arrive at the zendo and begin zazen you have to encourage yourself to sit well. These are just waves of your mind. In pure zazen there should not be any waves in your mind. While you are sitting these waves will become smaller and smaller, and your effort will change into some subtle feeling.

We say, "Pulling out the weeds we give nourishment to the plant." We pull the weeds and bury them near the plant to give it nourishment. So even though you have some difficulty in your practice, even though you have some waves while you are sitting, those waves themselves will help you. So you should not be bothered by your mind. You should rather be grateful for the weeds, because eventually they will enrich your practice. If you have some experience of how the weeds in your mind change into mental nourishment, your practice will make remarkable progress. You will feel the progress. You will feel how they change into self-nourishment. Of course it is not so difficult to give some philosophical or psychological interpretation of our practice, but that is not enough. We must have the actual experience of how our weeds change into nourishment.

Strictly speaking, any effort we make is not good for our practice because it creates waves in our mind. It is impossible, however, to attain absolute calmness of our mind without any effort. We must make some effort, but we must forget ourselves in the effort we make. In this realm there is no subjectivity or objectivity. Our mind is just calm, without even any awareness. In this unawareness, every effort and every idea and thought will vanish. So it is necessary for us to encourage ourselves and to make an effort up to the last moment, when all effort disappears. You should keep your mind on your breathing until you are not aware of your breathing.

We should try to continue our effort forever, but we should not expect to reach some stage when we will forget all about it. We should just try to keep our mind on our breathing. That is our actual practice. That effort will be refined more and more while you are sitting. At first the effort you make is quite rough and impure, but by the power of practice the effort will become purer and purer. When your effort becomes pure, your body and mind become pure. This is the way we practice Zen. Once you understand our innate power to purify ourselves and our surroundings, you can act properly, and you will learn from those around you, and you will become friendly with others. This is the merit of Zen practice. But the way of practice is just to be concentrated on your breathing with the right posture and with great, pure effort. This is how we practice Zen.

The marrow of Zen
In our scriptures (Samyuktagama Sutra, volume 33), it is said that there are four kinds of horses: excellent ones, good one, poor ones, and bad ones. The best horse will run slow and fast, right and left, at the driver's will, before it sees the shadow of the whip; the second best will run as well as the first one does, just before the whip reaches its skin; the third one will run when it feels pain on its body; the fourth will run after the pain penetrates to the marrow of its bones. You can imagine how difficult it is for the fourth one to learn how to run!

When we hear this story, almost all of us want to be the best horse. If it is impossible to be the best one, we want to be the second best. This is, I think, the usual understanding of this story, and of Zen. You may think that when you sit in zazen you will find out whether you are one of the best horses or one of the worst ones. Here, however, there is a misunderstanding of Zen. If you think the aim of Zen practice is to train you to become one of the best horses, you will have a big problem. This is not the right understanding. If you practice Zen in the right way, it does not matter whether you are the best horse or the worst one. When you consider the mercy of Buddha how do you think Buddha will feel about the four kinds of horses: He will have more sympathy for the worst one than for the best one.

When you are determined to practice zazen with the great mind of Buddha, you will find the worst horse is the most valuable one.

In your very imperfections you will find the basis for your firm, way-seeking mind. Those who can sit perfectly physically usually take more time to obtain the true way of Zen, the actual feeling of Zen, the marrow of Zen. But those who find great difficulties in practicing Zen sit easily.

When we reflect on what are doing in our everyday life, we are always ashamed of ourselves. One of my students wrote to me saying, "You sent me a calendar, and I am trying to follow the good mottoes which appear on each page. But the year has hardly begun, and already I have failed!" Dogen-zenji said, "*Shoshaku jushaku.*" *Shaku* generally means "mistake" or "wrong." *Shoshaku jushaku* means "to succeed wrong with wrong," or one continuous mistake. According to Dogen, one continuous mistake can also be Zen. A Zen master's life could be said to be so many years of *shoshaku jushaku*. This means so many years of one single-minded effort.

We say, "A good father is not a good father." Do you understand? One who thinks he is a good father is not a good father; one who thinks he is a good husband is not a good husband. One who thinks he is one of the worst husbands may be a good one if he is always trying to be a good husband with a single-hearted effort. If you find it impossible to sit because of some pain or some physical difficulty, then you should sit anyway, using a thick cushion or a chair. Even though you are the worst horse you will get to the marrow of Zen.

Suppose your children are suffering from a hopeless disease. You do not know what to do; you cannot lie in bed. Normally the most comfortable place for you would be a warm comfortable bed, but now because of your mental agony you cannot rest. You may walk up and down, in and out, but this does not help. Actually the best way to relieve your mental suffering is to sit in zazen, even in such a confused state of mind and bad posture. If you

have no experience of sitting in this kind of difficult situation
you are not a Zen student. No other activity will appease your
suffering. In other restless positions you have no power to accept
your difficulties, but in the zazen posture which you have
acquired by long, hard practice, your mind and body have great
power to accept things as they are, whether they are agreeable or
disagreeable.

When you feel disagreeable it is better for you to sit. There is no
other way to accept your problem and work on it. Whether you are
the best horse or the worst, or whether your posture is good or bad
is out of the question. Everyone can practice zazen, and in this way
work on his problems and accept them.

When you are sitting in the middle of your own problem, which
is more real to you: your problem or you yourself? The awareness
that you are here, right now, is the ultimate fact. This is the point
you will realize by zazen practice. In continuous practice, under a
succession of agreeable and disagreeable situations, you will realize
the marrow of Zen and acquire its true strength.

No dualism

We say our practice should be without gaining ideas, without any
expectations, even of enlightenment. This does not mean, however,
just to sit without any purpose. This practice free from gaining ideas
is based on the Prajna Paramita Sutra. However, if you are not careful the sutra itself will give you a gaining idea. It says, "Form is
emptiness and emptiness is form." But if you attach to that statement, you are liable to be involved in dualistic ideas: here is you,
form, and here is emptiness, which you are truing to realize
through your form. So "form is emptiness, and emptiness is form"
is still dualistic. But fortunately, our teaching goes on to say, "Form
is form and emptiness is emptiness." Here there is no dualism.

When you find it difficult to stop your mind while you are sitting and when you are still trying to stop your mind, this is the stage of "form is emptiness and emptiness is form." But while you are practicing in this dualistic way, more and more you will have oneness with your goal. And when your practice becomes effortless, you can stop your mind. This is the stage of "form is form and emptiness is emptiness."

To stop your mind does not mean to stop the activities of mind. It means your mind pervades your whole body. Your mind follows your breathing. With your full mind you form the mudra in your hands. With your whole mind you sit with painful legs without being disturbed by them. This is to sit without any gaining idea. At first you feel some restriction in your posture, but when you are not disturbed by the restriction, you have found the meaning of "emptiness is emptiness and form is form." So to find your own way under some restriction is the way of practice.

Practice does not mean that whatever you do, even lying down, is zazen. When the restrictions you have do not limit you, this is what we mean by practice. When you say, "Whatever I do is Buddha nature, so it doesn't matter what I do, and there is no need to practice zazen," that is already a dualistic understanding of our everyday life. If it really does not matter, there is no need for you even to say so. As long as you are concerned about what you do, that is dualistic. If you are not concerned about what you do, you will not say so. When you sit, you will sit. When you eat, you will eat. That is all. If you say, "It doesn't matter," it means that you are making some excuse to do something in your own way with your small mind. It means you are attached to some particular thing or way. That is not what we mean when we say, "Just to sit is enough," or "Whatever you do is zazen." Of course whatever we do *is* zazen, but if so, there is no need to say it.

When you sit you should just sit without being disturbed by your painful legs or sleepiness. That is zazen. But at first it is very difficult to accept things as they are. You will be annoyed by the feeling you have in your practice. When you can do everything, whether it is good or bad, without disturbance or without being annoyed by the feeling, that is actually what we mean by "form is form and emptiness is emptiness."

When you suffer from an illness like cancer, and you realize you cannot live more than two or three years, then seeking something upon which to rely, you may start practice. One person may rely on the help of God. Someone else may start the practice of zazen. His practice will be concentrated on obtaining emptiness, of mind. That means he is trying to be free from the suffering of duality. This is the practice of "form is emptiness and emptiness is form." Because of the truth of emptiness he wants to have the actual realization of it in his life. If he practices in this way, believing and making an effort, it will help him, of course, but it is not perfect practice.

Knowing that your life is short, to enjoy it day after day, moment after moment, is the life of "form is form and emptiness is emptiness." When Buddha comes, you will welcome him; when the devil comes, you will welcome him. The famous Chinese Zen master Baso, said, "Sun-faced Buddha and moon-faced Buddha." When he was ill, someone asked him, "How are you?" And he answered, "Sun-faced Buddha and moon-faced Buddha." That is the life of "form is form and emptiness is emptiness." There is no problem. One year of life is good. One hundred years of life are good. If you continue our practice, you will attain this stage.

At first you will have various problems, and it is necessary for you to make some effort to continue our practice. For the beginner, practice without effort is not true practice. For the beginner, the practice needs great effort. Especially for young people, it is necessary to try very hard to achieve something. You must stretch out your arms and legs as wide as they will go. Form is form. You must be true to your own way until at last you actually come to the point where you see it is necessary to forget all about yourself. Until you come to this point, it is completely mistaken to think that whatever you do is Zen or that it does not matter whether you practice or not. But if you make your best effort just to continue your practice with your whole mind and body, without gaining ideas, then whatever you do will be true practice. Just to continue should be your purpose. When you do something, just to do it should be your purpose. Form is form and you are you, and true emptiness will be realized in your practice.

Bowing

After zazen we bow to the floor nine times. By bowing we are giving up ourselves. To give up ourselves means to give up our dualistic ideas. So there is no difference between zazen practice and bowing. Usually to bow means to pay our respects to something which is more worthy of respect than ourselves. But when you bow to Buddha you should have no idea of Buddha, you just become one with Buddha, you are already Buddha himself. When you become one with Buddha, one with everything that exists, you find the true meaning of being. When you forget all your dualistic ideas, everything becomes your teacher, and everything can be the object of worship.

When everything exists within your big mind, all dualistic relationships drop away. There is no distinction between heaven and earth, man and woman, teacher and disciple. Sometimes a man bows to a woman; sometimes a woman bows to a man. Sometimes

from Zen Mind, Beginner's Mind

the disciple bows to the master; sometimes the master bows to the disciple. A master who cannot bow to his disciple cannot bow to Buddha. Sometimes the master and disciple bow together to Buddha. Sometimes we may bow to cats and dogs.

In your big mind, everything has the same value. Everything is Buddha himself. You see something or hear a sound, and there you have everything just as it is. In your practice you should accept everything as it is, giving to each thing the same respect given to a Buddha. Here there is Buddhahood. Then Buddha bows to Buddha, and you bow to yourself. This is the true bow.

If you do not have this firm conviction of big mind in your practice, your bow will be dualistic. When you are just yourself, you bow to yourself in its true sense, and you are one with everything. Only when you are you yourself can you bow to everything in its true sense. Bowing is a very serious practice. You should be prepared to bow even in your last moment; when you cannot do anything except bow, you should do it. This kind of conviction is necessary. Bow with this spirit and all the precepts, all the teachings are yours, and you will possess everything within your big mind.

Sen no Rikyu, the founder of the Japanese tea ceremony, committed *hara-kiri* (ritual suicide by disembowelment) in 1591 at the order of his lord, Hideyoshi. Just before Rikyu took his own life he said, "When I have this sword there is no Buddha and no Patriarchs." He meant that when we have the sword of big mind, there is no dualistic world. The only thing which exists is this spirit. This kind of imperturbable spirit was always present in Rikyu's tea ceremony. He never did anything in just a dualistic way; he was ready to die in each moment. In ceremony after ceremony he died, and be renewed himself. This is the spirit of the tea ceremony. This is how we bow.

Shunryu Suzuki

My teacher had a callus on his forehead from bowing. He knew he was an obstinate, stubborn fellow, and so he bowed and bowed and bowed. The reason he bowed was that inside himself he always heard his master's scolding voice. He had joined the Soto order when he was thirty, which for a Japanese priest is rather late. When we are young we are less stubborn, and it is easier to get rid of our selfishness. So his master always called my teacher "You-lately-joined-fellow," and scolded him for joining so late. Actually his master loved him for his stubborn character. When my teacher was seventy, he said, "When I was young I was like a tiger, but now I am like a cat!" He was very pleased to be like a cat.

Bowing helps to eliminate our self-centered ideas. This is not so easy. It is difficult to get rid of these ideas, and bowing is a very valuable practice. The result is not the point; it is the effort to improve ourselves that is valuable. There is no end to this practice.

Each bow expresses one of the four Buddhist vows. These vows are: "Although sentient beings are innumerable we vow to save them. Although our evil desires are limitless, we vow to be rid of them. Although the teaching is limitless, we vow to learn it all. Although Buddhism is unattainable, we vow to attain it." If it is unattainable, how can we attain it? But we should! That is Buddhism.

To think, "Because it is possible we will do it," is not Buddhism. Even though it is impossible, we have to do it because our true nature wants us to. But actually, whether or not it is possible is not the point. If it is our inmost desire to get rid of our self-centered ideas, we have to do it. When we make this effort, our inmost desire is appeased and Nirvana is there. Before you determine to do it, you have difficulty, but once you start to do it, you have none. Your effort appeases your inmost desire. There is no other way to attain calmness. Calmness of mind does not mean you should stop your activity. Real calmness should be found in activity itself. We say, "It is easy to have calmness in inactivity, it is hard to have calmness in activity, but calmness in activity is true calmness."

After you have practiced for a while, you will realize that it is not possible to make rapid, extraordinary progress. Even though you try very hard, the progress you make is always little by little. It is not like going out in a shower in which you know when you get wet. In a fog, you do not know you are getting wet, but as you keep walking you get wet little by little. If your mind has ideas of progress, you may say, "Oh, this pace is terrible!" But actually it is not. When you get wet in a fog it is very difficult to dry yourself. So there is no need to worry about progress. It is like studying a foreign language; you cannot do it all of a sudden, but by repeating it over and over you will master it. This is the Soto way of practice. We can say either that we make progress little by little, or that we do not even expect to make progress. Just to be sincere and make our full effort in each moment is enough. There is no Nirvana outside our practice.

Nothing special

I do not feel like speaking after zazen. I feel the practice of zazen is enough. But if I must say something I think I would like to talk about how wonderful it is to practice zazen. Our purpose is just to keep this practice forever. This practice started from beginningless time, and it will continue into an endless future. Strictly speaking, for a human being there is no other practice than this practice. There is no other way of life than this way of life. Zen practice is the direct expression of our true nature.

Of course, whatever we do is the expression of our true nature, but without this practice it is difficult to realize. It is our human nature to be active and the nature of every existence. As long as we are alive, we are always doing something. But as long as you think, "I am doing this," or "I have to do this," or "I must attain something special," you are actually not doing anything. When you give up, when you no longer want something, or when you do not try to do anything special, then you do something. When there is no gaining idea in what you do, then you do something. In zazen what you are doing is not for the sake of anything. You may feel as if you are doing something special, but actually it is only the expression of your true nature; it is the activity which appeases your inmost desire. But as long as you think you are practicing zazen for the sake of something, that is not true practice.

If you continue this simple practice every day you will obtain a wonderful power. Before you attain it, it is something wonderful, but after you obtain it, it is nothing special. It is just you yourself, nothing special. As a Chinese poem says, "I went and I returned. It was nothing special. Rozan famous for its misty mountains; Sekko for its water." People think it must be wonderful to see the famous range of mountains covered by mists, and the water said to cover all the earth. But if you go there you will just see water and mountains. Nothing special.

It is a kind of mystery that for people who have no experience of enlightenment, enlightenment is something wonderful. But if they attain it, it is nothing. But yet it is not nothing. Do you understand? For a mother with children, having children is nothing special. That is zazen. So, if you continue this practice, more and more you will acquire something—nothing special, but nevertheless something. You may say "universal nature" or "Buddha nature" or "enlightenment." You may call it by many names, but for the person who has it, it is nothing, and it is something.

When we express our true nature, we are human beings. When we do not, we do not know what we are. We are not an animal, because we walk on two legs. We are something different from an animal, but what are we? We may be a ghost; we do not know what to call ourselves. Such a creature does not actually exist. It is a delusion. We are not a human being anymore, but we do exist. When Zen is not Zen, nothing exists. Intellectually my talk makes no sense, but if you have experienced true practice, you will understand what I mean. If something exists, it has its own true nature, its Buddha nature. In the Parinirvana Sutra, Buddha says, "Everything has Buddha nature," but Dogen reads it in this way: "Everything *is* Buddha nature." There is a difference. If you say, "Everything has Buddha nature," it means Buddha nature is in each existence, so Buddha nature and each existence are different. But when you say, "Everything is Buddha nature," it means everything is Buddha nature itself. When there is no Buddha nature, there is nothing at all. Something apart from Buddha nature is just a delusion. It may exist in your mind, but such things actually do not exist.

So to be a human being is to be a Buddha. Buddha nature is just another name for human nature, our true human nature. Thus even though you do not do anything, you are actually doing something. You are expressing yourself. You are expressing your true nature. Your eyes will express; your voice will express; your demeanor will express. The most important thing is to express your true nature in the simplest, most adequate way and to appreciate it in the smallest existence.

While you are continuing this practice, week after week, year after year, your experience will become deeper and deeper, and your experience will cover everything you do in your everyday life. The most important thing is to forget all gaining ideas, all dualistic ideas. In other words, just practice zazen in a certain posture. Do not think about anything. Just remain on your cushion without expecting anything. Then eventually you will resume your own true nature. That is to say, your own true nature resumes itself.

mindfulness

—◇—

from

WHEREVER YOU GO,
THERE YOU ARE

by Jon Kabat-Zinn

This excerpt from Jon Kabat-Zinn's second book offers a firm reminder that meditation is not a way to escape difficulties, but rather a way to face and work with present circumstances. Meditate with that intention, and you will find your home here and now.

—◇—

Have you ever noticed that there is no running away from anything? That, sooner or later, the things that you don't want to deal with and try to escape from, or paper over and pretend aren't there, catch up with you—especially if they have to do with old patterns and fears? The romantic notion is that if it's no good over here, you have only to go over there and things will be different. If this job is no good, change jobs. If this wife is no good, change wives. If this town is no good, change towns. If these children are a problem, leave them for other people to look after. The underlying thinking is that the reason for your troubles is outside of you—in the location, in others, in the circumstances. Change the location, change the circumstances, and everything will fall into place; you can start over, have a new beginning.

The trouble with this way of seeing is that it conveniently ignores the fact that you carry your head and your heart, and what some would call your "karma," around with you. You cannot escape yourself, try as you might. And what reason, other than pure wishful thinking, would you have to suspect that things would be different or better somewhere else anyway? Sooner or later, the same problems would arise if in fact they stem in large part from your patterns of seeing, thinking, and behaving. Too often, our lives cease working because we cease working at life, because we are unwilling to take responsibility for things as they are, and to work with our difficulties. We don't understand that it is actually possible to attain clarity, understanding, and transformation right in the middle of what is here and now, however problematic it may be. But it is easier and less threatening to our sense of self to project our involvement in our problems onto other people and the environment.

It is so much easier to find fault, to blame, to believe that what is needed is a change on the outside, an escape from the forces that are holding you back, preventing you from growing, from finding happiness. You can even blame yourself for it all and, in the ultimate escape from responsibility, run away feeling that you have made a hopeless mess of things, or that you are damaged beyond repair. In either case, you believe that you are incapable of true change or growth, and that you need to spare others any more pain by removing yourself from the scene.

The casualties of this way of looking at things are all over the place. Look virtually anywhere and you will find broken relationships, broken families, broken people—wanderers with no roots, lost, going from this place to that, this job to that, this relationship to that, this idea of salvation to that, in the desperate hope that the right person, the right job, the right place, the right book will make it all better. Or feeling isolated, unlovable, and in despair, having given up looking and even making any attempt, however misguided, to find peace of mind.

331

By itself, meditation does not confer immunity from this pattern of looking elsewhere for answers and solutions to one's problems. Sometimes people chronically go from one technique to another, or from teacher to teacher, or tradition to tradition, looking for that special something, that special teaching, that special relationship, that momentary "high" which will open the door to self-understanding and liberation. But this can turn into serious delusion, an unending quest to escape looking at what is closest to home and perhaps most painful. Out of fear and yearning for someone special to help them to see clearly, people sometimes fall into unhealthy dependency relationships with meditation teachers, forgetting that no matter how good the teacher, ultimately you have to live the inner work yourself, and that work always comes from the cloth of your own life.

Some people even wind up misusing teacher-led meditation retreats as a way to keep afloat in their lives rather than as an extended opportunity to look deeply into themselves. On retreat, in a certain way everything is easy. The bare necessities of living are taken care of. The world makes sense. All I have to do is sit and walk, be mindful, stay in the present, be cooked for and fed by a caring staff, listen to the great wisdom that is being put out by people who have worked deeply on themselves and have attained considerable understanding and harmony in their lives, and I will be transformed, inspired to live more fully myself, know how to be in the world, have a better perspective on my own problems.

To a large extent, this is all true. Good teachers and long periods of isolated meditation on retreat can be profoundly valuable and healing, *if* one is willing to look at everything that comes up during a retreat. But there is also the danger, which needs to be looked out for, that retreats can become a retreat from life in the world, and that one's "transformation" will, in the end, be only skin deep.

Perhaps it will last a few days, weeks, or months after the retreat ends, then it's back to the same old pattern and lack of clarity in relationships, and looking forward to the next retreat, or the next great teacher, or a pilgrimage to Asia, or some other romantic fantasy in which things will deepen or become clearer and you will be a better person.

This way of thinking and seeing is an all-too-prevalent trap. There is no successful escaping from yourself in the long run, only transformation. It doesn't matter whether you are using drugs or meditation, alcohol or Club Med, divorce or quitting your job. There can be no resolution leading to growth until the present situation has been faced completely and you have opened to it with mindfulness, allowing the roughness of the situation itself to sand down your own rough edges. In other words, you must be willing to let life itself become your teacher.

This is the path of working where you find yourself, with what is found here and now. This, then, really is it . . . this place, this relationship, this dilemma, this job. The challenge of mindfulness is to work with the very circumstances that you find yourself in—no matter how unpleasant, how discouraging, how limited, how unending and stuck they may appear to be—and to make sure that you have done everything in your power to use their energies to transform yourself before you decide to cut your losses and move on. It is right here that the real work needs to happen.

So, if you think your meditation practice is dull, or no good, or that the conditions aren't right where you find yourself, and you think that if only you were in a cave in the Himalayas, or at an Asian monastery, or on a beach in the tropics, or at a retreat in some natural setting, things would be better, your meditation stronger . . . think again. When you got to your cave or your beach or your retreat, there you would be, with the same mind, the same body, the very same breath that you already have here. After fifteen minutes or so in the cave, you might get lonely, or want more light, or the roof might drip water on you. If you were on the beach, it might be raining or cold. If you were on retreat, you might not like the teachers, or the food, or your room. There is always something to dislike. So why not let go and admit that you might as well be at home wherever you are? Right in that moment, you touch the core of your being and invite mindfulness to enter and heal. If you understand this, then and only then will the cave, the monastery, the beach, the retreat center, offer up their true richness to you. But so will all other moments and places.

answers

—◇—

from
THE MIRACLE OF MINDFULNESS
by Thich Nhat Hanh

What is important? Thich Nhat Hahn's (born 1926) discussion of Leo Tolstoy's story "The Emperor's Three Questions" offers answers grounded in a Buddhist monk's perspective.

—◇—

To end, let me retell a short story of Tolstoy's, the story of the Emperor's three questions. Tolstoy did not know the emperor's name . . .

One day it occurred to a certain emperor that if he only knew the answers to three questions, he would never stray in any matter.

What is the best time to do each thing?
Who are the most important people to work with?
What is the most important thing to do at all times?

The emperor issued a decree throughout his kingdom announcing that whoever could answer the questions would receive a great reward. Many who read the decree made their way to the palace at once, each person with a different answer.

In reply to the first question, one person advised that the

emperor make up a thorough time schedule, consecrating every hour, day, month, and year for certain tasks and then follow the schedule to the letter. Only then could he hope to do every task at the right time.

Another person replied that it was impossible to plan in advance and that the emperor should put all vain amusements aside and remain attentive to everything in order to know what to do at what time.

Someone else insisted that, by himself, the emperor could never hope to have all the foresight and competence necessary to decide when to do each and every task and what he really needed was to set up a Council of the Wise and then to act according to their advice.

Someone else said that certain matters required immediate decision and could not wait for consultation, but if he wanted to know in advance what was going to happen he should consult magicians and soothsayers.

The responses to the second question also lacked accord.

One person said that the emperor needed to place all his trust in administrators, another urged reliance on priests and monks, while others recommended physicians. Still others put their faith in warriors.

The third question drew a similar variety of answers.

Some said science was the most important pursuit. Others insisted on religion. Yet others claimed the most important thing was military skill.

The emperor was not pleased with any of the answers, and no reward was given.

After several nights of reflection, the emperor resolved to visit a hermit who lived up on the mountain and was said to be an enlightened man. The emperor wished to find the hermit to ask him the three questions, though he knew the hermit never left the mountains and was known to receive only the poor, refusing to have anything to do with persons of wealth or power. So the emperor disguised himself as a simple peasant and ordered his attendants to wait for him at the foot of the mountain while he climbed the slope alone to seek the hermit.

Reaching the holy man's dwelling place, the emperor found the hermit digging a garden in front of his hut. When the hermit saw the stranger, he nodded his head in greeting and continued to dig. The labor was obviously hard on him. He was an old man, and each time he thrust his spade into the ground to turn the earth, he heaved heavily.

The emperor approached him and said, "I have come here to ask your help with three questions: When is the best time to do each thing? Who are the most important people to work with? What is the most important thing to do at all times?"

The hermit listened attentively but only patted the emperor on the shoulder and continued digging. The emperor said, "You must be tired. Here, let me give you a hand with that." The hermit thanked him, handed the emperor the spade, and then sat down on the ground to rest.

After he had dug two rows, the emperor stopped and turned to the hermit and repeated his three questions. The hermit still did not answer, but instead stood up and pointed to the spade and said, "Why don't you rest now? I can take over again." But the emperor continued to dig. One hour passed, then two. Finally the sun began to set behind the mountain. The emperor put down the spade and said to the hermit, "I came here to ask if you could answer my three questions. But if you can't give me any answer, please let me know so that I can get on my way home."

The hermit lifted his head and asked the emperor, "Do you hear someone running over there?" The emperor turned his head.

They both saw a man with a long white beard emerge from the woods. He ran wildly, pressing his hands against a bloody wound in his stomach. The man ran toward the emperor before falling unconscious to the ground, where he lay groaning. Opening the man's clothing, the emperor and hermit saw that the man had received a deep gash. The emperor cleaned the wound thoroughly and then used his own shirt to bandage it, but the blood completely soaked it within minutes. He rinsed the shirt out and bandaged the wound a second time and continued to do so until the flow of blood had stopped.

At last the wounded man regained consciousness and asked for a drink of water. The emperor ran down to the stream and brought back a jug of fresh water. Meanwhile, the sun had disappeared and the night air had begun to turn cold. The hermit gave the emperor a hand in carrying the man into the hut where they laid him down on the hermit's bed. The man closed his eyes and lay quietly. The emperor was worn out from a long day of climbing the mountain and digging the garden. Leaning against the doorway, he fell asleep. When he rose, the sun had already risen over the mountain. For a moment he forgot where he was and what he had come here for. He looked over to the bed and saw the wounded man also looking around him in confusion. When he saw the emperor, he stared at him intently and then said in a faint whisper, "Please forgive me."

"But what have you done that I should forgive you?" the emperor asked.

"You do not know me, your majesty, but I know you. I was your sworn enemy, and I had vowed to take vengeance on you, for during the last war you killed my brother and seized my property. When I learned that you were coming alone to the mountain to meet the hermit, I resolved to surprise you on your way back and kill you. But after waiting a long time there was still no sign of you, and so I left my ambush in order to seek you out. But instead of finding you, I came across your attendants, who recognized me, giving me this wound. Luckily, I escaped and ran here. If I hadn't met you I would surely be dead by now. I had intended to kill you, but instead you saved my life! I am ashamed and grateful beyond words. If I live, I vow to be your servant for the rest of my life, and I will bid my children and grandchildren to do the same. Please grant me your forgiveness."

The emperor was overjoyed to see that he was so easily reconciled with a former enemy. He not only forgave the man but promised to return all the man's property and to send his own physician and servants to wait on the man until he was completely healed. After ordering his attendants to take the man home, the emperor returned to see the hermit. Before returning to the palace the emperor wanted to repeat his three questions one last time. He found the hermit sowing seeds in the earth they had dug the day before.

The hermit stood up and looked at the emperor. "But your questions have already been answered."

"How's that?" the emperor asked, puzzled.

"Yesterday, if you had not taken pity on my age and given me a hand with digging these beds, you would have been attacked by that man on your way home. Then you would have deeply regretted not staying with me. Therefore the most important time was the time you were digging in the beds, the most important person was myself, and the most important pursuit was to help me. Later, when the wounded man ran up here, the most important time was the time you spent dressing his wound, for if you had not cared for him he would have died and you would have lost the chance to be reconciled with him. Likewise, he was the most important person, and the most important pursuit was taking care of his wound. Remember that there is only one important time and that is now. The present moment is the only time over which we have dominion. The most important person is always the person you are with, who is right before you, for who knows if you will have dealings with any other person in the future? The most important pursuit is making the person standing at your side happy, for that alone is the pursuit of life."

Tolstoy's story is like a story out of scripture: it doesn't fall short of any sacred text. We talk about social service, service to the people, service to humanity, service for others who are far away, helping to bring peace to the world—but often we forget that it is the very people around us that we must live for first of all. If you cannot serve your wife or husband or child or parent—how are you going to serve society? If you cannot make your own child happy, how do you expect to be able to make anyone else happy? If all our friends in the peace movement or of service communities of any kind do not love and help one another, whom can we love and help? Are we working for other humans, or are we just working for the name of an organization?

Service
The service of peace. The service of any person in need. The word service is so immense. Let's return first to a more modest scale: our families, our classmates, our friends, our own community. We must live for them—for if we cannot live for them, whom else do we think we are living for?

Tolstoy is a saint—what we Buddhists would call a Bodhisattva. But was the emperor himself able to see the meaning and direction of life? How can we live in the present moment, live right now with the people around us, helping to lessen their suffering and making their lives happier? How? The answer is this: We must practice mindfulness. The principle that Tolstoy gives appears easy. But if we want to put it into practice we must use the methods of mindfulness in order to seek and find the way.

I've written these pages for our friends to use. There are many people who have written about these things without having lived them, but I've only written down those things which I have lived and experienced myself. I hope you and your friends will find these things at least a little helpful along the path of our seeking: the path of our return.

acknowledgements

Many people made this anthology.

At Marlowe & Company: Editorial Director Matthew Lore's enthusiasm, intelligence and critical instincts were essential to the development of this book.

At Avalon Publishing Group:
Neil Ortenberg and Susan Reich offered vital support and expertise.

At Balliett & Fitzgerald Inc.:
Sue Canavan created the book's look with important contributions from Mike Walters and Patti Ratchford. Maria Fernandez oversaw production with superb care and attention, with help from Paul Paddock.

At the Writing Company:
Nate Hardcastle helped with research and organization. Mark Klimek, Lee Rader, Taylor Smith and March Truedsson took up slack on other projects.

At Shawneric.com:
Shawneric Hachey handled permissions with his usual aplomb.

Among friends and family:
Jennifer Schwamm Willis and Will Balliett deserve special thanks. Harper Willis and Abner Willis made me laugh.

Finally, I am grateful to the writers whose work appears in this book.

343

From *The Accidental Buddhist* by Dinty W. Moore. Copyright © 1997 by the author. Reprinted by permission of Algonquin Books of Chapel Hill, a division of Workman Publishing. ✦ From *Pilgrim at Tinker Creek* by Annie Dillard. Copyright © 1974 by Annie Dillard. Reprinted by permission of HarperCollins Publishers. ✦ From *Teachings on Love* by Thich Nhat Hanh. Reprinted with permission of Parallax Press, Berkeley, California. ✦ From *Sacred Hoops* by Phil Jackson and Hugh Delehanty. Copyright © 1995 by Phil Jackson and Hugh Delehanty. Reprinted by permission of Hyperion. ✦ From *Nine-Headed Dragon River* by Peter Matthiessen. Copyright © 1985 Zen Community of New York. Reprinted by arrangement with Shambhala Publications, Inc., Boston, www.shambhala.com. ✦ From *Long Quiet Highway* by Natalie Goldberg. Copyright © 1993 by Natalie Goldberg. Used by permission of Bantam Books, a division of Random House, Inc. ✦ From *The Tibetan Book of Living and Dying* by Sogyal Rinpoche. Copyright © 1993 by Rigpa Fellowship. Reprinted by permission of HarperCollins Publishers, Inc. ✦ From *Voluntary Simplicity* by Duane Elgin. Copyright © 1981 by Duane Elgin. Reprinted by permission of William Morrow, a division of HarperCollins Publishers, Inc. ✦ From *Lovingkindness* by Sharon Salzberg. Copyright © 1995 by Sharon Salzberg. Reprinted by arrangement with Shambhala Publications, Inc., Boston, www.shambhala.com. ✦ From *Everyday Blessings* by Myla and Jon Kabat-Zinn. Copyright © 1997 by Myla and Jon Kabat-Zinn. Reprinted by permission of Hyperion. ✦ From *When Things Fall Apart* by Pema Chödrön. Copyright © 1997 by Pema Chödrön. Reprinted by arrangement with Shambhala Publications, Inc., Boston, www.shambhala.com. ✦ From *Awakening the Heart* by John Wellwood. Copyright © 1983 by John Welwood. Reprinted by agreement with Shambhala Publications, Inc., Boston, www.shambhala.com. ✦ From *Full Catastrophe Living* by Jon Kabat-Zinn. Copyright © 1990 by Jon Kabat-Zinn. Reprinted by permission of Delacorte Press, a divi-

bibliography

The selections used in this anthology were taken from the editions listed below. In some cases, other editions may be easier to find. Hard to find or out-of-print titles often can be acquired through inter-library loan services or through Internet booksellers.

Chödrön, Pema. *When Things Fall Apart: Heart Advice for Difficult Times.* Boston: Shambhala Publications, 1997.

Delehanty, Hugh and Phil Jackson. *Sacred Hoops.* New York: Hyperion, 1995.

Dillard, Annie. *Pilgrim at Tinker Creek.* New York: HarperCollins Publishers, 1988.

Elgin, Duane. *Voluntary Simplicity.* New York: William Morrow & Company, 1993.

Goldberg, Natalie. *Long Quiet Highway.* New York: Bantam New Age Books, 1994.

Hanh, Thich Nhat. *Teachings On Love.* Berkeley, CA: Parallax Press, 1997.

Hanh, Thich Nhat. *The Miracle of Mindfulness.* Boston: Beacon Press, 1987.

Kabat-Zinn, Jon. *Full Catastrophe Living.* New York: Delta, 1990.

Kabat-Zinn, Jon. *Wherever You Go, There You Are.* New York: Hyperion, 1994.

Kabat-Zinn, Jon and Kabat-Zinn, Myla. *Everyday Blessings.* New York: Hyperion, 1997.

Kapleau, Roshi Philip. *The Three Pillars of Zen.* New York: Bantam Books, 1980.

Levine, Stephen. *Who Dies?* New York: Anchor Books, 1982.

Matthiessen, Peter. *Nine-Headed Dragon River*. Boston: Shambhala Publications, 1985.

Moore, Dinty W. *The Accidental Buddhist*. Chapel Hill, NC: Algonquin Books, 1997.

Salzberg, Sharon. *Loving-Kindness*. Boston: Shambhala Publications, 1995.

Sogyal Rinpoche. *The Tibetan Book of Living and Dying*. New York: HarperCollins Publishers, 1992.

Suzuki, Shunryu. *Zen Mind, Beginner's Mind*. New York: Weatherhill, 1970.

Watts, Alan. *The Way of Zen*. New York: Vintage Books, 1989.

Welwood, John. *Awakening the Heart*. New York: Random House, 1983.